THE STORY
OF
THE GUARDS

THE HOUSEHOLD DIVISION

THE LIFE GUARDS

THE BLUES AND ROYALS

GRENADIER GUARDS

COLDSTREAM GUARDS

SCOTS GUARDS

IRISH GUARDS

WELSH GUARDS

THE STORY
OF
THE GUARDS

JULIAN PAGET

PRESIDIO PRESS
SAN RAFAEL · CALIFORNIA

Published in 1977 by
PRESIDIO PRESS
1114 Irwin Street
San Rafael, California 94901

First published in 1976 by
Osprey Publishing Limited, London, England

Reprinted in 1977

Designed by Behram Kapadia

Library of Congress Catalog Card Number 77–89606
ISBN 0–89141–035–X

Printed in Great Britain

Dedicated
by gracious permission to
Her Majesty The Queen
Colonel-in-Chief
of the seven Regiments

Foreword

by His Royal Highness The Duke of Edinburgh

This book tells the story of an unique body of fighting men. Throughout history, every Monarch or Head of State has had a special military guard, but there can be few such bodies with a more colourful or gallant history. Their guard duties, although demanding, have fortunately never been vital; on the other hand, their military duties have taken Regiments of the Guards to most of the major battlefields of the British Army in the last 300 years.

It is natural to expect higher standards from Guards Regiments and, as these pages show, they have more than lived up to these expectations. Viewed with a mixture of envy and awe by the rest of the army, they have never failed to provide a yardstick of excellence in every department, be it turnout, drill, smartness, loyalty, courage or sacrifice. With a self-confidence bred of success and a never failing attention to detail and professional competence, they have weathered ridicule and adulation, malice and envy through all the changing fortunes of war and peace.

At a time when we all seem to be hesitant and uncertain about the future, this remarkable story of what British people can achieve with leadership, discipline and devotion comes with a resounding message of encouragement and hope.

Preface

It is a great privilege indeed to have been asked to write 'The Story of the Guards', and also a great challenge to do justice to the subject.

It is a vast canvas covering more than three centuries of service and striving, achievements and personalities, in peace and war. Inevitably, the problem has been what to omit, from a wealth of fascinating material. It has also been a matter of careful judgement to achieve the right balance between past history and more current events, between war and peace, and between matters military and civilian; nor is it easy to write an account of events that will satisfy seven different Regiments, each quite rightly 'jealous of its honour'.

I have not sought to whitewash or condemn, or indeed to pass judgement. This is an account simply of how the Guards have lived and died during three centuries, and how they have tried to play their part in the history of our country.

This is not an 'official' or even a 'Regimental' history, dutifully recording every date and detail. It is a picture, painted with a very broad brush, in which I have tried to present a 'readable' story, picking out the high-lights, and also including something of what Field Marshal Slim called 'unofficial history'.

It is a story that is of interest, I hope, not only to Guardsmen, but also to others, who may want to know more about the Guards. I have tried to write in a manner that suits both military and civilian readers. The former may feel that some military points are either over-simplified or are not given adequate coverage. This is, I fear, inevitable, if the civilian reader is not to be baffled and bored by matters which mean much to soldiers but little perhaps to others.

It has proved impossible to avoid military terms and titles completely, but they have been kept to a minimum, and the more complex points are explained in a Glossary at the end of the book.

No attempt has been made to describe in detail the many changes of uniforms, arms and equipment through the ages; that is a subject in itself. But the illustrations have been so chosen and arranged that they show the main developments over the years.

I am much indebted to many people who have helped me, and without whose support, this book would not have been completed.

Colonel Richard Crichton in particular has been responsible not only for collecting the illustrations, but also for much valuable comment, and Corporal Major Frearson of the Household Cavalry Museum has also provided much material and help. Headquarters, Household Division, have given every assistance, as have the Regimental Headquarters of all the Regiments. I am grateful too to the authors and others who have allowed me to use their material, and have also given me their help and advice. I hope that the many friends who have contributed in one way or another will accept my sincere thanks, even though I cannot mention them all by name. I am greatly indebted to those who have kindly allowed me to reproduce pictures in their possession. Acknowledgements for all pictures are made on page 297.

In conclusion, my hope is that this story may perhaps contribute towards a fuller understanding of the Guards, what they have done in the past, and what they are doing today.

July 1975   JULIAN PAGET

Contents

List of Illustrations

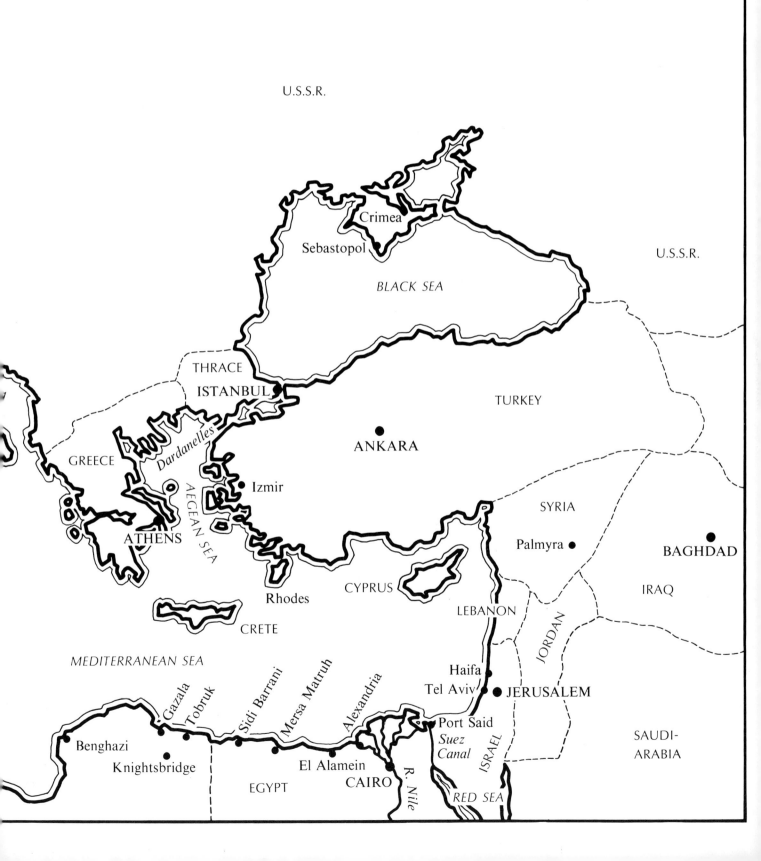

Europe and the Middle East

BALTIC SEA

U.S.S.R.

Crimea

Sebastopol

BLACK SEA

U.S.S.R.

THRACE

ISTANBUL

TURKEY

Dardanelles

GREECE

ANKARA

SYRIA

AEGEAN SEA

Izmir

Palmyra

BAGHDAD

ATHENS

CYPRUS

IRAQ

Rhodes

LEBANON

CRETE

JORDAN

MEDITERRANEAN SEA

Haifa

Tel Aviv

JERUSALEM

Gazala

Tobruk

Sidi Barrani

Mersa Matruh

Alexandria

Port Said

SAUDI-ARABIA

Benghazi

Suez Canal

Knightsbridge

El Alamein

CAIRO

R. Nile

ISRAEL

EGYPT

RED SEA

Chapter 1

The Guards

The Guards are essentially a part of the traditional pageantry of Britain, and are so portrayed worldwide on television, tourists' transparencies, films and postcards. The image inevitably emerges of peacetime soldiers, impressive in their drill, turnout and bearing, but hardly operational troops, geared to the military requirements of a nuclear age.

Most people probably associate the words 'The Guards' with the Changing of the Guard at Buckingham Palace, the unique splendour of the Queen's Birthday Parade, and the whole spectrum of the ceremonial scene in Britain. But this image, is of course, very much one side of the coin only.

Those who have fought alongside the Guards, or indeed against them, have a very different impression. They have memories of Guardsmen in battle in two World Wars, and in a score of campaigns round the world since 1945.

The many nations of the North Atlantic Treaty Organisation have seen Guardsmen training in Europe for nuclear and other types of warfare, or keeping the peace in Berlin.

In Malaya, the Communist terrorists remember the Guards battalions who fought there. The inhabitants of 'Kampong Coldstream' and many other villages may also remember the 'big men' who looked after them during the Emergency, and even helped them to build their homes. The citizens of Ulster know them too, either as friend or foe, according to taste.

Historians write of the Guards primarily as fighting men, who have

(*Opposite*) A State Visit to Windsor. The Royal Procession in the quadrangle of Windsor Castle, with a Guard of Honour and Band drawn up in the centre. The procession is led by the Household Cavalry Mounted Bands (top right), followed by the King's Troop, Royal Horse Artillery who, when on parade with their guns, take precedence even over the Household Cavalry.

16

taken part in most of the campaigns fought by the British Army since 1650, particularly such famous battles as Fontenoy, Waterloo and Inkerman.

The official title of the Guards today is the 'Household Division', which consists of two Regiments of Household Cavalry (The Life Guards, and The Blues and Royals) together with five Regiments of Foot Guards (Grenadier, Coldstream, Scots, Irish and Welsh Guards). These five Regiments of Foot Guards are today officially called 'The Guards Division', but are probably better known by their former title of 'The Brigade of Guards'. The nomenclature is involved and confusing, so, for simplicity, the Foot Guards will be referred to throughout this book as the Foot Guards. A Glossary of Military Terms is included on page 294 to explain some of the more complicated terminology.

It is not proposed in this book to become involved in the details or long history of the uniforms of the seven Guards Regiments through the ages. But it is perhaps of interest and value to give some idea of the ceremonial dress of each Regiment today, if only so that it is possible to distinguish one from another.

The two Regiments of Household Cavalry wear clearly contrasting uniforms, and are easily distinguished (see illustration, opposite). The five Regiments of Foot Guards may at first sight all look alike, but it is possible to identify them by three main features, the plume on the bearskin, the spacing of the buttons on the tunic (but not on the greatcoat), and the regimental badges on the collars and shoulders of the tunics.

The easiest way to illustrate the differences is perhaps to tabulate these points, which can also be seen in the picture opposite.

			Badges	
Regiment	*Plume*	*Buttons*	*Collar*	*Shoulder*
Grenadier Guards	White worn on the left	Singly	Grenade	Royal Cypher
Coldstream Guards	Red worn on the right	Pairs	Garter Star	Rose
Scots Guards	None	Threes	Star of the Order of the Thistle	Thistle
Irish Guards	Blue worn on the right	Fours	Shamrock	Star of the Order of St Patrick
Welsh Guards	White-Green-White worn on the left	Fives	Leek	Leek

The history of the Guards dates back to the time of King Charles II, in whose lifetime all the present Regiments were formed, except the Irish and Welsh Guards. The original Regiments are thus among the oldest in the British Army.

The Guards have always been the personal troops of the Sovereign, with the particular privilege of guarding the Royal Family in both war and peace. This was a very real duty in the days when the King personally led

(*Opposite above*) The Queen's Life Guard. The Guard changes in the yard of the Horse Guards building. The Blues are in the foreground with blue tunics and red plumes. Facing them are The Life Guards with scarlet tunics and white plumes. The Trumpeters (who wear red plumes in both Regiments) are mounted on greys, as ordered by King James II so that they would be easily distinguishable in battle when required to sound a call. Both the Old and New Guards have a Squadron Standard.

(*Opposite below*) Foot Guards Uniforms, 1975. A Warrant Officer from each of the five Regiments of Foot Guards. They are standing in the order in which their Regiments form up when on parade together– i.e. Grenadier Guards on the right flank, then Scots, Welsh and Irish Guards; with the Coldstream on the left flank.

The Prince of Wales, as Colonel of the Welsh Guards, presents leeks to the Regiment on St David's Day, which is celebrated as a Regimental occasion.

his troops into battle, as when William III, for instance, was saved from capture at Landen in 1693 by The Life Guards. But as recently as 1940 a special force called Coats Mission was formed from the Coldstream Guards to protect the Royal Family in the event of invasion.

In peacetime too, until the police force was formed in 1829, the Guards had the task of protecting the Monarch against the plots and intrigues of his enemies. In those times, the mounted Escorts, still provided today by the Household Cavalry on State occasions, were a necessary precaution, as were the Foot Guards lining the Royal route.

The links with the Throne remain very close today. The Sovereign is Colonel-in-Chief of all seven Guards Regiments, an honour granted to few other regiments or corps in the British Army. Also, three members of the Royal Family are Colonels of Regiments of the Household Division; the Duke of Edinburgh is Colonel of the Grenadier Guards and also Senior Colonel of the Household Division, the Prince of Wales became Colonel of the Welsh Guards in 1975, and the Duke of Kent of the Scots Guards the year before.

The Queen and all the Royal Family take a very personal interest in the day-to-day affairs of the Household Troops, not only on official occasions, such as the Queen's Birthday Parade, but also at many informal, purely Regimental occasions.

For their part, the Guards have particular responsibilities and privileges relating to the Monarchy. In addition to guarding the Sovereign and the Royal Palaces, there are many State occasions when they play a major part in the pageantry at which this country is unsurpassed.

Because these ceremonial duties are such a tourist attraction, they are inevitably the most publicised role of the Household Division. But all Guardsmen are trained first and foremost as operational troops, and this is their main task. Indeed, the Guards have taken part in most of the operations in which the British Army has found itself involved in the thirty years of so-called 'peace' since 1945.

At least half the Household Division is usually stationed overseas at any one time, either in Europe as part of the NATO forces, or on operations anywhere in the world from Belfast to Hong Kong.

The Household Cavalry consists today of three units. One operational armoured regiment, equipped with Chieftain tanks, is stationed in Germany; one armoured reconnaissance regiment, based at Windsor, is liable to be sent to any trouble spot at any time, while a mounted regiment remains in London to carry out ceremonial duties.

The Troopers seen mounting the Queen's Life Guard, or providing mounted Escorts to The Queen and foreign Heads of State, are serving only temporarily with the Household Cavalry Mounted Regiment, which is permanently stationed in Hyde Park Barracks for this purpose. After two years or so in London, these officers and men exchange their horses for tanks or armoured cars again, and return to their operational role.

The Foot Guards do not have any one unit specialising in ceremonial duties, but all their battalions rotate between tours of duty at home and

The Queen talking to Coldstream Guardsmen and their families at a Regimental gathering of past and present members.

abroad, changing from one role to the other every two or three years.

The time-gap between being engaged on London duties and being on active operations overseas is normally only about six weeks, including leave, which does not allow much time to adapt from patrolling in Ulster or Malaya to taking part in the Queen's Birthday Parade – or vice versa.

This dual commitment explains why, for example, some mystified American Air Force pilots in British Guiana (now Guyana) in 1963 saw the Guards battalion stationed there on internal security duties making strange white marks on the tarmac of the airfield, just before they were due to return home. The answer was that they were marking out the shape of the forecourt of Buckingham Palace, so that they could begin rehearsals for mounting the Queen's Guard.

The Foot Guards are best known as infantry, but throughout their history, they have shown themselves to be remarkably versatile. In the seventeenth century, they fought on board ship with the Royal Navy in the Dutch Wars; in Queen Victoria's time they fought in South Africa as 'Mounted Infantry', and actually rode into battle in the Sudan on camels.

In the Second World War, they formed an armoured division, their own Commando and a Guards Patrol in the Long Range Desert Group. Until 1975, they maintained a Parachute Company, and there is still a Guards Squadron of the Special Air Service (SAS); today they fly helicopters, and drive their own armoured cars and tanks as well as training for arctic or jungle warfare, Ulster or Cyprus.

22

It is no easy task to reconcile these two conflicting commitments of operational and ceremonial efficiency, and to maintain the highest standards in both. It is achieved however, and the answer lies largely in one basic Guards principle, which is that nothing is acceptable that is in any way second-rate.

This simple rule of life is inculcated into all Guardsmen, officers and men alike, from the moment they join until the end of their service. It has remained a guiding principle for the three centuries of their existence, in which time they have made an impressive contribution to the history of our country, both in peacetime and on the field of battle.

The Guards

Training in NATO. Chieftain tanks, manned by The Blues and Royals, train in Germany as part of the NATO forces there.

Chapter 2
Formation
(1642–62)

The earliest part of the story begins in one of the most troubled periods of British history, covering the Civil War (1642–8), the flight of Charles II in 1650, and his Restoration to the throne in 1660.

It was a time when the whole country was agonisingly split by political, religious and national differences. It was certainly not a United Kingdom, for English, Irish and Scots were all fighting bitterly against each other. And within England itself, the people were torn between loyalty to the King or to Parliament, so that even individual members of the same families sometimes found themselves fighting on opposite sides.

But from this period of strife and dissension sprang the beginnings of Britain's first standing army, and also the formation of all of the present Guards Regiments except for the Irish and Welsh Guards.

It is an involved story, complicated still further by rival claims by each Regiment as to their seniority and precedence. In this connection, it is important to make a clear distinction between the date on which a particular Regiment was formed as a *Regiment*, and the date on which that Regiment was granted the status of being *Household Troops*, with the duty and privilege of guarding the Sovereign in London. The two dates are not necessarily the same, and this has led to some controversy and confusion over the years.

A further complication is that some of the Regiments changed their identity several times, and some may be said to have broken the continuity of their service.

24

No attempt is made here to pass judgement, but only to tell the story with all possible accuracy, leaving readers to form their own opinions – according to their own loyalties and inclinations.

The Civil War (1642–8)

The story starts in the troubled year of 1642. Charles I was on the throne, but England was on the verge of the Civil War, and Ireland was in a state of rebellion. In this situation, Parliament were naturally reluctant to send English troops to quell the Irish rebels, and so they decided to raise ten Scottish regiments for this purpose.

King Charles I intended to lead the campaign himself, and one of these regiments, raised and commanded by the Marquess of Argyll, was designated to act as his Royal Guard while he was in Ireland. It is to them that the **Scots Guards** trace their ancestry as a Regiment.

In the event, the King never went to Ireland, but these ten Regiments, including Argyll's, served there for seven years, returning to Scotland in 1649. They had by then been reduced to such low numbers that they were on return formed into one unit, known as the 'Irish Companies'.

Meanwhile, in England, the Civil War tore the country apart for six bitter years, until the New Model Army, created in 1645, finally brought about the defeat of the Royalists, and so led to the execution of Charles I, the Martyr King, on 30 January 1649.

Events of 1650

With the Civil War ended, Oliver Cromwell held unprecedented power in England. But the Irish were still in revolt, and in 1649, he himself sailed for Ireland to settle the trouble there once and for all. While there he was much impressed by the military qualities of a certain Colonel George Monck, and determined to give him a regiment of his own to command.

But a problem arose, for Monck had originally been a Royalist, and had changed sides after being captured by the Roundheads and imprisoned for two years. By chance, the regiment that Cromwell offered to Monck turned out to be the very one that had taken him prisoner, and they were not unnaturally reluctant to accept him now as their new Commanding Officer.

Not to be thwarted, Cromwell created a completely new regiment, specially for Colonel Monck, by taking five companies from the regiment of George Fenwick and five from the regiment of Sir Arthur Hazelrigg, then Governor of Newcastle. Both these regiments had been formed originally in 1645 as part of the New Model Army.

The new regiment was formed on 13 August 1650, and was given the title of 'Monck's Regiment of Foot'.

'Thus was formed,' to quote Sir John Fortescue,[1] 'the oldest of our existing national regiments,[2] the one complete relic of the famous New

25

Model, the one surviving corps which fought under Oliver Cromwell, itself more famous under its later name of the **Coldstream Guards**.'

(*Opposite*) General George Monck, Duke of Albemarle.

Scotland meanwhile had retained strong loyalties towards the Royalist cause, and when Charles Stuart, exiled son of the Martyr King, landed at Speymouth on 23 June 1650 to reclaim the throne of England, he was welcomed by the Scots, who offered a Scottish army to help him.

One of the first Scottish units to declare their support was the Earl of Argyll's regiment. Charles gratefully accepted their services, and on 30 July, bestowed upon them the title of his 'Lyfe Guard of Foot' or 'Regiment of Scottish Foot Guards'.

On hearing the news of Charles's arrival, Oliver Cromwell, now back from Ireland, marched north, and decisively defeated Charles's army at the Battle of Dunbar on 3 September 1650.

Monck's Regiment of Foot took part under Cromwell, and a special medal was struck and awarded to all officers and men of the New Model Army who had been present at this great victory. It bore Oliver Cromwell's head on one side, and on the other, a scene of the House of Commons in session.

The Dunbar Medal, the first campaign medal awarded in the British Army. The Coldstream Guards are the only surviving Regiment to have earned it, and a specimen belonging to them is in the Guards Museum.

Charles's 'Regiment of Scottish Foot Guards' fought on the losing side, and was reduced to two companies by the end of the battle. Despite this reverse, Charles re-formed his army, and in July 1651 set off south on a desperate invasion of England. He was pursued by Cromwell, however, and was routed again at the Battle of Worcester on 3 September 1651, a year to the day after Dunbar.

This time his army, including his Scottish Foot Guards, was virtually destroyed, and Charles himself made his famous escape to France with a few loyal supporters, leaving Cromwell and his New Model Army in undisputed control of England.

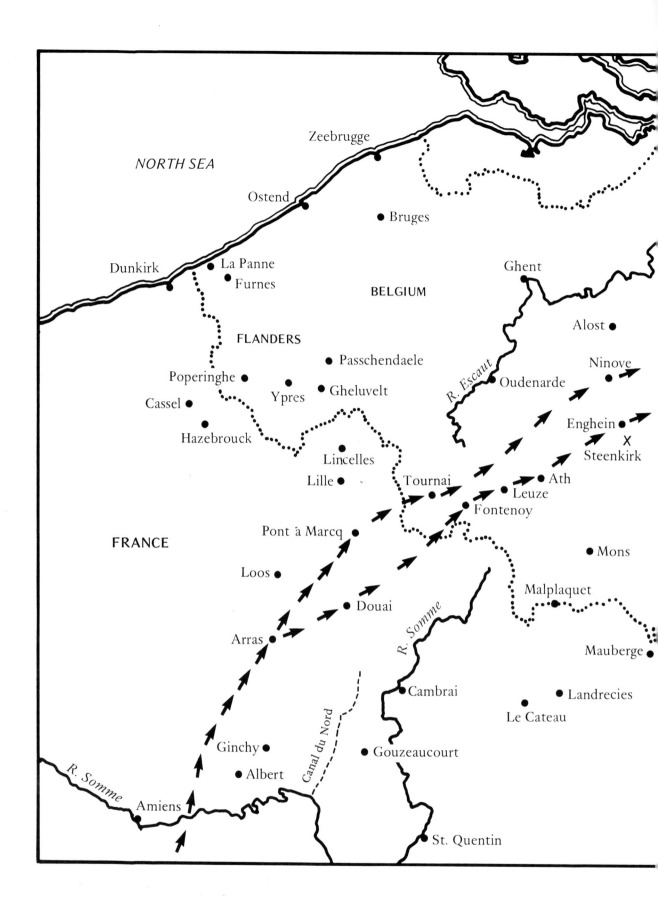

NORTH SEA

Zeebrugge

Ostend

Bruges

Dunkirk

La Panne

Furnes

BELGIUM

Ghent

Alost

FLANDERS

Passchendaele

Ninove

Poperinghe

Ypres

Gheluvelt

R. Escaut

Oudenarde

Cassel

Enghein

Hazebrouck

Steenkirk

Lincelles

Lille

Tournai

Ath

Leuze

Fontenoy

FRANCE

Pont à Marcq

Mons

Loos

Malplaquet

Douai

R. Somme

Arras

Mauberge

Cambrai

Landrecies

Le Cateau

Canal du Nord

Ginchy

Gouzeaucourt

Albert

R. Somme

Amiens

St. Quentin

28

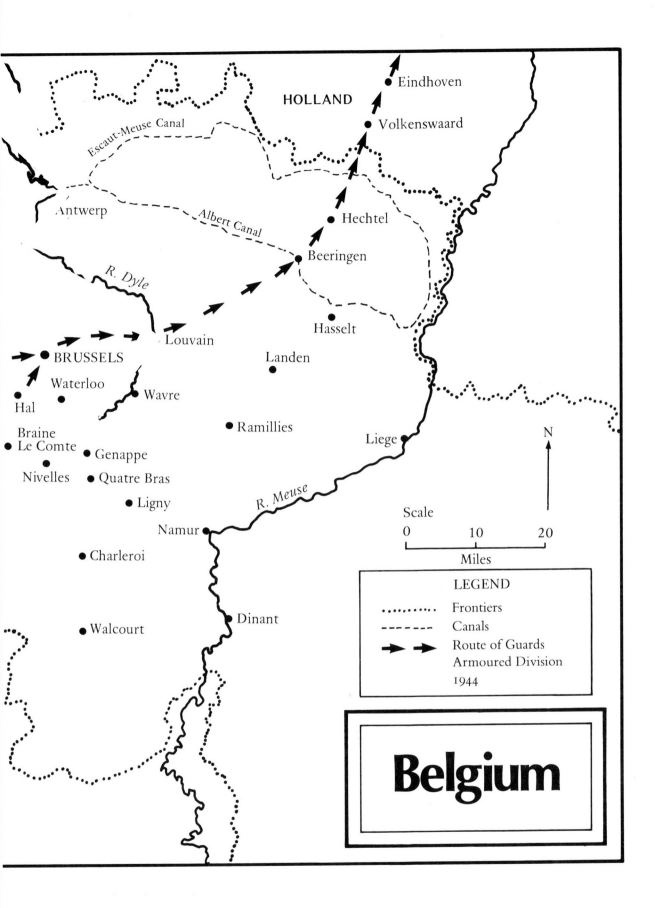

HOLLAND

• Eindhoven

• Volkenswaard

Escaut-Meuse Canal

Antwerp

Albert Canal

• Hechtel

• Beeringen

R. Dyle

Louvain

• Hasselt

Landen

BRUSSELS

Waterloo

• Wavre

Hal

Braine
Le Comte

• Genappe

Nivelles

• Quatre Bras

• Ligny

• Ramillies

Liege

R. Meuse

Namur

• Charleroi

Dinant

• Walcourt

N

Scale

0   10   20

Miles

LEGEND

.... Frontiers

- - - - - - Canals

➤ ➤ Route of Guards
Armoured Division
1944

Belgium

Scotland, however, remained steadfast in its loyalty to the exiled Charles, and Cromwell therefore appointed George Monck as Commander-in-Chief of the 6,000 Parliamentary troops in Scotland, which included Monck's own Regiment of Foot. His orders were to bring Scotland firmly under his control, and he carried out this task effectively.

The scene now shifts to the exiled Charles who, after nearly three years of wandering round Europe, finally established himself with his loyal Royalist followers at Bruges. He was still determined to regain his English throne and, to this end, he managed in the summer of 1656 to form round him in Flanders, five infantry regiments (one English, one Scottish and three Irish).

The English regiment was some 400 strong and consisted entirely of officers, most of whom had at great personal cost followed him into exile. Such was their devotion that many of them now accepted commissions in his service in ranks lower than those they had held previously in the Royalist forces during the Civil War.

Command of this new regiment was conferred in September 1656 on Lord Wentworth, and it was given the title of 'The Royal Regiment of Guards', to whom the **Grenadier Guards** trace their origins.

It is from this moment that the Grenadier Guards acquired the status of Household Troops, and so are recognised as the senior regiment of Foot Guards. The title of 'First Guards' was not in fact adopted until 1685, but for convenience the regiment will be referred to henceforward as the 'First Guards' until we reach 1815, when they became known as 'Grenadier Guards'.

One of the companies of the regiment was commanded by Colonel William Carless (or Carlos). He it was who guided Charles into the branches of the famous Boscobel Oak, so that he escaped from the Roundheads pursuing him after the Battle of Worcester. Charles assumed as a Royal badge to commemorate his escape an oak tree with his own crowned head peering out from it. This badge still continues today as the XXth Company Colour of the Grenadier Guards.

This famous occasion is also commemorated by the Household Cavalry, who wear an oak leaf and acorn motif on their helmets, and on the tips of their aiguillettes.

Like the Scots Guards, the Grenadiers found themselves fighting their first battle against the Parliamentary forces. Charles II had allied himself with Spain, and in 1658 Cromwell sent 6,000 troops to join the French and capture the port of Dunkirk, which then belonged to Spain.

Charles's Royal Regiment therefore joined in its defence and they distinguished themselves at the Battle of the Dunes on 24 May 1658 by fighting on when all others had retreated. As the battle died down, a French officer rode forward and summoned the Royal Regiment to surrender, explaining that resistance was useless.

'We are not accustomed to believe our enemies,' came the reply.

'Then look for yourselves,' retorted the Frenchman.

He then led their commander to a sand-dune, and showed him the retreating Spaniards. Only then did they agree to lay down their arms.

On the death of Oliver Cromwell in 1658, Charles's hopes of returning to England brightened, and he decided to strengthen his personal army in exile by forming his own 'Royal Mounted Bodyguard', in addition to his Royal Regiment.

He therefore created in 1659, from among the Royalist gentlemen with him in Bruges, a 'Troop of Horse Guards' commanded by Lord Gerard of Brandon. Their title is confusing, as they were in fact the forerunners of the present **Life Guards**, and not of the Royal Horse Guards as might be expected. For clarity, they will therefore be referred to hereafter as The Life Guards.

Just as the Grenadier Guards were to become the senior Regiment of Foot Guards on the strength of their loyalty at this time to the future King of England, so The Life Guards were to be recognised as the senior regiment in the Household Cavalry, and indeed in the Army List.

The Restoration (1660)

So we come to the momentous year of 1660, which saw the Restoration of Charles II as King of England, and the drawing together at last of the threads of our national life, that had been so tragically twisted and broken as a result of the Civil War.

The drama began to unfold on the very first day of the year in the little town of Coldstream on the Scottish border, where General Monck had assembled a large part of his troops, including his own new Regiment of Horse, formed in 1656.

Although most of Cromwell's generals believed in a military dictatorship, George Monck had different ideas. It is difficult to judge just what was in his mind, but it is clear that he felt strongly, not only that a change was called for from the military 'junta' which then ruled the country, but also that he should do something about it.

He decided therefore to march on London, and on 1 January 1660, he left Coldstream and set off south.

He had with him, in addition to his own Regiments of Horse and Foot, a further two cavalry and three infantry regiments, making a total force of about 7,000 men. His route lay via York, Nottingham, Leicester and St Albans, and as he and his men strode the length of the country, he received enthusiastic support for his cause.

But he 'kept his own counsel and none knew his intentions'.[3]

The march took five weeks, and Monck entered the capital on 3 February 1660, quartering his own Regiment in and around St James's, for the first time in their history.

In London, he found growing unrest, political conflict and confusion. Crowds roasted 'rumps' in the streets at one stage to show their discontent with the 'Rump' Parliament, and his troops were a decisive factor at a time of great uncertainty.

Despite some opposition to his ideas, Monck managed, without blood-shed, to break the Army's domination of the Government and to bring about the election of a freely-chosen Parliament, which met on 25 April 1660. Monck himself took his seat as the member for his native county of Devon, and one of the first acts of the new House of Commons was to vote for the return of the Monarchy, to which he gladly agreed.

So it happened that the Restoration of Charles II was achieved primarily by a Roundhead general at the head of part of the New Model Army. The result was to set the history of our country on a new course.

On 25 May 1660, the King landed at Dover, where he was welcomed by General Monck and they exchanged warm greetings.

Charles had brought with him from Bruges as his personal escort, the King's Troop of his own Life Guards, eighty strong. He had left behind in Flanders a second troop of his Life Guards (The Duke of York's Troop), and also his Royal Regiment of Guards, though their commander, Lord Wentworth himself accompanied the King.

The Royal party set off immediately for London, escorted by the King's Troop, and also by Monck's own Troop of Horse. The latter were within a year to join the King's Life Guards, and so it can be said that on this historic journey, the King had in fact the first 'Sovereign's Escort' ever provided by the present Life Guards, although they were not yet officially recognised as such.

The journey to London took four days, and on the 27th, when the Royal party stopped at Canterbury, the King showed his gratitude to General Monck by bestowing on him the Order of the Garter, which is now the basis of the badge of the Coldstream Guards.

He followed this on 7 July by creating him Duke of Albemarle, and appointing him Lord General of the Land Forces.[4] His regiment of foot now became known also as the 'Duke of Albemarle's Regiment', or 'The Lord General's Regiment', but for simplicity they will continue to be called 'Monck's Regiment', until they become Coldstream Guards about 1670.

So the King was back on his throne, but the situation was far from secure. A substantial part of the New Model Army was still under arms and their loyalty to Charles was, to put it mildly, decidedly questionable. Apart from his one Troop of Life Guards and Monck's Regiments of Horse and Foot, the King had no troops on whom he could really rely. The country was still in a state of turmoil, and he was highly vulnerable to attacks on his life and threats to his throne.

Not surprisingly, the King decided that the whole army must be rapidly and thoroughly purged of doubtful elements, and then be reorganised. As a first move, he dismissed all officers whose loyalty was in doubt, replacing them by Royalists.

He then looked around for any other regiment that he could trust, and picked on Colonel Unton Crook's Regiment of Horse to join his Royal troops.

He replaced their Roundhead Colonel by a staunch Royalist called Colonel Daniel O'Neale, who had the distinction of having escaped from the Tower of London, when imprisoned there. This done, the regiment' was given the new title of 'The Royal Regiment of Horse', later the **Royal Horse Guards** (**The Blues**). Hereafter the Regiment will, for simplicity, be referred to in this book as 'The Blues'.

By a strange coincidence, Colonel Unton Crook's Regiment had originally been formed in 1650 by the same Sir Arthur Hazelrigg, who produced the five infantry companies that became 'Monck's Regiment'. We thus owe to a staunch Roundhead, the creation of two Guards Regiments, The Royal Horse Guards and the Coldstream Guards.

Charles would have liked to retain a small standing army, but Parliament, with memories of the Civil War still very much in their minds, were firmly opposed to any form of permanent military power in the hands of the Monarch. They therefore passed an Act on 26 August 1660 ordering the disbandment of the entire New Model Army. No exceptions whatsoever were allowed, and all units in England, including even General Monck's Regiments, were listed for disbandment.

One concession only was made, and that was that Monck's Regiments of both Horse and Foot should, in recognition of their services to the King, be the last to disappear. This seemed at the time to be a somewhat dubious honour, but as events turned out, it was to have far-reaching results, for it was to lead to both regiments not only surviving, but also joining the Household Division.

By the middle of December 1660, the New Model Army had virtually ceased to exist. Those paid off included even Colonel O'Neale's 'Royal Regiment', which was disbanded at Bath in December after an existence of only six months as Royal troops; but they need not have worried, for within two months, they would be re-formed.

About this time, several plots against the throne came to light and as a result, Parliament agreed reluctantly that the Sovereign must be allowed to maintain adequate personal troops for his protection in England.

The King's Troop of Life Guards was already in England, and he was now allowed to send for the Duke of York's Troop as well. He was also authorised to raise in England a second 'Regiment of Guards', similar to Lord Wentworth's Regiment, which was to remain in Flanders as part of the garrison of Dunkirk. So on 23 November 1660, Colonel John Russell, son of the Earl of Bedford, raised twelve new companies, the first of which was to be known as the 'Sovereign's Company'.

Then on Sunday 6 January 1661, two days before Monck's two Regiments were due to be disbanded, came a minor event that was to have major repercussions both for the Household Division and for the British Army of the future.

On that day, a London wine cooper called Thomas Venner led some sixty fanatical, armed supporters in a revolt against the King and Parliament. His followers called themselves the 'Fifth Monarchy Men', or 'Millenarians', and they managed to cause so much trouble that neither the City Trained Bands nor Colonel John Russell's newly-recruited regiment could cope with the situation.

33

Parliament was forced somewhat reluctantly to call on 'Monck's Regiment of Foot' for help, whereupon these veterans, supported by some of the King's Life Guards, soon rounded up the rebels, and the Venner Riots were over.

The incident served however, to make two points clear to both Parliament and the King. The first was that there was definitely a need to maintain a larger, professional standing army in the country, both to protect the Sovereign and to maintain law and order. The second was that Monck's two regiments were too valuable to lose, and they should be retained as part of any such permanent force.

Creation of the Standing Army

So the disbandment of these two regiments was averted, and on 26 January 1661, King Charles II signed what has been called 'the birth certificate of the British Army'. It was a Royal Warrant authorising the establishment of the first Standing Army in the country, as opposed to the armies which had until then been raised only as required.

The Act of Parliament disbanding the New Model Army was however still on the Statute Book and had to be formally complied with. So it came about that at 10 o'clock on the morning of St Valentine's Day, 14 February 1661, Monck's Regiment of Horse and his Regiment of Foot, both paraded at Tower Hill. There they symbolically laid down their arms as units of the New Model Army, and were immediately ordered to take them up again as Royal troops in the new Standing Army, and as 'an extraordinary guard to his Royal person'.

Monck's Regiment of Horse was at once renamed 'Lord Albemarle's Troop of His Majesty's Life Guards', and became the Third Troop, after the King's and the Duke of York's. As such, they became Household Cavalry from that moment.

Monck's Regiment of Foot received the title of 'The Lord General's Regiment of Foot Guards', later to become known as the Coldstream Guards. They too are considered to have become Household Troops from this moment, with seniority immediately after Lord Wentworth's and Colonel John Russell's Regiments.

The Coldstream, of course, accepted the Royal Command as to their seniority, but nevertheless, just to make their views quite clear, they took as their Regimental motto 'Nulli Secundus' or 'Second to None'. To this day, they do not accept that they should ever be referred to as the 'Second Guards', and this was officially confirmed by the Secretary of War in January 1830. Also when the Grenadier and Coldstream Guards are both on parade and the Grenadiers stand undisputedly on the right of the line, the Coldstream then traditionally take position on the left of the line with other Regiments between, so that they are still 'Second to None'.

The 'Royal Regiment of Horse', which had been disbanded under Colonel O'Neale on 23 December 1660, also joined the new standing army, and on 16 February, 1661, they were paraded at Tothill Fields, Westminster, (now

Ceremonial and Operational.
(*Opposite above*) An autumn scene as a State Procession rides down the Mall.
(*Opposite below*) The same Household Troops exchange their ceremonial dress for combat clothing as helicopter pilots . . .
. . . and as mobile troops training in Armoured Personnel carriers in Germany.

34

Vincent Square), and were for the second time taken on as Royal troops. This time, the King gave the appointment of Colonel of the Regiment to Aubrey de Vere, Earl of Oxford, with Colonel Daniel O'Neale serving under him.

The Regiment wore uniforms which were Oxford blue in colour, from which came their ultimate title of the Royal Horse Guards ('The Blues'). But it is uncertain whether the uniform was in fact introduced by the Earl of Oxford, as there is evidence that the regiment wore blue when it formed part of the New Model Army.

They took precedence next after The Life Guards, and the first Troop was given the title of 'His Majesty's Own Troop'. But they were not yet granted the right of acting as the personal guard of the Sovereign in London, i.e. the status of Household Cavalry. They were however generally recognised as Household Troops from 1661, and the buckles on their standard belts still carry the date '1661'.

Charles II was crowned on St George's Day 1661, and among the many orders issued for the occasion was one 'that for the prevention of disorder, no person whatever does on that day ride upon any unruly or striking horse' – an order doubtless repeated often since, but inevitably issued on a basis of 'easier said than done'.

Having succeeded in creating his standing army in England, Charles now had to consider the position of Scotland, and on 1 May 1662, he signed a Warrant for the establishment of 'a New Regiment of Foot Guards to His Majesty', consisting of six hundred soldiers, with the Earl of Linlithgow as their Colonel. In 1666 a further seven companies were recruited, and they were then officially established as 'The Scottish Regiment of Foot Guards', now the Scots Guards. Thus the Regiment that had been scattered at the Battle of Worcester in 1651 was re-formed. It was still however, on the strength of the Scottish Army, and was not to be brought into the British Army until 1686.

Another regiment raised at this time and destined over 300 years later to join the Household Division was the 'Royal Dragoons (1st Dragoons)'. They were formed by Charles II at Southwark on 21 October 1661, as a troop of horse to be sent to reinforce the garrison of Tangier, where they remained from 1662 to 1683, acquiring the title of the 'Tangier Horse'. On their eventual return to England, they were reorganised as the Royal Dragoons, later known as '**The Royals**', but did not join the Household Division until they amalgamated with 'The Blues' in 1969.

(*Opposite above*) Coldstream Guards, 1661. The Coldstream Guards, then known as Monck's Regiment, salute King Charles II at the Tower of London. The Ensign lowers the Colonel's Colour, and doffs his hat, which was the customary manner of saluting at that time. To the left are Musketeers and to the right, Pikemen. (From a painting by H. Oake-Jones.)
(*Opposite below*) Foot Guards Uniforms, 1670 A Musketeer, Pikeman and a Drum Major.

The Household Troops in 1662

So by 1662, all but two of the present Guards Regiments were in existence. Most of them bore other titles at that time, but they were all personal troops of the King of England, who was now on his throne.

The regiments recognised at this time as Household Troops (with their present titles shown for clarity) were as follows:

His Majesty's Horse Guards (now The Life Guards)
    The King's Troop
    The Duke of York's Troop
    The Duke of Albemarle's Troop
The Royal Regiment of Horse (The Blues until 1969)
The Royal Regiment of Foot Guards (now Grenadier Guards)
    Colonel John Russell's Regiment
    Lord Wentworth's Regiment
The Lord General's Regiment of Foot Guards (now Coldstream Guards)
The Scottish Regiment of Foot Guards (now Scots Guards)

In November 1662, Charles II, always short of cash, sold Dunkirk to the French for £385,000. There was now no longer any need for a garrison there, and so in 1664, Lord Wentworth's Regiment of Foot Guards at last returned to England, where they were allotted to various garrisons.

The existence of two regiments with similar titles inevitably led to confusion, and when Lord Wentworth died in February 1665, the King incorporated the two regiments into one under Colonel John Russell – the first of many 'amalgamations' that the British Army would have to accept in the future.

The new regiment consisted of twenty four companies, and was called 'The King's Regiment of Foot Guards', a title that was changed in 1685 to 'The First Regiment of Foot Guards'.

By 1662, therefore, the existence of the Household Division that we know today was clearly established in fact, if not in name. It had yet to prove itself in battle, and that would soon come.

Its formation was a remarkable event, for it was composed initially of a number of completely unrelated regiments, some of which had indeed been fighting against each other only a few years previously.

But with the Restoration, the past was forgotten. Roundhead and Royalist became united by the common bond of service and loyalty to the Crown, and at the same time to their country – something which had proved tragically impossible during the trauma of the Civil War.

From now onwards, the various Guards Regiments were to start building up the standards and traditions that would inspire many future generations of Guardsmen.

Chapter 3

Early History (1662–1700)

Strangely, the first actions in which the Guards were involved after 1662 were on the high seas. But this was not so surprising as it may sound, since it was normal practice in the seventeenth century for soldiers to fight on board ships of the Royal Navy, and both the First and Coldstream Guards provided troops for naval service in the war against the Dutch in 1665–7.

Army officers even commanded men-of-war on occasions, and General Monck certainly won several naval battles, despite his habit of ordering his fleet to 'Wheel to the Right' or to 'Charge'.

Lord Gerard, first Colonel of The Life Guards, also fought at sea, and it is intriguing that the present Colonel, Earl Mountbatten, is an Admiral of the Fleet, and was also Supreme Commander of the Allied forces, land, sea and air, in South-East Asia in the Second World War.

In 1664, the Coldstream Guards provided a detachment which had the distinction of taking part in the capture of what is now the city of New York. It was at that time called New Amsterdam, being the capital of the Dutch settlements in North America.

The expedition was led by Captain Robert Holmes of the Royal Navy, who was also a Captain in the Coldstream Guards, and he loyally re-named the enemy capital, New York, in honour of the King's brother, the Duke of York.

The First Guards fought in several naval actions, and it is in commemoration of this 'service at sea' that the Regiment adopted the custom of playing

Service at Sea

39

'Rule Britannia' before the National Anthem at Retreat. This privilege was granted originally to the 3rd Battalion, and when they were disbanded in 1960, the tradition was, with the approval of the Sovereign and the First Sea Lord, passed on to the 2nd Battalion of the Regiment.

The death of General Monck on 3 January 1670 led to changes in the titles of his regiments. His Troop of Life Guards was re-named 'The Queen's Troop'[5] and his Regiment of Foot Guards were now officially given the title, by which they were already generally known, of 'Coldstream Guards', or the Coldstream (but not the Coldstreams).

To date, Regiments had consisted of a varying number of companies, each named after the officer who commanded it,[6] but these companies now

began to be formed into 'battalions'.[7] The First Guards formed two battalions in 1672, and a Composite Battalion from both the First and Coldstream Guards was involved in the Second Dutch War of 1672–4.

This is of interest, because it was the first time that a Composite Battalion was formed from the different Guards Regiments. This practice has occurred regularly ever since with complete success, and is part of the strength and versatility of the Household Division; but it is not always realised that it dates back over 300 years.

The Life Guards were also involved in the war, and it was their first active service – ashore.

Another point of interest is that an Ensign in the King's Company of the

The Guards land at Tangier, prior to their successful campaign of 1680. The Moorish forces watch from their positions round the garrison.

41

First Guards on this campaign was one John Churchill, later 1st Duke of Marlborough.

The first Battle Honour of any of the Guards Regiments is 'Tangier', borne on the Colours of the Grenadier and Coldstream Guards. This chief city of Morocco had been given away as a wedding present to King Charles when he married Katherine of Braganza in 1662, and the Moors not unnaturally resented seeing it in infidel hands. They raided it constantly, and regularly cut off its water supply.

Finally, in 1680 the Governor called for reinforcements, in order to deal with the Moors once and for all. A Composite Guards battalion was sent out, called the 'King's Battalion', and commanded by Colonel Sackville of the First Guards. It joined the garrison of Tangier (which already included the Royal Dragoons), and the Moors were soon decisively defeated, and forced to make peace. The First and Coldstream Guards thus acquired the Battle Honour 'Tangier 1680'. The Blues and Royals however carry 'Tangier 1662–80' on their Standards, in recognition of eighteen years of active service there by The Royals.

Only four years later Charles decided that he could no longer afford to maintain this outpost; Tangier was therefore handed back to the Moors, and the garrison was withdrawn.

On their return after twenty-two years abroad, the Royal Dragoons were confirmed as Royal troops and re-named by Charles II as 'The King's Own Royal Regiment of Dragoons',[8] with precedence over all other regiments of horse except The Life Guards and The Blues. John Churchill, was appointed their first Colonel.

About this time, several other noteworthy changes of organisation occurred among the Household troops. First, in 1678, the two English Regiments of Foot Guards each received a 'grenadier company'.[9] These men were armed with hatchets and grenades, and they wore caps instead of broad-brimmed hats, so that they could easily sling their firelocks over either shoulder. Evelyn described them in his diaries as wearing 'furred hats with coped crowns, which gave them a fierce expression . . . their clothing was piebald yellow and red'. Their special role was to lead the assault on fortifications, which was a demanding task, and they were therefore normally men of above average height and physique. The Guards were pioneers of this development, and it was not till the reign of James II that all infantry regiments were similarly organised.

Secondly, the three English troops of The Life Guards were similarly strengthened by the raising of three troops of 'Horse Grenadier Guards', who were in effect mounted infantry. Each troop consisted of three officers and 90 other ranks, and their tactics were that they rode into battle, and then 'dismounted, linked their horses, fired, screwed their daggers into the muzzles of their fusils, charged, returned their daggers, fired, and threw their grenades by ranks.'[10] They were described by Evelyn as 'very fierce and fantastical' (see illustration on page 44).

It was about this period too that 'double rank' became more general. This arrangement had always existed in The Life Guards, because many of their officers, who held high rank in the Royalist Army in the Civil War, loyally joined the King in exile in a junior rank. To compensate them, Charles II ordered in 1661 that they should be allowed to hold one rank above that of their actual appointment in the army.

The privilege was extended to the Foot Guards in 1687, when Captains were granted the 'double rank' of Lieutenant Colonel; four years later Lieutenants received 'double rank' too, but it was not granted to the junior rank of Ensign until 1815. The system continued for almost two centuries, not being abolished until the Cardwell reforms of the Army in 1871.

Charles II died in 1685, and was succeeded by his brother, James. There now followed a second period of religious and political dissension in the country almost comparable to the Civil War.

It began with the rebellion by the Duke of Monmouth and his defeat at the Battle of Sedgemoor on 7 July 1685, in which all the Guards Regiments were involved.

1686 was a notable year, because the Scottish Regiment of Foot Guards came onto the strength of the English Army for the first time. They also formed their fourteen companies into two battalions, one of which came south and joined the training camp set up by the King on Hounslow Heath. Being the junior Guards Regiment present, they were greeted with the nickname of 'The Kiddies', which has remained with them ever since.

The Abdication (1688)

1688 saw the loyalties of the country, and of the Royal troops in particular, tested severely. The King's failings, and above all his determination to convert Britain to Catholicism, had alienated him from a large part of the population, including many Army officers, some of whom he had dismissed on religious grounds. Others, including the Earl of Oxford, had resigned on grounds of conscience, because they refused to appoint Catholic officers as demanded by the King.

The final test came when the Protestant Prince William of Orange landed in Devon on 5 November 1688, at the instigation of several leading figures in the country. His aim was to drive James from the throne, and restore Protestantism to the country. This situation forced all ranks of the Household troops to make the hard choice between loyalty to their unpopular, Catholic-minded Sovereign and loyalty to a foreign, Protestant invader.

In the event, most of the Guards Regiments stood by their King, though some of the Scots Guards, because of their opposition to Catholicism, went over to Prince William. Happily, the whole Regiment was reunited after James fled.

Some individuals also deserted the King, notably Lieutenant General the Earl of Grafton, who had succeeded Colonel John Russell as Colonel of the First Guards. This drew the comment from the old Marshal Schomberg, serving with Prince William, that this was 'the first lieutenant general he had heard of that deserted his colours'.

GRENA. G.

In the event, no blood was shed, although James II ordered a substantial force, which included both Life Guards and some Foot Guards, to Salisbury, to prevent the invaders from reaching the capital.

Then, on the night of 11 December, James made his historic flight from London, throwing the Great Seal into the Thames on the way. He was recognised, however, when he reached Sheerness, and was almost captured by Protestant supporters. He was rescued just in time by Lord Feversham, who conducted him back to London with an escort of 240 loyal Life Guards and Horse Grenadiers.

But James was not prepared to fight for his throne, and when the 82-year-old Earl of Craven, Colonel of the Coldstream Guards, wanted to send his Regiment to halt Prince William's forces as they approached London, the King personally forbade him to do so.

Finally, on 18 December 1688, James II fled and the Prince entered London, where he was crowned as King William III.

The new Monarch broke with tradition from the start by having his Coronation on 11 April, instead of on St George's Day, 23 April. In addition, he was actually crowned by Bishop Compton of London, because the Archbishop of Canterbury refused to officiate.

Bishop Henry Compton, youngest son of the Earl of Northampton, had in fact been an officer in The Blues before joining the Church. He was a firm and outspoken Protestant, and had consequently been 'suspended' by James II for two years from 1686. A man of deeds rather than words (James II complained that 'he talked more like a colonel than a bishop') he firmly put his signature to the 'invitation to invade', which was sent to Prince William of Orange.

He then helped King James's daughter, the future Queen Anne, to escape from her apartments in Whitehall, and, dressed now as a Colonel with a sword at his side, he rode off with her to support Prince William. Soon afterwards, he re-entered his see – riding happily at the head of a troop of horse in the best traditions of a fighting bishop.

Horse Grenadier, 1751. He wears the same cap as his counterpart on foot, and carries a fusil as well as a sword.

William and Mary (1688–1702)

Even though he was accepted as King, William found that his position was far from secure. He was faced not only by an England still sharply divided between Protestant and Catholic beliefs, but also by external threats from Jacobite supporters in Scotland and Ireland.

One of his first acts was to order all the English Guards Regiments out of London. The Life Guards were sent to Ireland and The Blues to Flanders. The Coldstream Guards were particularly suspect, as a result of the Earl of Craven's loyalty to James II, and within three months both their battalions were despatched to Flanders, while their Colonel was dismissed.

The Earl of Oxford, on the other hand, was restored to command of his Regiment, as was the Earl of Grafton.

Guard duties in the capital were handed over to the King's own Dutch Life Guards, who were mounted on grey horses. When the Dutch Guards departed in March 1689, their mounts were given to the 2nd Dragoons, who became known thereafter as 'The Greys'.

Strangely 'The Blues' in the British Army probably also owe their title to these Dutch cavalry, for the former were now increasingly called the 'Oxford Blues' to distinguish them from the 'Dutch Blues'.

The Jacobite War (1689–96)

In 1689 the King sent a force to Flanders under the command of Lieutenant General John Churchill, now Earl of Marlborough, and it is of interest as the first occasion on which all five Guards Regiments then in existence were together on active service. (See Map 2, page 28.)

There was little fighting for the first two years however, and in 1690, King William took an army of about 37,000, which included The Life Guards and The Blues, from Flanders to Ireland in an effort to settle the Jacobite rebellion there. On 1 July, he decisively defeated James II and his army at the Battle of the Boyne, and the threat from Ireland was removed for the moment.

One result of this defeat for the Irish was the formation of the Irish Brigade, which was to earn a great reputation fighting as mercenaries for France for the next century, and was to find itself opposed to the British Army on several future occasions, notably at the Battle of Fontenoy.

Having settled Ireland, the army now returned to Flanders, but no major engagement occurred until the Battle of Steenkirk on 3 August 1692.

This was an unfortunate affair. The Earl of Marlborough had been deprived of his command because of political intrigue at home, and he actually spent the summer of 1692 imprisoned in the Tower.

The King was in overall command, and he planned a surprise dawn attack, led by the 2nd Battalion of the First Guards. The initial success was not followed up, however, and the French soon brought up strong reinforcements, so that thirteen British battalions were finally faced by no less than 53 French battalions, including the Swiss and French Guards, supported by seven regiments of dragoons.

At the crucial moment, the British reserves could have won the day, but they were controlled by the Dutch general, Count Solmes, who had led the Dutch Guards into London in 1688, and had the remarkable distinction of hating the British. He refused to send the reserves forward, growling, 'Damn the English; if they are so fond of fighting, let them have a bellyful.'

Disaster was averted by the cavalry, but it was a defeat nevertheless, and is not a Battle Honour.

Another battle which ended in defeat but with honour for the Guards, was at Landen on 29 July 1693. Two Guards Brigades[11] were involved in this dour contest, as well as The Life Guards. This is the first occasion in which the Foot Guards fought as brigades, under their own Guards officers, a system followed from then onwards.

The English and Dutch were in a defensive position, to which the key was the village of Neerwinden, and the defence of the sector was given to the two Guards Brigades, together with a battalion of the Royal Scots, the Seventh Fusiliers and some Hanoverians.

All day, this force held out against a series of attacks by twenty-six French battalions, and only when their ammunition ran out, and they had lost 4,000 men, did they withdraw. They were saved by a series of fine last-minute charges by the heavy cavalry consisting of The Life Guards and five regiments of Dragoons.

It was a dramatic encounter, for the English Life Guards met their French equivalent – and routed them. The fine cavalry action could do no more, however, than avert complete disaster for the allied army, which retreated across the river that night. The King distinguished himself again under fire, and indeed was nearly captured at one moment, being rescued by the Third Troop of The Life Guards.

A victory, for a change, was the capture on 30 August 1695 of the fortress of Namur where the Guards formed the assault troops and also gained their second Battle Honour (although it was not awarded until 1910).

Preceded by their grenadier companies, the two Guards Brigades advanced steadily with shouldered arms across half a mile of flat, open country, against the concentrated fire of the French defenders. On reaching the palisades, they thrust their flintlocks through, fired one volley, then flung themselves over the ramparts and stormed the defences. A Marshal of France was captured in this action, which was a rare achievement indeed.

Both Guards Brigades were commanded on this occasion by Lord Cutts, Colonel of the Coldstream, an officer so renowned for his exceptional coolness and bravery under fire, that he was given the nickname throughout the Army of 'Salamander Cutts'.[12]

After the action, he was appointed a 'Brigadier of the Guards', an honour never previously enjoyed by any officer.

He became a major general in 1702, and died in 1707 while Commander-in-Chief in Ireland. Sadly, he was by then so impoverished that his staff had to contribute £10 each to have their general buried with due honours.

This story of the campaigns of the Guards began with a naval action, and it ends with another, for on 2 June 1694, a 'commando' raid was carried out against the port of Brest, as part of the campaign against France. A Composite Guards Battalion took part, but the operation failed, largely it was believed as a result of treachery. Major General Tolmach of the Coldstream Guards was in command of the expedition and himself died of wounds received in the action. He was a distinguished soldier, who featured as 'Talmash' in Laurence Sterne's 'Tristram Shandy'. His descendants have served almost constantly in the Coldstream Guards since, the family name being Tollemache.

The war finally ended with the Peace of Ryswick on 11 September 1697, and the two Guards Brigades returned home to London.

Home Service

Their primary task here was, of course, to ensure the safety of the King and his property. The protection of the Royal residence in Whitehall meant that men were usually on duty about one day in six. In addition, an Escort of 160 men was called for every time the King went out, and this responsibility, which was the sole prerogative of The Life Guards, kept them fully occupied. They did not as yet receive any help from The Blues, who were normally stationed in the provinces.

The Life Guards had also since 1664 had special responsibilities with regard to the protection of the Sovereign *within* his palaces, as well as outside. This was a very real commitment in those days, when there was neither a police force nor Special Branch, to guard against the constant plotting by political and religious bodies who sought to attack the Monarchy.

Following the threat to the King's life revealed by the Titus Oates affair in 1678, Charles II had decided that he and the Queen must have even closer protection at all times. He gave this duty to The Life Guards, and issued a Royal Order dated 1678[13] which stated that The Life Guards had the responsibility of:

attendance on the King's person on foot, wheresoever he walk, from his rising to his going to bed, and this is performed by one of the three Captains, who always waits immediately next to the King's own person, before all others carrying in his hand an ebony staff or truncheon with a gold head, engraved with His Majesty's cypher and crown ... near him also attends another principal Commissioned Officer, with an ebony staff and silver head, who is ready to relieve the Captain on occasions.

There were also two subordinate appointments called 'Ivory Sticks', but they were discontinued in 1760.

From this sprang the appointments, still very much in being today, of the Gold Stick-in-Waiting, and the Silver Stick-in-Waiting. In addition to his duty of being in constant attendance on the Sovereign, the Gold Stick-in-Waiting passed any wishes and orders of the Sovereign which involved the Household Cavalry, direct to the Regiments rather than 'through the usual Army channels'. It was not until the reign of William IV that the Household Cavalry accepted instructions from the Commander-in-Chief direct.

The appointment of Gold Stick-in-Waiting is today held, in rotation for a month at a time, by the Colonels of the two Household Cavalry Regiments. The Silver Stick is *ex officio* the serving officer holding the post of Officer Commanding the Household Cavalry. These officers are no longer in constant attendance on the Sovereign, but they are always present on State occasions, where the Gold Stick-in-Waiting takes precedence over all other officers of the Armed Forces.

So are customs and traditions born.

Chapter 4

France the Foe (1700–75)

The eighteenth century was a period of war, one campaign following another with grim regularity, as Britain and France struggled for power in Europe and overseas.

All three Regiments of Foot Guards were involved in most of the campaigns, and they now developed as normal procedure the custom, first seen at Landen in 1693, of fighting as Guards Brigades under the command of a Guards general.

Both The Life Guards and The Blues, however, spent one of their longest periods on home service, lasting from 1692 to 1742.

Marlborough's War (1702–13)

The first campaign was the War of the Spanish Succession which broke out in 1702. As so often, it found Britain militarily unprepared; the Army had been reduced to a mere 19,000, and more than half of them were in Ireland, where rebellion continued to smoulder.

The country did however have one great asset in the shape of John Churchill, Duke of Marlborough, formerly First Guards. He was now to lead the allied armies in a series of brilliantly successful campaigns against the French, with the First Battalion of his old Regiment under his command throughout.

Little happened in 1702 except for an abortive raid on Cadiz, in which the usual Composite Guards Battalion took part. A detachment of The Life

Guards was also present, escorting the Duke of Ormonde of The Life Guards, who was joint commander of the expedition with Admiral Sir George Rooke.

The main fighting occurred in Marlborough's campaign in central Europe, and here 1st Bn First Guards were the only representatives of the Household Division for the first six years.

The 'Forlorn Hope'

It was in July 1704 that Marlborough marched across Europe to attack the French and Bavarian forces on the Danube, and found them established on a fortified hill called the Schellenberg overlooking Donauwörth on the north bank of the river. Marlborough knew that they would be reinforced the next day, and he considered that his best, indeed his only chance of defeating them was therefore to attack at once. (See Map 1.)

Despite the protests of his allies, he gave orders that the assault must be launched that evening, even though the troops had only just completed a forced march of sixteen hours.

The force selected consisted of sixteen battalions, including the First Guards, whose grenadier company under Colonel Lord Mordaunt was made the spearhead of the attack.

It seemed a 'forlorn hope' that they could possibly succeed in capturing this strongly defended feature, and it is as such that their exploit has gone down in history.

Under intense fire, the force struggled up the steep hill, holding their own fire until they were within 80 yards of the enemy. At one moment, it seemed that the attack must fail, but they pressed on, gained their objectives, and even repelled a fierce counter-attack.

Casualties were heavy, and only 21 of 82 men in the grenadier company survived. Incredibly they included Lord Mordaunt, who escaped with three bullet holes through his clothing, while another officer, Colonel Munden had five through his hat.

Then just in time, the main body of Marlborough's army arrived and, attacking the French flank, drove them back in disorder. Unable to escape across the river, three quarters of the French Army were destroyed.

In a mere hour and a half, a decisive victory had been won; it was an event of great psychological significance, being the first real defeat suffered by the French and their allies for forty years.

Blenheim (13 August 1704)

Six weeks later on 13 August, Marlborough won his 'famous victory'[14] at Blenheim, and again the First Guards were the only Household troops to gain this Battle Honour.

Marlborough had discovered, in the course of the detailed reconnaissance that he always carried out before his battles, that the French positions were vulnerable in the centre, because the bulk of their forces were being used to fortify the key village of Blenheim on their right flank.

He allotted to the infantry the vital task of attacking Blenheim, as the prelude to a decisive cavalry attack which he planned against the weak French centre at a later stage.

The First Guards were normally held as Marlborough's personal reserve, but on this occasion he attached them to Row's Brigade, where they joined four battalions[15] of the Line. These five English battalions had the formidable task of advancing in the open against élite French battalions established in a strongly fortified position in Blenheim.

Under the leadership of General 'Salamander' Cutts, they attacked with great gallantry twice, but they could not penetrate the defences. They did, however, accomplish what was required of them, by paving the way for the cavalry, who successfully broke through the enemy centre and inflicted a crushing defeat on the French Army.

The cost was high on both sides. The allies lost 12,000,[16] but the enemy lost around 40,000 men, together with 100 guns and 300 colours and standards.

Most important of all, Blenheim shattered the bogey of French military supremacy, and raised the morale of the allies as could nothing else. For decades, the French had seemed invincible both for their generalship and for the valour and skill of their troops. But now they had been thoroughly trounced by Marlborough, not once but twice, and were in full flight back to France.

The war continued its course, with the victory of Ramillies (23 May 1706) in which the First Guards were again the only Guards Regiment involved. But in 1708 they were joined by a composite Battalion of First and Coldstream Guards, whereupon a Guards Brigade was formed, which took part in the successful battles of Oudenarde (11 July 1708) and Malplaquet (11 September 1709).

The war petered out, however, from then onwards, despite some further successes. In 1711, Marlborough was accused of political intrigue, and was removed from all public office, including his military command. Two years later the Treaty of Utrecht was signed, and the Guards returned home in March 1713.

Meanwhile the allies were also waging a secondary campaign in Spain, which was to lead to two severe blows for the Foot Guards. (See Map 1.)

The Rock of Gibraltar had been captured from Spain in 1704 by a detachment of Marines[17] under Admiral Sir George Rooke, but reinforcements were required to hold it against determined Spanish efforts to regain this prestige fortress.

The second draft sent there included another composite Guards Battalion (200 First Guards and 400 Coldstream Guards) who helped to repel several attacks on Gibraltar, and acquired another Battle Honour thereby. They then joined in the sortie into Spain which began with the capture of Barcelona

51

in 1705, but ended two years later with defeat at the Battle of Almanza, when the entire British force, including the composite Guards Battalion, was forced to surrender.

The disaster was repeated in 1710 when another allied force was besieged in Brihuega, and despite a gallant defence, finally surrendered. The Royal Dragoons and the 1st Battalion of the Scottish Foot Guards were both part of this force, and the latter earned high praise for their fighting qualities; but it was a bitter blow to them to suffer such a setback in their first campaign as part of the British Army.

This second defeat meant the end of allied operations in Spain, and comparative peace ensued for the next twenty-six years.

Home Service

The Act of Union in 1707 led to the Scottish elements of the Household troops being brought south. They now began to wear the badge of the Order of the Thistle, and changed their coat facings from white to the Royal blue already being worn by the First and Coldstream Guards.

In February 1712 the 2nd Bn of the Scottish Regiment of Foot Guards were ordered from Edinburgh to London, and from that date, the Regiment did not do duty in its native land again until 1911. Also in 1712, the Regiment was officially given the title of 'Third Regiment of Foot Guards', which it was to retain until 1831.

The Household Cavalry also received a Scottish element into their ranks, when the 4th or Scots Troop of Life Guards moved south and joined the remainder of the Regiment in London in 1712.

In 1714, George I came to the throne, and introduced several much-needed reforms into the Army. Annual inspections of units began to be carried out, and attempts were made to check some of the worst abuses, such as officers who drew their pay but seldom appeared on parade.

Sadly, this was neither a happy nor a creditable time for the Army, and relations between them and the nation were generally poor. As a result, pay and conditions were not improved, discipline became lax, and efficiency deteriorated; it was not till the middle of the century that the situation improved.

In 1750, the Horse Guards building was re-designed by William Kent, and the King opened it formally the next year, by riding through the Arch. It was occupied not only by the Guards, but also by the Secretary of War and his staff.

War of the Austrian Succession (1740–8)

The causes of this war are involved, and are largely irrelevant to our story. Suffice it to say that when Britain sent an expeditionary force to the Continent in 1742, it included not only a Household Cavalry Brigade, created for the first time, with The Life Guards, The Blues, and The Royals, but also a Guards Brigade consisting of the 1st Battalions of all three Regiments of Foot Guards.

Two battles, Dettingen and Fontenoy, are of particular interest for the part played by the Guards.

A Private, a Drummer, and an Officer of the First Guards in 1745.

BATTLE OF DETTINGEN (27 JUNE 1743) This battle is well-known as the last occasion on which a King of England personally led his army into action.

The allied army in Flanders was commanded initially by Lord Stair, but in the summer of 1743 King George II arrived to command his troops in person, and promptly led them into a trap carefully laid for him by the skilled French General Noailles.

On 27 June, the allied army of more than 40,000 found themselves marching into a narrow defile with the unfordable River Main on their left, and impenetrable woods and hills on their right. The next moment they discovered that the road ahead through the little village of Dettingen was blocked by a French force of 28,000, while others had closed in behind them.

Fortunately the French force in Dettingen attacked before the trap was properly closed, and the allies were able to survive, and indeed turn what might have been a disastrous defeat into a victory.

The Household Cavalry Brigade, under the Earl of Crawford, were more heavily engaged in the battle than the Guards Brigade, who formed the rearguard and were not committed until the final stages.

The cavalry made several charges mostly against the French and Swiss Guards, and finally drove the enemy back against the river.

During one charge by The Life Guards at the height of the battle, Lord Crawford's trumpeter urged his comrades on with the notes of 'Britons Strike Home' from Purcell's opera *Boadicea*, and The Life Guards trumpeters still play a fanfare version of this today.

The French finally suffered a severe defeat, losing 5,000 men, many of whom were drowned while trying to swim across the River Main as the only means of escape.

The King's tactical skill was limited, but he fully made up for this by considerable courage in the thick of the fighting. He was escorted by the Gold Stick and a detachment of thirty-six men from The Life Guards, several of whom became casualties. At one stage his horse ran away with him, but he seemed to revel in the excitement, and set a fine example. When his staff remonstrated with him for exposing himself unduly, he replied, 'Do you think I came here to be a poltroon?'

BATTLE OF FONTENOY (11 MAY 1745) In 1745, the King gave overall command to his twenty-five year old son, the Duke of Cumberland. Immediately under him was the Austrian General Graf von Königseck aged seventy-three; so Cumberland's youth should have been tempered somewhat by the age of his deputy. But it did not work out that way.

The Duke of Cumberland's first venture was the Battle of Fontenoy on 11 May 1745, which was one of the bloodiest fought to date. It was also grossly mismanaged, and ended in defeat, so that it is not recorded as a battle honour.

It is however worthy of recall for a historic encounter between the British Guards and their French counterpart, and for the exploits of Lieutenant Colonel Lord Charles Hay of the First Guards.

Cumberland's plan went astray from the start for various reasons, and he was finally reduced to launching a frontal attack against the enemy centre. On either flank were French strongpoints, which had not been captured, as they should have been, and the assault had therefore to be carried out across half a mile of open country, swept by point blank fire from both flanks.

The Guards Brigade were on the right of the leading line in their customary positions, that is the First Guards on the right, the Coldstream on the left and the Third Guards in the centre. The brigade was commanded by

Negro Trumpeter, 1750. Negroes were often engaged as military musicians until the middle of the nineteenth century.

54

Colonel George Churchill (Coldstream Guards), who had succeeded
Charles, 2nd Duke of Marlborough (First Guards).

With shouldered arms, the three Guards battalions marched steadily forward, shoulder to shoulder, ignoring the intense fire which swept great gaps
in the line. As they advanced further, this fire began to come from behind
them, while ahead, protected by a ridge, the massed French infantry awaited
them.

As the Foot Guards, now seriously reduced in numbers, topped the crest
ahead of them, they found themselves facing at a range of some thirty yards
four complete battalions of French Guards, as yet unscathed.

As the front rank halted, preparatory to opening fire for the first time,
Lord Charles Hay of the King's Company of the First Guards stepped forward and doffed his hat.

He then pulled out a flask, raised it and drank a toast to the astonished
French troops, a stone's throw from him.

'Gentlemen of the French Guard,' he called out, 'I hope you will wait for
us today, and not escape by swimming the Scheldt as you swam the Main at
Dettingen.'

He then turned to his own men, and continued:

'Men of the King's Company, these are the French Guards, and I hope you
are going to beat them today.'

His Guardsmen answered with a cheer, though one Private was heard to
mutter. 'For what we are about to receive, may the Lord make us truly
thankful.'

At this point, the French opened fire,[18] but they seem to have been so
distracted by Lord Charles's performance, that they fired high.

The turn of the British had come at last. Down came the muskets, and a
deadly volley rang out, which laid low nineteen French officers and 600
men.

Steadily, the British reloaded, firing in disciplined sequence, six platoons
at a time, so that the volleys never ceased. The muskets of those days had a
barrel that was 39 inches long, with a calibre equal to a modern 12 bore.
They were muzzle-loading and fired a ball $\frac{3}{4}$ inch in diameter and weighing
$1\frac{1}{4}$ oz. They tended to fire high, and so the officers kept tapping down the
muzzles with their canes to keep the men's aim straight.

French casualties mounted and the British infantry advanced steadily
right into the enemy camp. But their allies failed to move forward to their
support at this crucial moment, and before long both flanks were again
dangerously exposed.

Now the enemy cavalry appeared, and the French Life Guards charged
repeatedly. But for three hours, the Guardsmen stood firm.

Support was now urgent, and the Dutch could have saved the day, but
still they would not move.

The French threw in yet more reserves, including the Irish Brigade
(see also page 46) and finally the British were forced to withdraw, with the
Guards Brigade acting as rearguard.

The British cavalry had not been employed as early as they might have been, but at this crucial moment, they charged repeatedly in the face of fierce artillery fire, and so enabled the infantry to complete their withdrawal.

'You have gained as much honour,' declared Lord Crawford, 'in covering so great a retreat, as if you had won a battle.'

Nevertheless, it had been a bitter and a bloody defeat, in which the allied forces lost 6000 out of 15,000, and each Guards battalion lost almost half its strength.

Captain Lord Charles Hay was seriously wounded, but received many messages of congratulations for his behaviour. Sadly, though, his military career came to an untimely end later, when as a Major General, he was court-martialled for making insubordinate remarks in Canada about his superior officer, the Commander-in-Chief Lord Loudoun.

According to the charge sheet, he accused his Lordship of 'making sham sieges and planting cabbages, when he ought to have been fighting'. He was

The Battle of Fontenoy, 1745. Lord Charles Hay (centre, facing), exchanges courtesies with the Commander of the French Guards before the exchange of fire.

found guilty, and died while waiting for the sentence of cashiering to be confirmed by the King.

The '45

In July 1745, a new threat arose at home when Charles Stuart, grandson of James II, landed in Scotland, and stirred up rebellion there. Having defeated the English at Prestonpans in September, he advanced boldly towards London.

The grenadier companies of the Guards battalions in London joined a scratch force assembled to defend the capital, while the Guards Brigade in Flanders was hurriedly ordered home.

The threat faded, however, and Cumberland pursued the Jacobite army northwards, with a force of cavalry, supplemented by 1000 'mounted volunteers', 400 of whom were found by the Foot Guards – not the only occasion on which they have gone into action on horseback. (See also page 151.)

This mounted force returned after relieving Carlisle, but Cumberland continued into Scotland, and crushed the Jacobite threat for ever at the Battle of Culloden Moor on 16 April 1746, in which the Guards were not involved.

When Cumberland returned to Flanders in 1747, he took with him a fresh Guards Brigade composed this time of the second battalion of each Regiment; they returned home in 1748, when war was ended by the Treaty of Aix-la-Chapelle.

Seven Years War (1756–63)

The peace that followed lasted only eight years, and in 1756 trouble on the Continent led to yet another campaign against the French, the Seven Years War.

The Guards were not involved initially, but in 1758, a Guards Brigade, composed of the 1st Battalion of each Regiment, took part in several somewhat abortive raids on the French coast.

An attack against St Malo in September was a disaster, for the rearguard consisting of four companies of the 1st Battalion First Guards, together with the grenadier companies of all three Regiments, was cut off by superior enemy forces. They fought as long as their ammunition lasted, but finally surrendered; 800 were killed or wounded and the same number were taken prisoner.

For the remainder of the campaign, the limelight fell on The Blues, and in particular, on their flamboyant Colonel, John Manners, Marquess of Granby.

THE MARQUESS OF GRANBY In July and August 1758, a British force of 12,000 was sent to Germany to join the allied army which was commanded by Prince Ferdinand of Brunswick. The Foot Guards were not included, having been kept at home because of the threat of invasion. The Blues however formed part of a Cavalry Brigade under Major General The Marquess of Granby, who had just become their Colonel.

They were therefore the only Household Division troops involved in the great Battle of Minden on 1 August 1759, where six British battalions attacked and drove back forty French battalions, supported by sixty squadrons of cavalry.

The part played by the British cavalry that day was less glorious, owing to the failure of their British commander, Lord George Sackville, to commit them at the crucial moment.

Four aides were sent to Lord Sackville telling him to send forward the cavalry, but he did nothing. Finally the Prince sent a fifth aide direct to Lord Granby, remarking very rightly, 'I know he at least will obey me.'

He did indeed, and his brigade charged to support the hard-pressed infantry.

But now it was too late, for the Hanoverian cavalry had achieved what the British should have done, and the French were in full flight. Even now Lord Sackville[19] would allow no pursuit, and the magnificent achievements of the infantry were not exploited as they should have been.

The Marquess of Granby.

59

Minden is not a Battle Honour of The Blues, though it does appear, curiously, on the personal Guidon presented to the Regiment by King William IV.

The Blues distinguished themselves at the Battle of Warburg on 31 July 1760, a memorable day for the Regiment and for their Colonel.

On this occasion he was in command of all the British cavalry, in the place of the disgraced Lord Sackville, and he personally led them in three charges against the French. The Blues yielded their place on the right of the line, that was theirs by seniority, so that they could ride behind their Colonel who led in the centre.

Galloping at their head, Granby lost both his hat and his wig, and his bald head, gleaming in the sunlight, served effectively as a rallying point for The Blues, as they swept aside the French cavalry and infantry.

Three squadrons of French cavalry counter-attacked but were driven off, and finally the enemy retreated. Granby with ten squadrons and twelve battalions chased them hard, and the battle ended as a fine victory.

The bold leadership of Granby is remembered by the phrase 'going baldheaded for it' which originated from his exploits in this battle.

Also, because Lord Granby was hatless and wigless when he later saluted Prince Ferdinand, The Blues have ever since retained the custom of saluting their officers, even when bareheaded – a custom unique in the Army today.

A Guards Brigade under the command of a Coldstream General with the unusual name of Julius Caesar, and composed of the second battalion of each Regiment, had arrived in Germany in 1760. A year later, the grenadier companies of the three Regiments were formed into a composite Grenadier Battalion, which then became a fourth battalion of the brigade, a practice that was to be followed for the next fifty years.

The Guards Brigade was not however seriously engaged until the Battle of Wilhelmstal (24 June 1762) where the official despatch reported that 'Granby did the whole business . . . . His Blues did almost beyond anything that was ever done by a regiment of cavalry.'

The Guards Brigade returned home early in 1763, and Lord Granby was greeted very rightly as a national hero. He was at pains to look after members of his Regiment who were in need on leaving the Army, and he set many of them up as publicans, which accounts for the number of inns all over the country which still bear his name.

So ended sixty years, in which the British Army, including always some Guards units, had spent twenty-four years fighting the French somewhere on the Continent.

Their next campaign was to be on the other side of the Atlantic.

Chapter 5

Eighteenth Century Soldiering (1750–1802)

As a change from the continuous struggle against France, a new challenge materialised in 1775, when the dissatisfied settlers in the British territories in North America dared to defy Britain and to demand their Independence.

The War of American Independence (1775–83)

This early puff of the 'wind of change' produced a predictable response in Whitehall, and a force was despatched across the Atlantic to 'teach the rebels a lesson'.

The expedition included a composite Guards Battalion[20] drawn from all three Regiments, and they set sail for America in March 1776. The voyage took no less than five months, and it was August before the troops thankfully set foot on dry land.

Almost immediately, they were involved in the capture of New York, and no doubt the Coldstreamers present reminded the First and Third Guards that the Coldstream had already carried out that operation once before just 111 years earlier. (See page 39.)

The Guards contingent fought throughout the campaign, and were involved in most of the engagements of 1776–7. This was followed by two years of garrison duty in New York, before they were sent south to join General Cornwallis in Carolina.

Throughout this war, the British troops in their conspicuous uniforms found themselves at a distinct disadvantage against the unorthodox mobile tactics of the American settlers whose camouflaged sharp-shooters caused undue casualties to the 'redcoats.' In an attempt to counter this, the Guards formed a 'light company', consisting of men specially trained and equipped to act as skirmishers, and protect the vulnerable ranks of infantry. This was the first occasion on which the rigid parade ground manoeuvring of the last hundred years was modified, and it was to lead to the acceptance of 'light companies' as a normal part of regular infantry battalions.

In February 1781, the brigade distinguished itself when the troops waded waist high for 500 yards across the flooded Catawba River in North Carolina under heavy fire from the opposite bank, and then drove back the American defenders.

Six weeks later, on 15 March, both battalions took part in the Battle of Guildford Court House where they helped defeat a numerically superior American force. It was an expensive victory however, and they lost almost half their strength, a setback that Cornwallis could ill afford.

It was in fact the beginning of the end for the British Army in the south. Soon afterwards, Cornwallis found himself cornered in Yorktown, and after a brief defence, he surrendered on 19 October 1781 with his entire force of 6,000 men, including 500 men of the Guards Brigade.

The American colonies were granted their independence in November 1782, and the next year Britain also came to terms with France, Spain and Holland. A peace of exhaustion ensued, but within a decade, Europe was once again plunged into war.

Fighting Revolutionary France (1793–1800)

The French Revolution of 1789 altered the face of Europe militarily as well as politically. It marked the beginning of a war of over twenty years, that was to be the last between England and France, and was to end in a decisive defeat for the French.

It also produced for the first time the phenomenon of 'a nation at arms', as Napoleon built up a huge army of conscripts for his campaigns against the standing armies and the professional mercenaries of France's enemies.

Tactics too began to change from the rigid rules of war that had prevailed largely unaltered since the days of the Roman phalanx. The adoption of skirmishers in the French Revolutionary Army, together with the lessons learned in North America, led to the development of similar tactics in the British Army, and to the formation of the Light Infantry Regiments and the Rifle Brigade.

The Foot Guards had disbanded the skirmishers they had formed in America, but now in 1793 they formed six 'light companies' from the Second Battalion in each Regiment. They wore a form of shako with a green plume, and became the left flank companies, while the grenadier company continued to hold the right flank.

Britain's strategy, as planned by the Prime Minister, William Pitt, was to try to weaken the power of victorious France (who had just conquered Italy, Switzerland and Austria) by using Britain's sea power to attack France's overseas possessions. But an obligation to support our ally, Holland,

62

REG.^t of G^{ds}

COLDSTREAM GARDS

REG.^t of G^{ds}

led to an expeditionary force being earmarked to embark for operations there.

Prospects were not encouraging for any concerted action among the Allies. The Dutch were not particularly enthusiastic, and Spain was too weak and corrupt to be effective. The other two allies, Austria and Prussia, distrusted each other to the point of non-cooperation.

The British Army, too, was in a parlous state, for it had been allowed to decline to a shameful level during the last thirty years of comparative peace. It was only with the greatest difficulty that an expeditionary force could be raised at all, and it was then disgracefully ill-equipped and supplied.

Grenadiers from the First Guards, Coldstream Guards, and Third Guards in 1751. The 'grenadier company' was always the right flank company in each battalion. All the Foot Guards Regiments wore their buttons singly until 1774.

LIGHT INFANTRY *of the* FOOT GUARDS

Four of these new rais'd Companys Embarked to join the DUKE of YORK in the Siege of VALENCIENNES July 9.th 1793.

A private of the Light Company, 1793. The light company acted as skirmishers in battle, and normally stood in the left flank on parade.

The troops most available and ready for action were as usual the Foot Guards, and they were hurriedly formed into a Guards Brigade consisting of the First Battalion of each Regiment, together with a fourth, or Flank Battalion formed from the grenadier companies and the light companies.

They sailed for Holland in February 1793, and thus had the dubious honour of being among the first British troops to engage the armies of Revolutionary France on the Continent, in a struggle that was to be fought out in Flanders, Egypt, Portugal and Spain, and was to end twenty-two years later at Waterloo.

But in 1793, they were so ill-equipped, with no transport, no reserve ammunition and few stores, that victory seemed remote. Indeed, shipping was so short that they had to sail to Holland in Thames coal barges.

64

Nor was it any better when they finally reached Holland, for the allied commanders quarrelled among themselves and missed every opportunity of victory, while the French grew daily stronger.

It was an uninspiring start, but there was a moment of glory on 18 August 1793, when the Guards were sent to support the Prince of Orange whose troops had been driven from the village of Lincelles.

On arrival, the brigade commander, Major General Lake, found that some 5,000 French troops were strongly entrenched in the village, which was on a hill with both flanks protected by woods. But there was no sign of the Prince and his troops, who were supposed to support the Guardsmen in any action taken.

Boldly Lake decided that, as the light was failing, his only hope lay in launching a frontal attack, even though he had only 1100 men against the 5000 French.

Despite heavy artillery and musketry fire against them, the three Guards battalions steadily climbed the steep slope, stormed the defences and cleared the village, thereby earning one more Battle Honour – the first actually awarded at the time.

The campaign dragged on, and The Blues distinguished themselves at Beaumont in April 1794, where they were among nineteen allied cavalry squadrons who charged and routed 20,000 French infantry. A month later, they fought alongside the Foot Guards at the successful battle of Tourcoing.

But the allies were still at loggerheads and their slow advance into France that summer turned into a grim retreat across Northern Europe during one of the severest winters of the century. Finally, in April 1795, the British expeditionary force was withdrawn from the Continent and the Guards Regiments gladly returned home.

During the next three years, Napoleon established himself as supreme in Europe. He defeated Austria in a brilliant campaign in Italy in 1796–7, and forced them to make peace. Russia withdrew from the struggle when Catharine the Great died in 1796, while Holland and Spain both came to terms with the triumphant French.

So by 1797, Britain stood alone yet again, facing an apparently invincible Napoleon, who made it clear that he was determined now to crush this last, defiant opponent of Revolutionary France.

Set now on world domination, Napoleon planned an invasion of England. But although he assembled an invasion fleet at Dunkirk, he was effectively prevented by the British Navy from ever using it. In February 1797, the Spanish Fleet was destroyed at Cape St Vincent, and the Dutch fleet met the same fate at Camperdown in October.

So the landing barges never set sail from Dunkirk, and England breathed again, just as she was to do in 1805 and then in 1940.

Egypt (1798–1801)

Just as Hitler in 1940 attacked Russia and Egypt when he was thwarted in his plans to invade Britain, so Napoleon in 1798 struck in the Middle East. A comparison of the two campaigns is intriguing, for whereas Rommel was stopped in 1941 in Egypt by General Auchinleck, so Napoleon was halted in 1799 in Palestine by the defiant garrison of Acre under Sidney Smith.

Thwarted, and also isolated, by Nelson's destruction of the French fleet in Aboukir Bay on 11 August 1798, Napoleon left his army in Egypt to their fate and returned himself the next year to France, where he overthrew the Government and became First Consul.

His first action was to set out to restore the situation in Italy, where the French were suffering reverses. He also defeated the Austrians and forced them to make peace at Luneville in February 1801.

Yet again, Britain stood alone, facing a formidable league of France, Spain, Denmark and Sweden. It was a grim prospect, brought home by the levying of a new 'income tax' at what was considered the monstrous rate of $2\frac{1}{2}$ per cent. But Britain as always used her sea power to open up operations on widely-scattered fronts, and two events at opposite ends of Europe were to change the situation dramatically within the next twelve months.

In January 1801, Nelson destroyed the Danish fleet at Copenhagen, while in December 1800, Abercromby sailed from Minorca (captured two years earlier) on an expedition that was soon to drive the French from Egypt. He had only 16,000 men and they were deficient in much of their equipment and other essentials; moreover, the Turkish support promised to them never materialised.

Opposed to him was the French army in Egypt, numbering about 25,000; but their morale was low, and their commander, General Menou was indifferent.

Included in Abercromby's force was a Guards Brigade consisting of 1st Bn Coldstream Guards, and 1st Bn Third Guards. They had joined him originally in Gibraltar in September 1800, and now they sailed with him from Minorca to the Bay of Marmorice on the coast of Turkey near the island of Rhodes.

There the whole force was relentlessly trained in conjunction with the Royal Navy in carrying out opposed landings, till everything ran like clock-work – an early instance of thorough combined operations planning. It was a precaution that was to pay good dividends.

ABOUKIR BAY (8 MARCH 1801) In March 1801, the force sailed for the selected landing place, Aboukir Bay, a beach about two miles wide at the tip of a long, narrow peninsula, ten miles east of Alexandria. It was covered by the guns of Aboukir Fort, and was such a strong defensive position that the French commander had confidently allotted only 2,000 men to man it. (See Map 3 on page 70.)

As was his custom, Abercromby made a detailed personal reconnaissance, rowing close inshore in a ship's boat to inspect the beaches. He then made a bold, but simple plan.

During the night of 8 March, the assault force was formed up in three lines of assault boats, each containing fifty men. There was fifty foot between each boat, and the right of each line was marked by the camp colours of the grenadier companies, as if on parade.

The force consisted altogether of nine battalions in three brigades as follows:

> Right ...   Moore's Brigade[21] of five battalions of the Line;
> Centre ...   Ludlow's Guards Brigade[22] of two Guards Battalions;
> Left ...   Coote's Brigade of two battalions of the Line.

As dawn broke, the flotilla moved slowly forward in perfect formation, watched by some astonished French picquets at the beaches. There was no firing, for the British soldiers had been ordered not to load their muskets, so as to 'keep their powder dry'. The only sound was the rattle of the rowlocks.

Then, with a roar, the guns of Aboukir Castle opened up, and columns of water sprang up round the boats from a storm of grape shot, round-shot and chain-shot. A direct hit sank one boat of fifty Coldstreamers and then one from the Third Guards was hit. Soon musketry fire added to the casualties.

But without reply, the boats pushed steadily ahead, and at last they grounded. The men leapt ashore, formed up as if on parade, and prepared to advance up the beaches.

Initially, there was some confusion in the Guards Regiments, due to their losses, and a French cavalry charge against them before they had re-formed, threatened to drive them back into the sea. But a volley from the left hand battalion of Moore's Brigade (the 58th Foot) gave the Guards time to load.

The French cavalry were repulsed, and all three British brigades advanced in line, just as on their many exercises. The French withdrew and the bridgehead was finally established.

It had been a highly hazardous operation, but thanks to discipline, leadership and training, it was a victory.

On 21 March, Abercromby advanced on Alexandria, where a fierce battle was fought, in which the Third Guards suffered 186 casualties. But the most serious loss was the death of the gallant Sir Ralph Abercromby, who had continued to lead the fighting all day despite a wound in the thigh, which later turned gangrenous.

His successor, General Hutchinson, captured Cairo on 27 June, while 6,000 men, including the Guards Brigade (now under the Earl of Cavan, First Guards), occupied Alexandria on 2 September. It marked the end of a highly successful campaign which left Egypt in the hands of Britain, and in December, the Guards Brigade sailed for home.

For their 'conspicuous service' on this campaign, the two Guards Regiments involved, the Coldstream and Third Guards, were awarded the distinction of carrying on their Colours a badge of a sphinx, superscribed with the word 'Egypt'.

Back in Britain, the resignation of Pitt had left England under the weak Government of Addington, and in 1802 they signed the Treaty of Amiens. But the peace lasted less than a year.

(Overleaf) Aboukir Bay, 1801. The Guards Brigade land and begin to form up on the beach in the face of attacks by French cavalry.

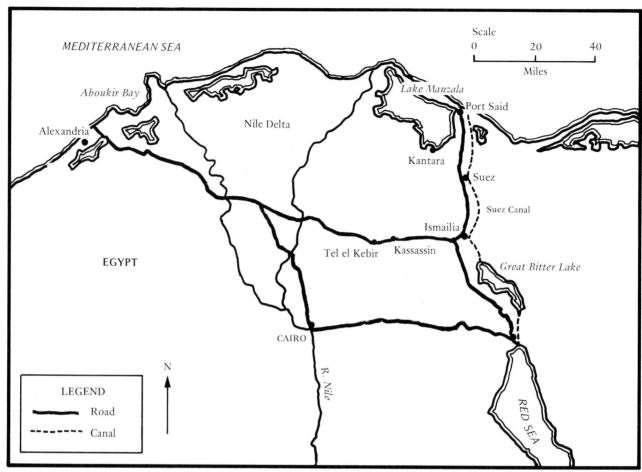

Home Service (1750–1800)

The eighteenth century will seem from the last two chapters to have been devoted entirely to campaigning overseas, but soldiering continued in Britain, particularly for the Household troops, who had the duty of protecting the Sovereign and maintaining law and order in the capital.

This was a very real commitment, for in 1795, for example, King George III was shot at while on his way to the House of Lords, and on the same day was stoned while driving between St James's Palace and Buckingham House.[23]

Major trouble developed in June 1780 when the somewhat eccentric Lord George Gordon stirred up such agitation against a pro-Catholic bill in Parliament that it developed into the famous Gordon Riots. For four days, mobs shouting 'No Popery!' rampaged through the streets of London, virtually controlling the city, until the King insisted that troops be employed to restore the situation.

Sergeant Pell, serving then with the First Guards, recorded in his diary that 'Regiments of Horse and Foot were daily pouring into London, so that it seemed like a seat of War.'

Twenty regiments were called in eventually, and the line of the River Thames was used to keep rioters on the south bank from crossing into Westminster and the City. A Guards Brigade was encamped in St James's Park and several other Regiments were in Hyde Park. Guards were mounted on key points, while detachments from the Foot Guards patrolled the streets.

Nevertheless, Newgate Prison was burned to the ground, and the Bank of England was attacked. The Lord Mayor had fortunately been granted 'some Horse and Foot in order to protect the Mansion House and the Bank', and they drove off the mob, inflicting several fatal casualties.

After almost a week of rioting, the troops were finally authorised to open fire to dispel the crowds, which they did to such effect that some 300 people were killed.

The Gordon Riots were over, but from then on the Foot Guards were called upon to provide a nightly picquet to guard the Bank of England, which they continued to do until 1973. (See illustration on page 73.)

Between 1763 and 1789, the whole Army had become increasingly disorganised, and the decline affected the Household troops too.

For some time, the ranks of The Life Guards had been filled largely by the sons of city merchants, for whom it provided a desirable entrée to society, and a secondary occupation after their business activities. This became increasingly unacceptable to the Regiment, particularly when they found themselves known as the 'Cheesemongers'. The final straw came when Queen Charlotte had on one occasion to tell her coachman to slow down, as two of her escort had fallen off.

The Duke of York described them in 1788 as 'the most useless and unmilitary troops that ever were seen'.

A drastic reorganisation of the regiments was therefore carried out that year. The Life Guards and The Horse Grenadier Guards[24] were transformed into the 1st and 2nd Regiments of Life Guards, and were made to become very much more professional.

Efforts were also apparently made to raise the standard of riding after this, as shown by the forfeits to be paid by officers of The Life Guards while under instruction in the Riding School in 1798:

(i) Half a guinea for a fall or involuntary separation of the Rider's body from the horse.
(ii) A crown for the dropping of a hat.
(iii) A half-a-crown for Dropping any other Appointment.

In 1793, the present Officers Mess was built at St James's Palace for the officers of the Household troops on guard duty there and at Horse Guards. Regulations allowed for 'a dinner for thirteen officers to be provided . . . to consist of two regular courses and a dessert, with port, sherry, madeira, wines, ale, porter and table beer.'

The thirteen officers entitled to partake of this meal were:

Officers of the Life Guards on duty	3
Officers of the Foot Guards on duty	5
The Silver Stick of the Life Guards	1
Field Officers and Adjutants of the Foot Guards in Brigade and parade waiting	4
	13

Barracks began to be provided for the Army from 1792, chiefly because of the threat of invasion; Hyde Park Barracks were built for the regiment of The Life Guards which was responsible for carrying out policing duties, while the quarters at Portman Square, near Regents Park, were used for the regiment mounting the Royal Guards.

At Windsor, some new cavalry barracks were completed in 1804 and occupied by The Blues, who were clearly favoured by poor mad King George III. He spent most of his time at Windsor Castle, and had his own Troop, frequently turning up for early morning parades, wearing the uniform of a Captain in the Regiment. He formed the Regiment's first Band, and personally presented them with a pair of solid silver kettle-drums, still used today.

Most men lived out in billets, usually ale houses, which had to be 'within trumpet call' of the barracks. The northern limit for Hyde Park Barracks in Knightsbridge was the present Praed Street, more than a mile away, which must have tested the lungs of the trumpeters, even in those quieter days.

The Foot Guards were also mostly billeted out, but did have some quarters in the Tower of London and in the Savoy area.

Living out was not necessarily more comfortable than barracks, for an Order of 1718 had laid down a scale of 'five beds for ten men in as little room as can well be allowed. Cost – £12 per man.' Sergeant Pell confirmed that it was still two men to a bed at the end of the century.

Cooking was carried out in the barrack rooms by the men themselves over coal fires. Lighting was by candles, washing facilities were scarce, and so the atmosphere must have been of impressive potency.

Despite these squalid conditions, the men were expected to pipe-clay white breeches for parade, and also to plait their hair into a queue, which had then to be greased and powdered, until it hung straight and stiff down the back like a rod. It was a tedious and unpopular task, which men had to do in pairs, and it might take up to two hours to get ready for a parade. When the Duke of York abolished queues in 1804 and ordered soldiers' hair to be cropped, it was a welcome change.

Pay was virtually the same as in the time of Queen Elizabeth, that is just over eightpence (3 new pence) a day. In 1797, it was increased to the famous 'shilling a day' (5p) which was to continue to be the rate for another century.

From this meagre sum, 'stoppages' were deducted for food and clothing, and as often as not, the soldier ended up with little or nothing for the week.

Complaints were not encouraged. Discipline throughout the Army was harsh to the point of brutality, with flogging as the standard punishment for every offence, however trivial. Twenty-five strokes was the minimum, and 100 was considered a light sentence, with some men receiving up to 1,000 lashes, from which they might suffer severe or even fatal injuries.

Brutal though it may seem today, it was in keeping with those times, and Royal Navy discipline was equally harsh. There were many hard ruffians in the fighting forces for whom flogging was an appropriate punishment, and certainly it was generally accepted as essential on active service.

The lashings were normally carried out at a ceremonial parade convened

for the purpose, and attended by the Commanding Officer, Adjutant, Medical Officer and all available men. The prisoner was stripped to the waist, tied to the triangles, and a drummer then applied the 'cat o' nine tails' to his back. Every twenty-five strokes a new drummer took over, until the sentence was completed.

The Medical Officer could stop the punishment, but seldom did, because it meant that the man had to have the balance of the sentence inflicted as soon as he had recovered.

From the time of the French Revolution, the justification for this brutal discipline began to be increasingly questioned, and Sir John Moore showed that there were other forms of leadership. From about 1806, flogging was imposed less often and the sentences became more lenient, while from 1815, it gradually lapsed into disuse, except on active service.

It was a tough life in the Army of this time, but the men who joined it were tough fighters, who had few equals on the field of battle, as they were to prove when they embarked on the Peninsular Campaign.

The Bank Picquet, seen by the cartoonist James Gillray (1757–1815). The Picquet traditionally marched along the pavement, which caused some resentment particularly when a Lord Mayor of London was among those pushed into the gutter.

Chapter 6

The Long Struggle

(1802–14)

The year 1802 saw Napoleon triumphantly dominating Europe, having forced England to make peace. In France he had been voted First Consul for life, with supreme powers. Indeed, he was almost a legend, and English tourists travelled to Paris to catch a glimpse of 'Boney'.

The moment peace was concluded, Britain as usual wasted no time in cutting down the size of her army, and even discharged 40,000 sailors as well. But within a year, it became clear that Napoleon had not abandoned his dreams of world domination, and by 16 May 1803 England and France were once more at war.

England alone stood now between Napoleon and his ambitions. Angrily, he declared that she must be crushed once and for all, and that meant invasion.

With furious energy, he assembled in the Channel ports the so-called 'Grand Army' of 160,000 of his finest troops, together with thousands of barges to lift them.

'Let us be masters of the Straits for six hours,' he told his admirals, 'and we shall be masters of the world.'

But Admiral Villeneuve could no more grant him those vital hours than Admiral Raeder, supported by Reichsmarschall Herman Goering, could grant them to Adolf Hitler, 137 years later.

Meanwhile in that defiant island across 'the ditch', John Bull was preparing to fight 'on the beaches . . . in the fields and in the streets . . . in the hills'.[25] Certainly he did not intend to surrender.

74

By the autumn almost a tenth of the population had joined the Volunteers, the equivalent of the Home Guard, only to find to their indignation that there were not enough muskets for everyone, and many were issued only with pikes.

The strategy for defeating the invaders was to rely on delaying tactics, guerilla warfare, and a slow withdrawal from the coast to defensive positions round the capital.

Among the regular forces defending the capital were three Guards Brigades, the 1st and 2nd formed from regular battalions, while the 3rd contained the depot battalion of each Regiment.

Careful plans were laid to give warning of any invasion threat. Round, stone Martello Towers were built to cover likely landing places, as were the concrete pill-boxes in 1940, while a chain of beacons could flash the news from the South Downs to the Scottish border in a matter of hours.

As the enemy advanced, they were to be watched, constantly harried, and delayed by the new-style light infantry being trained by Sir John Moore.

The threat reached a peak in the first days of 1804. The King resolved to move with the Prime Minister to Dartford, while the Queen and the Court were to be evacuated to Worcester, together with the gold from the Bank of England, which was to be stored in the Cathedral. All Press mention of troop movements was forbidden, and editors who disobeyed were to be arrested. The Volunteers hurried to their posts and the Navy waited with calm confidence.

'I do not say the French cannot come,' growled the First Sea Lord, 'I only say they cannot come by water.'[26]

And he was right. He knew that Napoleon must first defeat the Royal Navy before he could cross the Channel, and now Napoleon was realising it too. The French admirals had failed to break the inexorable blockade imposed round all their ports, and until they did, they could not concentrate their fleet to face the Royal Navy.

As 1804 passed by, Napoleon's hopes of a successful invasion dwindled. The Victory medals which he had ordered, with the inscription 'Struck in London in 1804', remained in the vaults, and the French and Spanish fleets remained in their ports. When, on 21 October 1805 Admiral Villeneuve's fleet finally ventured out from Cadiz, it was destroyed off Cape Trafalgar.

Now the threat of invasion was ended, and England could think again of taking the offensive.

'England has saved herself by her exertions,' declared the Prime Minister at the Lord Mayor's Banquet, 'and will, I trust, save Europe by her example.'

True to tradition, Britain used her sea power to strike at the enemy. A force which included 1st Guards Brigade sailed in 1805 to occupy the vital Mediterranean base of Sicily, where it remained till 1808; also in 1805, 2nd Guards Brigade took part in an abortive foray into Hanover.[27]

Somewhat further afield, redcoats were landed from men-of-war to capture the Cape of Good Hope in January 1806, and from there a mere 1600 of them crossed the Atlantic in September and seized Buenos Aires, the capital of a Spanish colony half the size of Europe.

But in Europe, England stood alone against a dictator in complete control of the continent. Undaunted, she used her sea power again, and in August 1807, 2nd Guards Brigade took part in a daring, but this time highly successful raid against Denmark. Copenhagen was captured, and the entire Danish fleet was removed, just ahead of Napoleon, who had had the same idea.

But Britain was not yet strong enough to face Napoleon's armies on the soil of Europe, and it was not until 1808 that the two opposing forces met.

The Peninsular Campaign (1804–14)

The confrontation was sparked off, when Napoleon turned against his old ally, Spain, and in February 1808 poured his armies across the Pyrenees. Having forced the King to abdicate, he placed his own brother Joseph on the throne. He then invaded Portugal as well, but not in time to prevent the Royal Navy from removing the entire Portuguese fleet, just as they had done in Denmark.

His plotting seemed successful for a while, but like Hitler after him, he underestimated the spirit of a nation oppressed by a foreign invader. The Spanish people rose in revolt, and waged a bitter guerilla war against the rape of their country. They also appealed to Britain for help, and Portugal followed suit.

Eager to encourage any resistance to Napoleon, the British Government sent an army under thirty-nine-year-old Lieutenant General Sir Arthur Wellesley to Portugal, as a prelude to larger-scale operations to support Spain as soon as possible. The Peninsular Campaign had begun. (See Map 1.)

Wellesley soon drove the French from Portugal and, encouraged by this, the Government ordered a force of 13,000 under General Baird to land at Corunna. There they were to be joined by 20,000 troops already in the Lisbon area, 300 miles to the south, the combined force being under the command of General Sir John Moore.

The Corunna force included 1st Guards Brigade, still consisting of 1st and 3rd Battalions First Guards, and they were soon marching inland towards a concentration area round Salamanca.

Moore united his two forces in November and then boldly marched north to attack Marshal Soult beyond Valladolid.

But then, on Christmas Day, came disastrous news. The Spanish armies that were supposed to support Moore had disintegrated, and Napoleon himself had marched into Spain at the head of 200,000 veterans. Having re-occupied Madrid, the Emperor was now heading north with 50,000 men and threatened to cut off Moore's entire army from its base at Corunna.

Outnumbered two to one, Moore had no option but to withdraw at once, in order to save what was not only virtually the entire British Army, but also the only allied force still effectively opposing Napoleon.

So on 26 December 1808 began the grim retreat to Corunna.

The glory of the magnificent rearguard action fought for the next three weeks belongs to Major General Crawford's Light Brigade, to the cavalry

under Lord Henry Paget,[28] and to the Reserve Division under his brother,
Edward Paget. The Guards were hardly involved, but they did distinguish
themselves by their discipline under conditions which turned many units of
Moore's force into a disorderly rabble.

In general, the British soldiers of the Peninsular Army were good fighting
material, even though many of them were recruited from the prisons, the
poorhouses, and the alehouses. Tough, tenacious, and at times brutal and
licentious, they were proud of their profession and scornful of their enemies.

Their life centred around the Regiment; they lived and fought for it and
its reputation, and were prepared to die for it too, particularly if well led.
Their morale depended on fighting, and they did not like retreating; and
this was a grim retreat indeed.

The staff work was abysmal, and there were almost no supplies, clothes or
comforts. Soon many troops were barefoot, famished and frozen. The
Spanish citizens, for whom the British were enduring all this, barred their
doors against them, while the Spanish troops thought more of looting and
drinking than of fighting. The snow was deep, the cold and wind intense,
and there was no shelter, no respite and no hope but to plod onwards.

Hungry, exhausted, shivering and dispirited, men looted, drank themselves into a stupor, died by the roadside, or swore and stumbled on. Only
when the French closed in, did they miraculously recover, show their anger
fiercely and effectively, and then trudge on again.

Then when at long last, on 11 January 1809, the famished and exhausted
troops came in sight of Corunna, it was to find that the fleet which was to
evacuate them had not yet arrived.

It was as Sir John Moore watched the 15,000 survivors of his ragged and
dispirited army plod down the slope towards Corunna that there occurred
a famous incident, much valued by all Guardsmen. It cannot be better
described than in the words of Sir John Fortescue himself:

A brigade caught the General's eye at a distance, for they were marching like
soldiers.
'Those must be the Guards,' he said, and presently the two battalions of the
First Guards, each of them still 800 strong, strode by in column of sections, with
drums beating, the drum major twirling his staff at their head and the men keeping
step as if in their own barrack yard . . . The senior regiment of the British infantry
had set an example to the whole army . . .[29]

A tradition was established that day, which was to help many Guardsmen
in years to come, not least on the retreat from Mons in 1914, and again on the
beaches of Dunkirk in 1940.

It was 14 January 1809 before the British fleet sailed into Corunna, and
embarkation could begin. On the same day, Soult's troops closed up to the
British positions round the town, but fortunately they did not press home an
attack. When they finally did attack two days later, the thin British line
held somehow, and at the end of the day, it was the French who withdrew.

But at the height of the battle, Sir John Moore was struck by a round shot,
which tore away his left arm. He died just before the fighting ended,

and was buried at dawn on 17 January, while the last of his troops embarked.

With the departure of Moore's army from Corunna, the only British troops left in the Peninsula were 10,000 men round Lisbon. They hung on grimly, and in April 1809 received welcome reinforcements which included 2nd Guards Brigade. They also welcomed back Sir Arthur Wellesley who was to lead them in a campaign that would over the next five years drive Napoleon's armies out of both Portugal and Spain.

Their first action was a highly successful crossing of the River Douro in May 1809, followed by the Battle of Talavera on 28 July. The Guards Brigade, as part of Sherbrooke's 1st Division, was in the centre of the British line, and after a severe artillery bombardment, they were attacked by at least 15,000 French infantry. They held their fire till the enemy were only fifty yards away, and then halted them with a volley. Before the French could recover, the whole division charged, and drove them back.

But the Guardsmen, among others, pressed on too far, and soon found themselves cut off. They were rescued by the 48th Foot (1st Battalion, Northamptonshire Regiment), whose intervention enabled them to rally, and resume their position in the British line.

The fighting ended with the French withdrawing during the night, but it had been a costly battle. British casualties were about 5,000, almost a quarter of their total strength, and the two Guards battalions each lost some 300 men out of about 1000.

It became a Battle Honour for both the Coldstream and Third Guards, and a special medal was struck for issue to 'meritorious officers'.

But despite this success, Wellesley had now to go over to the defensive, and he withdrew for the winter of 1809–10 to the famous defensive lines of Torres Vedras, which he had constructed that autumn.

Meanwhile, members of 1st Guards Brigade, back in England after the ordeal of Corunna, may well have attended the opening on 21 April 1809 of Mr William Lord's new cricket ground at St John's Wood.[30] But before the end of the season, they found themselves taking part in an unpleasant expedition to the Netherlands island of Walcheren.

Its purpose was to capture Antwerp, and so perhaps encourage some of England's allies to further efforts against Napoleon. But the attack failed, and then a terrible fever dominated the force. In September, the expedition was abandoned, and 1st Guards Brigade returned thankfully home.

It was not however the last that the Guards in England were to see of Holland, for exactly five years later in March 1814, a composite Guards Brigade from all three Regiments was to join another unsuccessful expedition against Antwerp. Again disaster struck, but this time it was due to an unsuccessful attack on the fortress of Bergen-op-Zoom, which ended in the death or capture of two thirds of the 1000 Guardsmen involved.

Meanwhile in the Peninsula the next two years, 1810–12, proved decidedly frustrating for 2nd Guards Brigade; their only real chance of action was on 8 May 1811 at Fuentes d'Onoro, near Ciudad Rodrigo, where both the Coldstream and Third Guards earned a Battle Honour.

There was training, of course, and also some sport to keep all ranks occupied. The officers managed to organise some hunting,[31] shooting and racing, and life seems to have been enlivened by the antics of a well-known practical joker, Captain Dan MacKinnon of the Coldstream Guards. Indeed it is related that on one occasion, when Wellesley, now Viscount Wellington, was taking tea with the Mother Superior in the parlour of Vizeu Convent, he was not a little surprised to see one of the nuns do a smart hand-stand, revealing not a prudish petticoat but the boots and trousers of Captain MacKinnon.[32]

Nor was this the only antic of this young officer, who on another occasion when he landed in Spain, impersonated the Duke of York. The local Mayor received him and his friends with full honours, including a grand banquet which culminated in the arrival of a huge bowl of punch. At this point, Mackinnon evidently thought the joke had gone far enough, for he plunged his head into the bowl of punch, which brought the festivities to an abrupt conclusion. He received a severe reprimand from Wellington, but was later forgiven.

He was also a great athlete, of whom the famous clown, Grimaldi said, later that he had 'only to put on the motley costume and he would totally eclipse me'.[33] He seems however to have settled down enough in later life to write a history of his Regiment, not usually a task for the flippant.

In March 1810, a composite Guards Brigade[34] arrived from England, but were promptly locked up for the next two and a half years as part of the garrison of the besieged port of Cadiz. Their only moment of glory came in 1811 when they joined a force which was withdrawn from Cadiz and landed further up the coast, with a view to attacking Marshal Victor's encircling army from the rear.

The 4,000 British troops of the sortie force, commanded by Major General Thomas Graham[35] became separated from their Spanish allies, however, and on 5 March 1811, found themselves faced by two French divisions totalling about 7,000.

The British had been marching for the last fifteen hours, but they charged the fresh French infantry and cavalry, almost twice their own numbers, and drove them from a strong position near Barossa.

The attack, headed by the First Guards, was costly, and the Guards lost one man in three, grim figures for a battle that lasted not more than an hour and a half. Fortescue describes it, 'as one of the bloodiest and one of the most creditable to British troops'. Certainly it was a worthy Battle Honour and a gold medal was awarded for it, as for Talavera.

General Graham said of the Guards after the battle that they 'had gloriously maintained the high character of His Majesty's household troops in an action where they had all distinguished themselves.'

Cadiz was still besieged, however, and the remnants of the force withdrew into the garrison.

By the end of 1811, Portugal was clear of the enemy, except for the frontier fortresses, and Wellington began to make secret plans to capture them by surprise attacks in mid-winter, when the French would expect his army to be resting in its winter quarters.

So on 4 February 1812, Wellington marched quietly out at the head of the 1st, 3rd, 4th and Light Divisions. With him went 2nd Guards Brigade, still in the 1st Division.

The plan worked, and by 19 January 1812 Ciudad Rodrigo had fallen, to be followed by the capture of Badajoz in April. On 22 July, Wellington attacked and took Salamanca, where 40,000 French were virtually beaten in forty minutes. This was followed by the capture of Madrid on 12 August.

This British success led the French to lift the two and a half year siege of Cadiz, whereupon the liberated garrison marched north, determined to miss no more fighting. They covered 400 miles in nineteen days, and joined the main army on 18 October.

At the same time, 1st Bn First Guards landed at Corunna, and also marched to the sound of the guns. But they all arrived just as Wellington withdrew in the face of overwhelming enemy force to the safety of Ciudad Rodrigo, where the Army settled into winter quarters for a much-needed period of rest and reorganisation.

On the very day that Wellington turned back from Burgos (21 October), Napoleon was turning back from the ruins of Moscow with the remnants of his army of a quarter of a million men, so few of whom would see France again. Russia and England thus continued to fight Napoleon to the bitter end.

A total of five Guards battalions were now serving in the Peninsular Army, and Wellington therefore formed them into two Guards Brigades[36] both of which were placed in 1st Division, commanded by General Graham of Barrosa fame.

The Guards element was also considerably strengthened by the arrival from England of a Household Brigade of Cavalry. It was commanded by Colonel Sir Robert Hill of The Blues, brother of General Lord Rowland Hill, and consisted of both The Life Guards and The Blues. The brigade came under the cavalry commander in Spain, General Sir Stapleton Cotton, later Lord Combermere, who gave his name to the Household Cavalry barracks at Windsor. It was the first time that a Household Brigade had been formed, and also the first time that Wellington found the Household Cavalry under his command,[37] so it was a precedent for all concerned.

It was some time before they were in action, for the winter of 1812–13 was a quiet one for Wellington's army, and the worst casualties were caused by an outbreak of low fever brought from Walcheren.

By the spring, the situation in the Pensinsular Campaign had swung in Wellington's favour. His army was stronger, and he had a total of 80,000 men, of whom 47,000 were British. They had had a good rest over the winter, and were better equipped and trained than ever before.

The French on the other hand, had been harried incessantly by Spanish guerillas, and King Joseph, sitting uneasily on the throne of Spain, had had to send so many men to replace Napoleon's casualties in Russia, that he now had a mere 40,000 left.

Wellington decided that the time had at last come when he could think of driving the French out of Spain altogether, and the most effective way of achieving this would be to strike at their communications where they were all concentrated at Bayonne, the main route through the Pyrenees.

Boldly, he divided his forces into two columns, and headed north in May. His plan succeeded, and on 4 June he was across the River Douro, which was the main obstacle in his way. Burgos, which had defied him the previous autumn, was abandoned by the French and blown up.

Continuing the advance, Wellington all but destroyed the French army on 21 June at Vittoria.

After this defeat, the French army fled across the mountains back into France, leaving unprecedented booty in the hands of the British troops. Wellington could not however, pursue them into France until he had dealt with the fortress of San Sebastian which stood in his way.

The siege was successful, but took three months, from July to September 1813, and resulted in heavy casualties, particularly to the Guards battalions, whose volunteer assault party of 200 suffered no less than 160 casualties.

This obstacle finally removed, Wellington thrust into France and both 1st and 2nd Guards Brigades were involved in a series of bold operations, including river crossings over the Bidassoa (7 October), the Nivelle (10 November), the Nive (9 December), and the Adour (23 February 1814).

2nd Guards Brigade distinguished themselves on this last operation when six companies of the Third Guards and two of the Coldstream crossed the river before dark, and held a precarious bridgehead all night, until relieved next morning. The operation is also of interest because this assault force used a new rocket battery against the French and, apparently, it had a very discouraging effect on them.

The End (1814)

On 5 April 1814, Napoleon abdicated, and was banished to the island of Elba. But it was not till a week later that the news reached either the French commander or Wellington, and as a result, Wellington launched an unnecessary attack on the town of Toulouse on 10 April, in ignorance of the fact that the war was over. Casualties were heavy on both sides, and Marshal Soult withdrew two days later, still unaware of Napoleon's abdication.

The Guards were not engaged in that battle, but they were closely involved in an equally tragic affair four days later, when the French commander of Bayonne, called Thourenot, made a last desperate sortie against the British. He had by then heard of the abdication, but refused to believe it, and attacked by night with 6,000 men.

He was met by 1st and 2nd Guards Brigades and after fierce, confused fighting in the dark, the French were finally repulsed. The last action of the war had been fought.

Sadly, it had been a bloody encounter, each side losing close on 1,000 men; the two Guards Brigades suffered 506 casualties, which was bitter indeed, eleven days after the peace had been declared. After the battle, the Guards set up their own military cemetery at Bayonne, which still exists today, and must be one of the earliest war cemeteries on record.

The Peninsular Campaign was over. It had been long and hard, and the troops had suffered severe hardships, worsened by the lack of trained staff. Transport, supplies, clothing, medicines and other essentials were usually totally inadequate, and it was a campaign of hard marches, and counter-marches, harsh winters and burning summers, costly battles and frustrating setbacks.

The Guards found it particularly frustrating, for although they were present at almost every battle, they had remarkably few opportunities to show their worth in action.

They had however shown very clearly how other military qualities beyond bravery are of importance in an army, particularly under adverse conditions. Discipline, of course, leadership and morale, were all essential on such a campaign, and the Guards set a standard in this respect. As Wellington wrote to the Duke of York in May 1809: '. . . the Brigade of Guards are in every respect the example and object of admiration of the whole army.'

Lest it be thought by any chance that the Guards can do no wrong and are *always* an example, mention should perhaps be made here, of the occasion when they incurred the Duke's displeasure. It occurred when Wellington visited a detachment of the First Guards occupying a redoubt towards the end of the Peninsular Campaign, and noticed to his surprise, 'a great many umbrellas under which sat the officers'.

A senior officer was promptly dispatched to the offenders with the clear and concise message that 'Lord Wellington does not approve the use of umbrellas during the enemy's firing and will not allow the gentlemen's sons to make themselves ridiculous in the eyes of the Army.'[38]

Chapter 7

The Guards at Waterloo (1815)

Life was just getting back to normal in the winter of 1815 when the news arrived that Napoleon had escaped from Elba and landed near Cannes. At first, it caused little concern, but when it became evident that he was being received with growing national enthusiasm as he made his way north towards Paris, dismay took over.

Louis XVIII fled to Ghent, and on 20 March, Napoleon returned in triumph to his capital. Within a month, he had assembled a formidable army of 360,000 seasoned troops, eager with him to re-establish the honour and glory of France.

Representatives of the Allies (England, Austria, Russia and Prussia), were at that moment assembled at Vienna, arguing about the dismemberment of the French Empire and the sharing out of the spoils. Now they anxiously agreed to place Wellington in overall command and to provide 150,000 men each, to settle with Napoleon once and for all.

But the raising of such a force was easier said than done. The Prussians, under that staunch seventy-three year-old campaigner, Marshal Blücher, produced an army of 116,000, but the Austrians and Russians took so long to mobilise that they made no effective contribution.

Wellington had no easy time building up his own army, and it was only after much argument and acrimony with Whitehall, that he managed to assemble around his headquarters in Brussels a British force of twenty five battalions of infantry and sixteen regiments of cavalry, totalling about

24,000 men. Half of them were the 2nd or 3rd Battalions of their Regiments, most of the 1st Battalions having been sent to fight in America. It was very much a make-shift army, although most of them had seen active service.

Comparing it with the highly professional and experienced force that had fought and won the Peninsular Campaign, it was hardly surprising that the exasperated Duke wrote to Whitehall, and complained:

I have got an infamous army, very weak and ill-equipped, and a very inexperienced Staff. In my opinion, they are doing nothing in England. They have not raised a man; they have not called out the Militia either in England or Ireland; are unable to send me anything and they have not sent a message to Parliament about the money. The war spirit is therefore evaporating as I am informed.[39]

Although the Allies had a total of 209,000 men, against Napoleon's 124,000, Wellington himself had only 93,000. All depended, therefore, on Blücher's 116,000 Prussians linking up with Wellington's army before Napoleon could attack each of them separately.

Nor was this Wellington's only worry. Many of the allied troops under his command were so unreliable that he made a point of positioning them between British regiments, in order to strengthen the line. He was also hampered by the necessity of being on the defensive, and thus allowing Napoleon the initiative. Finally, he suffered at the start from an almost complete lack of information as to the movements of the enemy, being forbidden for political reasons to cross the frontier into France.

He therefore positioned his forces in a line to the west and south of Brussels, with the Prussians on his left, so as to cover all likely approaches from France. (See Map 2, page 28.)

Wellington's army contained a strong contingent from both the Household Cavalry and the Foot Guards.

A Household Cavalry Brigade commanded by Major General Lord Edward Somerset, formed part of the allied cavalry under Lieutenant General Lord Uxbridge,[40] and consisted of:

> First Life Guards
> Second Life Guards
> Royal Horse Guards (The Blues)
> 1st King's Dragoon Guards

They had arrived from England in May and were now quartered at Ninove.

The Royals were also present as part of the Union Brigade commanded by Major General Ponsonby.

The Foot Guards provided 1st and 2nd Guards Brigades[41] both in 1st Division, which was commanded by Major General Sir George Cooke (First Guards).

On the evening of Thursday 15 June, the two Guards Brigades were encamped round Enghien, with the role of ensuring that Napoleon did not advance on Brussels from the west, which would cut Wellington's lines of communication with the Channel ports.

In fact, Napoleon had that very day occupied Charleroi and driven the Prussians back on Ligny, but the news had not yet reached Wellington, who, with many of his officers, was preparing to attend the Duchess of Richmond's ball in Brussels that night.

Certainly, several Guards officers were there and one of them, Captain George Bowles of the Coldstream Guards, described the dramatic moment when Wellington, at about an hour after midnight, received information at last of Napoleon's whereabouts, and learned that the French were within two and a half miles of Quatre Bras.[42]

Quietly ordering all officers to return immediately to their units, Wellington himself withdrew to the Duke of Richmond's study, where they both looked at a map, and discussed the situation briefly.

'Napoleon has humbugged me, by God,' declared Wellington. 'He has gained 24 hours march on me.'

'What do you intend doing?' asked the Duke.

'I have ordered the army to concentrate at Quatre Bras; but we shall not stop him there, and if so, I must fight him here.'

He then marked the battlefield of Waterloo on the map with a thumb nail, bade his host goodnight, and went off to bed.

Quatre Bras (16 June 1815)

At about the same early hour in the morning of 16 June, the two Guards Brigades were hurriedly packing up. An order to move, issued about 2200 hours, had not reached them till 0130 hours, but they were ready nevertheless by 0400 hours, and set off as ordered for Braine-le-Comte, arriving five hours later. Here they should have received orders from the Prince of Orange, in command at Quatre Bras, to hurry on and join him there.

The message never arrived, but General Cooke, commanding 1st Division, boldly decided to 'march to the sound of the guns'.

It was as well that he did, for as dawn broke on 16 June, there were only about 8000 allied troops, mostly Dutch and Belgian, with sixteen guns, in position to defend the vital cross roads at Quatre Bras against a French corps, 20,000 strong, under the dashing Marshal Ney, and supported by 3,000 cavalry and sixty guns.

But Ney for once did not press the attack as he might have, and the allied forces just managed somehow to hold out all day, being saved several times only by the arrival of new troops, who were thrown into the struggle piecemeal the moment they appeared.

The two Guards Brigades meanwhile marched steadily through the heat of a flaming June day, and finally arrived at Quatre Bras at 1700 hours. It was then a crucial moment in the battle, for the French had just gained possession of the vital Bossu Wood. So threatening was this that first the light companies, and then the two leading battalions (2nd and 3rd Battalions of the First Guards), were flung straight into the battle, company by company, as they arrived.

They had been marching for thirteen hours, covering 26 miles in extreme

85

heat, but they drove the French steadily back out of the thick wood. Their losses were heavy, but their intervention helped to halt the French attack, and Quatre Bras remained in allied hands.

The Household Cavalry did not take part in this battle, but spent the whole day on a fifty-mile approach ride from their billets near Ninove to Quatre Bras, where they spent the night of 16 June. There was little hope of sleep, however, for there were no picquet lines, and they could only lie on the ground, wrapped in their cloaks, and holding on to their restless horses.

Meanwhile, the Prussians to the east had also been heavily attacked by the French during 16 June, at Ligny, but withdrew in reasonably good order to Wavre, some ten miles from Waterloo.

At the height of the battle, the gallant Marshal Blücher was thrown from his horse, and then twice ridden over by cavalry charges, first by the French and then by his own troops. He was retrieved, bruised but unbroken, and remained firmly in command.

This was just as well, for he later made the vital decision, against the advice of his Chief of Staff, Gneisenau, that he would withdraw northwards towards Wellington, rather than east towards Prussia. This honourable decision undoubtedly influenced the outcome of the Battle of Waterloo.

17 June 1815

The 17th of June was spent by both sides in reorganising and preparing for the next round.

Soon after daybreak, Captain Bowles, now with his battalion, found himself talking to the Duke of Wellington at Quatre Bras, when a staff officer, Lt Colonel Gordon (Third Guards), rode up with the first news of the Prussian defeat at Ligny.

'The Duke, without the least change of countenance gave him some orders and dismissed him. He then turned round to me and said: "Old Blücher has had a damned good licking, and gone back to Wavre, eighteen miles. As he has gone back, we must go too. I suppose in England they will say we have been licked. I can't help it, as they are gone back, we must go too."

'He made all the arrangements for retiring without moving from the spot on which he was standing, and it certainly did not occupy him five minutes.'[43]

The withdrawal was to a position that the Duke had first noted a year before round Mont St Jean. He also sent a message to Blücher telling him that the British would have to withdraw even further unless the Prussians could promise him one corps.

Colonel Hardinge, Wellington's liaison officer with the Prussians, went to see the old man and found him in bed, rubbing his bruises with brandy, and dosing himself with his favourite medicine of gin and rhubarb. Blücher greeted him with a grin and the undeniable comment, 'Ich stinke etwas.' ('I smell somewhat.') But he swore he would get his whole army to Wellington, even if he had to be held on his horse.

Meanwhile, the Guards, together with the rest of Wellington's army, were plodding back from Quatre Bras towards their new positions at Mont St Jean just south of the village of Waterloo. The withdrawal was covered by the cavalry, and The Life Guards had a lively and successful skirmish at Genappe, where Wellington's headquarters had been the night before.

Some French Chasseurs attacked the British rearguard, and a charge by some British light cavalry failed to check them.

'The Life Guards shall have this honour,' declared Lord Uxbridge, and ordered them to charge, which they did in his own words 'with right good will'.

The enemy were routed, and His Lordship wrote later that it had been 'the prettiest Field Day of Cavalry and Horse Artillery that I have ever witnessed.'

The withdrawal was completed according to plan, and the troops made themselves as comfortable as they could in the heavy rain which had begun to fall at midday.

The Battlefield at Waterloo

The battlefield of Waterloo consisted of two ridges some 1,200 yards apart, and the two armies faced each other across the shallow intervening valley along a front of some 4,200 yards. The allied positions centred on Mont St Jean, with the village of Waterloo just behind it. (See map on page 88.)

The low ground between the two armies was soggy and heavy after the rain, and this was to be a significant factor in the battle, in that it slowed up the French cavalry charges, and so robbed them of their impetus and impact, particularly as they were attacking uphill.

There were three key points forward of the British positions, which were used by Wellington to break up any enemy attack. They were:

		Held by
Right	Hougoumont	2nd Guards Brigade
Centre	La Haye Sainte	King's German Legion
Left	Papelotte	Nassau Brigade

On 17 June, just before dusk, General Cooke, commanding 1st Division, had been ordered by Wellington to send a force forward to secure the Chateau of Hougoumont as this would strengthen the British line. He detailed the four light companies of both Guards Brigades for the task which was carried out just in time, for Napoleon had also appreciated the tactical value of Hougoumont, and the troops sent by him to occupy it were only just forestalled.

As a result, 8,000 Frenchmen were to die next day trying to capture it.

Immediately behind Hougoumont were 2nd Guards Brigade, with 1st Guards Brigade on their left, towards the centre of the British line.

Along his main line of defences, Wellington posted most of his troops out of view on the reverse slope of the ridge, as was his custom. This not only reduced casualties from the heavy French artillery bombardments, but also to some extent served to conceal their strength and dispositions.

87

The French troops, on the other hand, were positioned on a forward slope, where their manoeuvring could be closely watched by Wellington.

The Battle of Waterloo – 18 June 1815

It was still raining at dawn on Sunday, 18 June, and 68,000 allied troops awoke, cold, wet and muddy. A gin ration helped, but not much, as they looked across the valley at the equally sodden 72,000 French on the opposite slope.

At about 0800 hours, the rain stopped, and Wellington's army prepared for the French attack, which everyone felt must surely come at any moment.

But Napoleon had decided that he would not launch his main assault until noon, so that the sodden ground could dry out. Meanwhile, as a diversion, he ordered Reille to use his corps to capture Hougoumont; it seemed a simple operation, which should make Wellington weaken his centre, where the main French attack was to be launched later.

The attack on Hougoumont thus became the first of four distinct phases in the battle, in all of which the Guards played a key part:

a. The defence of Hougoumont;
b. The attack by d'Erlon's Corps against the allied centre;
c. The French Cavalry charges;
d. The defeat of the French Imperial Guard.

4 The Battle of Waterloo

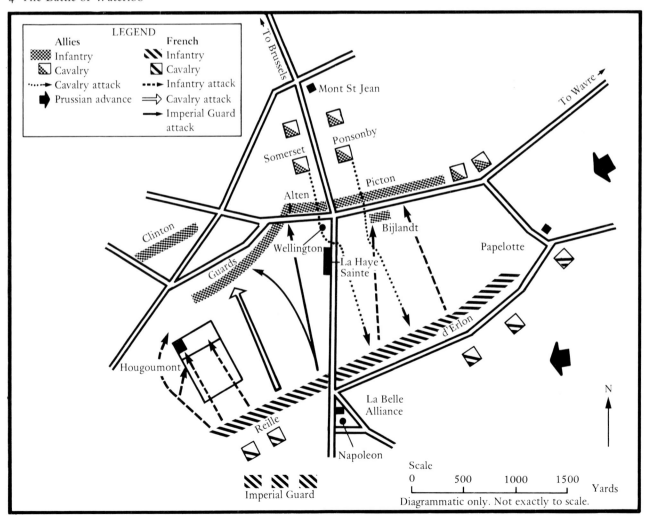

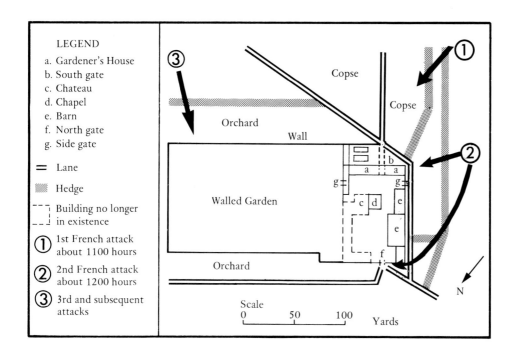

LEGEND

a. Gardener's House
b. South gate
c. Chateau
d. Chapel
e. Barn
f. North gate
g. Side gate

= Lane

Hedge

Building no longer in existence

① 1st French attack about 1100 hours

② 2nd French attack about 1200 hours

③ 3rd and subsequent attacks

Copse

Copse

Orchard

Wall

Walled Garden

Orchard

N

Scale
0   50   100
Yards

HOUGOUMONT As can be seen from Map 5, Hougoumont covered a rectangular area some 500 yards square. The buildings consisted of a house along the south, or enemy side, with a gateway through it; the great barn to the west; and in the centre, a small chateau, with a chapel attached. In the north-west corner was the main gateway.

The night of the 17th was spent by the men of all three Regiments fortifying the buildings, loopholing the walls, and building platforms to enable them to fire over the parapets. All entrances to the position were barricaded, except the north gate (f on Map 5), which was left open, so that ammunition and reinforcements could be brought in.

The defence of Hougoumont rested on two Guards officers, who were already known for their coolness and bravery in battle. Lt Colonel Lord Saltoun of the First Guards, aged thirty, was in command of the light companies of 2nd and 3rd Bns First Guards, who were responsible for the defence of the garden and orchard. He had fought at Corunna and Walcheren, and in the Peninsular Campaign, and was to distinguish himself throughout the day at Waterloo, so that Wellington described him as 'a pattern to the army, both as a man and a soldier'.

The task of holding the buildings of Hougoumont, with the light companies of 2nd Bn Coldstream Guards and 2nd Bn Third Guards, lay with Lt. Colonel James Macdonnell of Glengarry who was, despite his name, a Coldstreamer. He too had fought in the Peninsula, and he evidently had the confidence of Wellington, for when General Müffling, who was Marshal Blücher's liaison officer with the Duke, remarked that Hougoumont was a difficult place to defend, Wellington replied: 'Ah, but you do not know Macdonnell'.

By dawn on the 18th, the defenders of Hougoumont were ready, but the first French attacks did not come till after 1100 hours. Lord Saltoun's force

Hougoumont today
(*Above*) The north gate, with the chapel visible behind. It is of interest to compare this with the painting on the back cover taken from the same angle. A Scots Guards plaque is on the wall.

(*Opposite below left*) The south gate.
(*Opposite top*) A tree at Hougoumont showing the bullet marks of 1815.
(*Opposite below right*) The charred figure of Christ in the chapel.

in the copse had by then been replaced by some German troops, but the latter were driven back soon after and the light companies of the First Guards had then to be recalled to restore the situation. This they did and then remained there for the rest of the morning.

Although this first French attack was repulsed, it was soon followed by another, and this time the enemy swept round both flanks, so that the buildings were under attack from three sides. The south gate came under heavy pressure, but held, and was in fact never forced open.

To the north and west of Hougoumont, the Guardsmen still outside the walls now withdrew through the north gate. Sergeant Fraser of the Third Guards rode back however on a charger belonging to Colonel Cubières, commanding the French 1st Light Regiment, whom he had unhorsed in personal combat.

As the last men entered, the great gate was swung shut. But before it could be properly barricaded, it was rushed by a party from the 1st Light Regiment, led by a Lieutenant Legros, a huge man to match his name. Armed with an axe, he forced open the gate, and at the head of about a dozen men fought his way into the courtyard. After a desperate hand-to-hand struggle, all the Frenchmen were killed.

But more French troops were now attacking the gate, which had to be closed if Hougoumont was to be held. Led by Colonel Macdonnell himself, a party from both the Coldstream and Third Guards fought to push back the wall of enemy that was pressing forward into the gap.

While some stabbed and thrust at the desperate attackers, others heaved at the heavy doors. Slowly, very slowly, they forced them back, pushing aside the pile of dead and dying Frenchmen on the other side.

At last the gates were closed tight, and barricaded with anything heavy within reach. The crisis was over for the moment.

The names of the men who shut the gates at Hougoumont have been recorded and they are:

Coldstream Guards:
Lt Colonel James Macdonnell
Captain Henry Wyndham
Ensign James Hervey
Ensign Henry Gooch
Sergeant James Graham
Corporal Graham (his brother)

Third Guards:
Sergeant Fraser
Sergeant Brice McGregor
Sergeant Alston
Private Lister

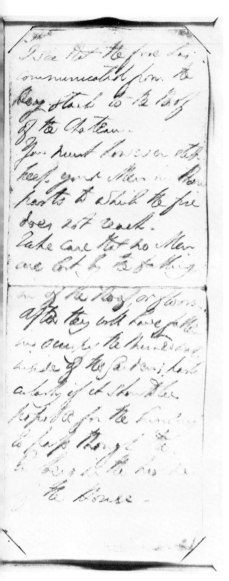

Wellington's message to Colonel Macdonnell, one of many such messages written in his own hand during the battle and sent by hand of officer to various commanders.

(*Opposite*) A Private in the Life Guards, 1751. Most Troopers in The Life Guards at this time were indeed 'private gentlemen', and the title of 'Private' continued until 1906.

(*Overleaf*) The Coldstream defending the garden of Hougoumont. (From a painting by D. Dighton.)

The French attacks continued on all sides, and at about 1230 hours, Colonel Woodford of 2nd Bn Coldstream Guards led a counter-attack on the west side of Hougoumont where the light companies were again in grave danger. This achieved, he used his men to reinforce the defenders of Hougoumont itself. This meant that the whole of his battalion was now there (less two companies left to guard the Colours), and he therefore took over command from Lt Colonel Macdonnell.

Yet another assault on the orchard at 1300 hours was repulsed, this time thanks to a counter-attack by the 2nd Bn Third Guards, under Lt Colonel Home, and to the steady accurate fire from the walls of Hougoumont.

The Third Guards now replaced the First Guards light companies in the orchard, and the latter returned to 1st Guards Brigade, who were now completely clear of Hougoumont. The whole of 2nd Guards Brigade (less the two Coldstream companies) had however been drawn into its defence. This brigade was now commanded by Lt Colonel Hepburn of the Third Guards, who was to be responsible for the defence of Hougoumont for the remaining six hours of the battle.[44]

The defence continued, but now to add to the horror, the buildings of Hougoumont had been set on fire, and wounded put there for cover were burned alive or crawled out of the barns with their uniforms alight.

Some of the buildings were eventually gutted, but in the chapel, the flames, having charred the feet of a wooden figure of Christ crucified, strangely burned no further.

The accurate musketry from Hougoumont never slackened, and even when Reille in desperation flung in two complete divisions, they could not gain a foothold.

Nevertheless, the situation was now critical, and two battalions of the King's German Legion were sent forward to counter-attack outside Hougoumont. With this support, the French were repulsed for the last time.

So ended this 'battle within a battle'.

For eight hours a force of never more than 2000 (and initially it was a mere 500) had withstood continuous attacks by almost a third of Napoleon's infantry. By so doing, they prevented one corps from supporting Napoleon's four major attacks during the day, and this must have influenced the battle to no small degree. Eight thousand Frenchmen fell trying to capture Hougoumont, while the Guards lost some 540 all ranks.

Later in the day Wellington rode past the blackened ruins, when the battle was won, and remarked to General Müffling, who was again with him, 'You see, Macdonnell held Hougoumont'.[45]

ATTACK BY D'ERLON'S CORPS Two elements of Napoleon's plan had now gone wrong. Hougoumont had not been eliminated, and Wellington had not weakened his centre to reinforce Hougoumont, as Napoleon had hoped he would. Now the Prussians were approaching and the French attack could not be delayed much longer.

So at 1300 hours Napoleon ordered d'Erlon's corps of four divisions,

HORSE.Gds

supported by a brigade of heavy cavalry, to advance against the British centre.

Since noon, eighty-four guns had been pounding the main British positions with 'a fire so terrible as to strike with awe the oldest veteran in the field'.

Confident that no troops could withstand sixty minutes of such a storm of round shot and shell, Napoleon watched the 18,000 men of d'Erlon's corps closing in on the 8,500 British and Hanoverians covering the main road to Brussels.

At one moment it seemed that Napoleon's confidence might be justified, for the Netherlands Brigade showed signs of breaking; but Picton's division, positioned just behind it, not only stood firm, but even counter-attacked.

The French heavy cavalry now charged the British positions, and for a while the battle hung in the balance. It was a critical moment, and Lord Uxbridge in command of the allied cavalry saw his opportunity. Having some time before been given complete freedom of action by the Duke, he now decided to launch both his heavy cavalry brigades against the French columns. It was a bold move to send 2,000 horsemen against an unbroken force of infantry still many times their own number, but he did not hesitate.

Having formed both cavalry brigades into line, the Union Brigade to the east of the road and the Household Cavalry on the west, he placed himself at the head of the Household Brigade, and led their charge himself. It was a gallant and typical gesture, but in fact it was to prove a costly mistake, for by joining in the attack when he was in overall command, he lost control of the cavalry as a whole, and particularly of The Blues, and The Greys, who formed the reserve.

As they were forming up, Wellington rode by and called out, 'Now, gentlemen, for the honour of the Household Brigade.'

It was about 1430 hours when the bugles sounded the 'Charge'. The impetus of their attack not only halted the French advance, but scattered the attackers, including the brigade of French Cuirassiers.

Carried away by their success, The Life Guards, with the rest of the heavy cavalry,[46] charged on through the infantry and on to the French gun lines. But they went too far, and were soon dangerously scattered. Napoleon threw in more of his cavalry and the British began to suffer heavy casualties.

Too late, Uxbridge realised the danger and galloped back to regain control. He looked for The Blues, his reserve, and saw that they, receiving no orders, had joined in the charge and were now in the thick of it. But, although their Colonel had fallen wounded, they had retained their formation, and were able, with the help of the light cavalry, to support The Life Guards, and enable them to re-form.

While this reorganisation was taking place, Wellington, on the spot as always, called out, 'Thank you, Life Guards.'

This costly charge had deprived Wellington of a quarter of his cavalry and The Life Guards lost nearly half their strength. But it had broken Napoleon's main assault, and repulsed his strongest corps. The French lost 3,000 prisoners, in addition to over 2,000 killed and wounded.

97

The Guards at Waterloo (1815)

(*Opposite above*) The Battle of Talavera, 1809. The Third Guards in action (left) with their Colours visible as a rallying point. (From a painting by C. C. P. Lawson.)

(*Opposite below*) The Heavy Cavalry Charge at Waterloo. The Life Guards (left) charge the French infantry and cuirassiers at Waterloo.

(*Overleaf*) Hougoumont, the day after the battle.

There were many deeds of gallantry that afternoon, but the exploits of Corporal John Shaw of The Life Guards stand out. While stationed in England, he had shown himself to be an outstanding prize fighter; he had defeated Edward Painter over thirty-five rounds in 1815, and had been booked to fight Tom Cribb, heavyweight champion of Britain, but the war intervened. He stood six feet three inches tall, and weighed fifteen stone, with a magnificent physique. Charles Dickens mentioned him in *Bleak House*, with the words '. . . Old Shaw, the Lifeguardsman? Why he's the model of the whole British Army in himself.'

Shaw used his strength well at Waterloo, where he cut down eleven Frenchmen in this charge, splitting one man's skull and decapitating another.

Later he found himself battling dismounted against ten Frenchmen. He dealt with five, but then his sword broke. He fought on using first the hilt of his sword and then his helmet as weapons, until he was himself killed by a bullet from a French sniper.

Another hero was Lt Colonel Samuel Ferrier, (1st Life Guards) who is said to have led no less than eleven charges personally, most of them after he had been wounded twice.

Private Tom Evans of The Blues also distinguished himself. He had been told by his Commanding Officer, Sir Robert Hill, that he was too fat for active service, but he managed nevertheless to account for five French Cuirassiers single-handed in the course of rescuing his Commanding Officer, who had been wounded. When he retired, he opened a pub in Old Windsor called 'The Oxford Blue' which is still there today.

THE DEFEAT OF THE FRENCH CAVALRY Foiled in his main assault, Napoleon now ordered another intensive artillery bombardment of the British centre, beginning soon after 1530 hours. As was his custom, Wellington ordered his forward troops to move back behind the crest, out of the direct line of fire.

Marshal Ney, who was watching the bombardment, noticed the British infantry pull back, and also saw some allied wounded, moving to the rear, together with some prisoners and empty ammunition wagons. Mistaking this for a crumbling of Wellington's defence, he ordered an attack by 5,000 cavalry, to take advantage of this supposed 'retreat'.

The first attack, carried out by a corps of Cuirassiers, came in at about 1600 hours. They advanced between Hougoumont and La Haye Sainte which meant that their front was narrowed to a mere 500 yards.

The scene has been vividly described by Captain Gronow of the First Guards:

You perceived at a distance what appeared to be an overwhelming, long moving line which, ever advancing, glittered like a stormy wave of the sea when it catches the sunlight . . . They were the famous Cuirassiers, almost all old soldiers, who had distinguished themselves on most of the battle-fields of Europe. In an almost incredibly short period they were within twenty yards of us shouting 'Vive L'Empéreur'. The word of command 'Prepare to receive cavalry' had been given, every man in the front ranks knelt, and a wall bristling with steel, held together by steady hands, presented itself to the infuriated Cuirassiers.

Five times the French attacked, and five times they were beaten off. The squares stood firm, and Captain Gronow described the noise of the bullets striking the enemy's cuirasses as being like 'a violent hail-storm beating upon panes of glass'.[47]

He watched, too, as Wellington, accompanied only by an aide-de-camp moved into the square formed by the 2nd Battalion First Guards. 'The Duke sat unmoved, mounted on his favourite charger.[48] I recollect his asking Lt Colonel Stanhope what o'clock it was, upon which Stanhope took out his watch and said it was twenty minutes past four.'

'To which the Duke replied: "The battle is mine; and if the Prussians arrive soon, there will be an end of the war".'[49]

The comment seems remarkably confident, but it was accurate, for in fact, the Prussians' advance guard was to emerge from the Bois de Paris not long after.

For over an hour, the French cavalry charged with the utmost gallantry and determination, but they were frustrated again and again by the stubborn squares that refused to break, and by the steady accurate musketry that struck both them and their mounts with deadly effect. They also suffered severely from the grape-shot fired at a range of fifty paces by Captain Mercer's Troop of Horse Artillery, as well as from several counter-charges made by the cavalry under Lord Uxbridge.

Even when Napoleon threw in yet more cavalry, including the heavy cavalry of the Guard, the ever-dwindling squares still stood firm, until finally, at about 1800 hours, it was the French who withdrew.

DEFEAT OF THE IMPERIAL GUARD Having failed to capture Hougoumont or to break through in the centre, Napoleon now attacked the allied left, and by about 1830 hours, his infantry had captured the key positions of La Haye Sainte and Papelotte, despite a most gallant defence by the King's German Legion and the Nassauers.

This brought Wellington's centre under devastating close-range artillery and musketry fire, and several formations began to waver under the strain.

Ney realising this, asked Napoleon for reinforcements to seize the opportunity for a decisive blow. But Napoleon was not yet prepared to commit his precious Imperial Guard, and having nothing else to offer Ney, he gave the famous retort: 'Des troupes? Où voulez-vous que j'en prenne? Voulez-vous que j'en fasse?'★

Half an hour later Napoleon decided at last to commit his Imperial Guard. But it was half an hour too late. Wellington had used those precious minutes to re-form his line, and to move units from his left flank to the centre, which he could afford to do, now that the Prussians had at last begun to arrive on the battlefield.

Now came the climax of the battle, as Napoleon himself led forward five battalions of his famous Imperial Guard. In the valley between the two

---

★ 'Troops? Where do you think I am to get them from? Do you expect me to create them?'

101

armies, Napoleon handed them over to Ney for the final assault that would surely decide the day in his favour.

The French artillery opened up with yet another bombardment, whereupon Wellington again ordered his exhausted regiments to move back just behind the crest and lie down, so that they were not only out of the direct line of fire, but were completely hidden from view. They rested gladly and some of the First Guards even slept as cannon balls hummed a few feet over their heads.

At about 1930 hours, the final French assault began, as 6,000 veterans of the Imperial Guard advanced steadily through the heavy mud. For 1,000 yards they marched forward, as if on a review, 'their red epaulettes and cross-belts put on over their blue great-coats [giving] them a gigantic appearance, which was increased by their high hairy caps and long red feathers, which waved with the nod of their heads as they kept time to a drum in the centre of their column.'[50]

Ney rode at their head until, for the fourth time that day his horse was killed under him; even then he continued on foot.

The Guard advanced in two massive columns, each on a frontage of 70–80 men shoulder to shoulder. It was an awe-inspiring sight, and behind them the heavy cavalry of the Guard waited to exploit the expected breakthrough.

It was an historic moment, with the future of Europe at stake.

The battle was nearing its climax, as the two great commanders, both aged forty-six, made their final bid for victory. A mere thousand yards apart, each watched and waited. Between them, two corps of élite troops closed in on each other for the final, decisive confrontation.

One column of the Imperial Guard, some 3,000 strong and composed of two battalions of Grenadiers and two of Chasseurs advanced directly at 1st Guards Brigade, reduced by now to only about 1,000 men of the First Guards.

The Guardsmen, lying down as ordered just over the crest, could not at first see the enemy advancing on them. But they could hear the tramp of their feet, getting ever closer, and the confident roars of 'En avant. Vive l'Empéreur'.

Wellington however, on horseback just behind them, could see the Imperial Guard closing in steadily, while across the valley, Napoleon stared through the smoke, watching them fade into the dusk.

Wellington waited calmly until the enemy were only some forty paces from the ranks of Guardsmen just over the crest.

Then he called out to the Brigade Commander:

'Now Maitland. Now's your time.'

And a few seconds later:

'Stand up, Guards. Make Ready; Fire.'[51]

As the Guardsmen sprang to their feet, the two sides saw each other for the first time.

There was the briefest pause – but no exchange of courtesies this time as there had been at Fontenoy.

The Guards were, on Wellington's orders, in four ranks to gain maximum fire effect, and they overlapped the frontage of the French column. The first deadly volley struck the packed ranks of the Imperial Guard, and 300 of them fell.

Two hundred yards to a flank, Bolton's battery joined in with a barrage of grape-shot, which did terrible damage.

Packed so close, it was almost impossible for the French to retaliate or to deploy. For about ten minutes, they tried to advance, but could not. The devastating fire thudded into the packed ranks.

Then at last, they wavered.

'Now's the time, my boys,' called Lord Saltoun, and the First Guards charged with fixed bayonets. For a moment the French faced them, but then they turned. As at Fontenoy, the First Guards saw the coat tails of their French counterparts.

Meanwhile, the left hand column of the Imperial Guards was advancing further to the right of the Guards, whose flank was suddenly exposed. To counter this, Maitland ordered his right-hand battalion (2nd Bn First Guards) to re-form.

But the order was misunderstood, and some confusion arose. A gap was created which could have become highly dangerous. Just in time they managed to reorganise and the threat was averted.

Meanwhile, Colonel Colborne, commanding the 52nd (the Buckinghamshire Light Infantry), the next Regiment on the right, managed by a brilliant manoeuvre, to wheel his whole battalion to the left, so that they could enfilade the entire enemy column. One deadly volley into the left flank of the Chasseurs took them by surprise and stopped them. A bayonet charge, led by Colonel Colborne himself, then drove them back in disarray, pursued by both Adam's Brigade, and the 2nd Battalion First Guards.

Unbelieving, British and French alike watched the impossible happen. The Imperial Guard were in retreat; they had been beaten. The invincible Grenadiers of France had been repulsed, they had failed.

'La Garde recule.'★

These three words spelt, in effect, the defeat of France. Napoleon had gambled all, and had lost. Nothing was left now.

The cry swept through the French Army. The panic spread. On all sides, the French turned and fled. Wellington saw it and raising his hat, he waved it in an unmistakable signal towards the French lines.

With a resounding cheer, the entire British line, now only 40,000 strong, swept forward and drove the demoralised enemy headlong down the slope into the valley below, and then up the opposite slope, where Napoleon had so confidently surveyed the scene that morning.

The cavalry took up the pursuit, hacking and slashing at the fleeing infantry. Even the exhausted defenders of Hougoumont joined in.

'Sauve qui peut,' went up the cry, and the retreat became a rout.

Napoleon himself was forced to shelter at one moment inside a square

---

★ 'The Guard is retreating.'

formed briefly by two battalions of his Imperial Guards which he had kept in reserve. But finally he too turned and rode back towards France, having been forced to abandon his carriage.

It was now just 2030 hours, and the sun was setting, blood-red through the thick smoke.

So ended more than twenty years of war, and with it the Empire that Napoleon Buonaparte had built up in that time. That morning he had been a triumphant Emperor; now he was a fugitive.

The British were too exhausted to pursue far, and they left that task to the Prussians, who had arrived on the battlefield in strength, just after the Imperial Guard were repulsed. Eager to avenge their past defeats, they hunted and harried the French ruthlessly throughout the night, giving them no chance to rally.

It was as Wellington sat on his horse watching the defeat of the French that another of the well-known incidents of Waterloo occurred. One of the last cannon shots of the day struck Lord Uxbridge who was beside him, and shattered his right knee.

'By God Sir, I've lost a leg!' exclaimed Uxbridge.

'By God Sir, so you have', replied Wellington.

The actual words are perhaps apocryphal, but they are certainly characteristic of both men.[52]

The leg was in fact not removed by the shot, but was amputated later, in the house of a local Belgian, called Monsieur Paris.

The severed limb was, with Lord Uxbridge's agreement, buried by Monsieur Paris in his garden in a wooden coffin with an inscribed tombstone.

Lord Uxbridge was said to have made a point, when he visited this house several years later, of dining with his two sons at the very table where he had lain during the operation.

Lord Uxbridge himself recovered, and had an artificial leg fitted; it was specially designed to enable him 'to ride like a gentleman', and was among the earliest articulated artificial limbs. One is now in the Household Cavalry Museum at Windsor, and another in the Anglesey Museum.

At about 2115 hours, the celebrated meeting took place between Wellington and Blücher at La Belle Alliance, which had been the centre of Napoleon's position.

They rode towards each other as a Prussian band nearby played 'God Save The King'.

'Mein lieber Kamerad,' exclaimed the gallant Marshal, embracing the Duke. 'Quelle affaire,' he added, which Wellington commented later was 'pretty much all he knew of French.'

It had been 'an affair' indeed. Some 40,000 men and 10,000 horses lay dead or wounded on the battlefield that night, within an area of two square miles. The Guards Division losses amounted to 1,034 and the Household Cavalry to 320, roughly half their effective strength.

The issue had been in the balance on several occasions, and continued in doubt till the very last moment. Few battles had ever been fought so fiercely for so long.

The final word came very properly from Wellington himself, when he discussed the battle next morning with that well-known columnist of the day, Thomas Creevey, who described it for posterity.

'It has been a damned serious business,' he said. 'Blücher and I have lost 30,000 men. It has been a damned nice thing – the nearest run thing you ever saw in your life . . .'. Then as he walked about, he praised greatly those Guards who kept the farm [Hougoumont] against the repeated attacks of the French; and then he praised all our troops, uttering repeated expressions at our men's courage.

He repeated so often its being 'so nice a thing – so nearly run a thing' that I asked him if the French had fought better than he had ever seen them do before:

'No,' he said. 'They have always fought the same since I first saw them at Vimiero.'
Then he said:
'By God! I don't think it would have done if I had not been there.'[53]

Following the victory at Waterloo, the Allied Armies advanced into France, and Paris capitulated on 3 July.

Most of the Guards regiments returned home, but 2nd Guards Brigade remained near Paris as part of the Army of Occupation. It was commanded by Major General Sir John Byng (Third Guards), and consisted of 3rd Bn Grenadier Guards and 2nd Bn Coldstream Guards.

The Battle Honour of Waterloo was awarded within four weeks[54] and all ranks who took part received a Waterloo medal, the first general issue made to the British Army. In addition, they had the letters 'W.M.' (Waterloo Man) put in red after their names in the records, and, of more significance, this was entitled to count as two years extra service.

Foot Guards officers benefited too, in that the privilege of 'double rank' was extended to Ensigns, who were given the rank of Lieutenant.

The Household Cavalry received the special favour that the Prince Regent declared himself Colonel-in-Chief of the Household Cavalry as a mark of his august appreciation of their gallantry at the Battle of Waterloo. He also sent a consignment of crowns out to Paris for the NCO's to wear above their chevrons as a mark of his approbation, and this custom is continued still today, on undress uniform.

The First Guards also received special recognition, and the London Gazette of 29 July 1815 stated: 'His Royal Highness has also been pleased to approve of the First Regiment of Foot Guards being made a Regiment of Grenadiers and styled The First or Grenadier Regiment of Foot Guards in commemoration of their having defeated the Grenadiers of the French Imperial Guard on this memorable occasion.'

The Grenadier Guards is the only regiment in the British Army that has directly gained its title from the part it played in action. It is in recognition of this that the grenade is worn as a badge on the forage cap, on the tunic, and on the Colours of the Regiment.

The bearskin cap, which had since 1778 been worn by the grenadier companies only in each regiment, was now adopted as the headdress of the whole Regiment of Grenadier Guards, but not as yet by the Coldstream or Third Guards.

Sergeant Graham of the Coldstream Guards and Sergeant Fraser of the Third Guards were both awarded a special medal for their gallantry at Hougoumont. Sergeant Graham was also nominated by Wellington for an annuity of £10 a year, which had been offered by a patriotic citizen, the Reverend John Norcross of Framlingham Rectory in Suffolk, to 'one of his brave countrymen, who fought in the late tremendous but glorious conflict.'

Unfortunately after only two years, the annuity ceased when the Rector went bankrupt. But when he died, he left £500 to be given to 'the bravest man in England'. Wellington was now asked to nominate this individual, and he wrote: 'The success of the battle of Waterloo turned on the closing of the gates [at Hougoumont]. These gates were closed in the most courageous manner at the very nick of time by the efforts of Sir J. Macdonnell.'[55]

So the Colonel received the £500, but promptly shared it with Sergeant Graham.

Chapter 8

The Long Peace (1816–54)

I n 1818, 2nd Guards Brigade which had formed part of the Allied Army of Occupation in France returned home, and the Household troops then settled down to 'the long peace' as it was called. For the Foot Guards it continued until the outbreak of the Crimean War in 1854, while the Household Cavalry were to have their longest-ever period of home service, lasting sixty-seven years.

It was the dawn of the 'age of elegance', with George IV setting the pace as 'the First Gentleman of Europe'. The extravagant social round of the Court was centred not only on London and Windsor, but also on Brighton, which became almost a second capital.

Both the Household Cavalry and the Foot Guards had to be in attendance on the King wherever he was, including Brighton, and a Life Guards Order of 1822 states that 'During the period of His Majesty's residence [in Brighton], officers are required never to appear in the town otherwise than in Full Dress.'

The Monarch delighted in extravagant uniforms, and the Household Cavalry in particular were called upon to try out a variety of fanciful headgear. Full dress for the King's Coronation, for example, on 19 July 1821, meant an enormous plumed bearskin 23 inches tall, which made it somewhat dangerous to ride in a strong wind. For 'Field Days', including some Escort duties on which they were expected to trot, they wore a 'bearskin crested helmet' which weighed 4 lbs 2 oz (as against the 2 lbs 12 oz of the present day helmet).

The Age of Elegance

Cuirasses, not worn since the time of William III, were now re-introduced as ceremonial dress, and uniforms changed in style almost annually, to the delight of the military tailors and the cartoonists.

The Foot Guards too made changes and adopted virtually the uniform that is worn for ceremonial duties today. The scarlet coatee was introduced, with grey or white trousers, and in 1832, bearskin caps became the official head-dress of all three Regiments.

The grenadier companies had always worn white plumes on the left of their head-dress and this custom was continued by the Grenadier Guards from 1815. The Coldstream Guards in 1832 therefore adopted red plumes. The Grenadier plumes were worn on the left of the bearskin and the Coldstream on the right, so that the plumes faced inwards and were visible when both Regiments were in line in battle or on parade. The Scots Guards being in the centre of the line, wore no plumes.

Not surprisingly, it was somewhat costly to hold a commission in the Guards. Officers were expected to pay for their own uniforms, whereas today all ceremonial dress is held centrally by Regiments and issued as needed to officers and men stationed at home. It cost a Household Cavalry officer at least £600 to equip himself, which was a great deal of money in those days, and that did not include the cost of the two black chargers that he had also to provide for himself.

But officer status gave an entrée into society and so to a way of life, that was, at least in peacetime, the ambition of many, but the privilege of few. Some might 'purchase' their commission, in accordance with the accepted custom, but surprisingly perhaps, there were also instances of selected men rising from the ranks to become officers.

In 1821, The Blues were at long last granted by the King the status of Household Cavalry, with the privilege, denied them until then, of mounting the King's Life Guard in London. They moved, therefore, from Windsor to the new barracks at Albany Street, near Regents Park, which had been completed that year to replace those in Portman Square. From there, they now took on the Royal Guards which were the responsibility of the regiment at Regents Park, while those at Hyde Park Barracks had the less enviable task of maintaining law and order in the capital.

Ceremonial duties were a continuing commitment for the Foot Guards as well as the Household Cavalry.

During the reign of William IV, the Buckingham House Detachment of the King's Guard was a Sergeant's Guard only, but in 1837, when Queen Victoria took up residence there, the Guard was increased to one officer and forty-four men. It has always been, and still is today, a detachment of the Queen's Guard which is based at St James's Palace.

An intriguing problem of tradition occurred on 9 November 1841, when the future King Edward VII was born at 1048 hours. By tradition, the Captain of the Queen's Guard on the day when an heir to the throne was born was granted a brevet majority, but at that moment both the Old and the New Guards were on parade, the New Guard having arrived at 1045 hours. Both guard commanders therefore claimed promotion, and it

(*Opposite*) A farrier of the First Life Guards, 1828. The axe, used for several purposes including despatching wounded horses, is still carried today on ceremonial parades. In the background, a Private on barrack sweeping fatigue.

Foot Guards Uniforms, 1832. From left to right, a Cymbalist, Scots Fusilier Guards; a Private, Grenadier Guards; a Lieutenant/Captain, Grenadier Guards; and a Sergeant, Grenadier Guards.

seems that the decision went in favour of the Captain of the Old Guard, found that day by the Grenadier Guards.

Life at this time was governed by rigid social laws. One of them decreed that smoking was a highly undesirable vice, in which no self-respecting member of society would indulge in public. The Army took the matter seriously, and when the Duke of Wellington was Commander-in-Chief he urged Commanding officers to discourage the habit, particularly among young officers. He actually issued a General Order,[56] which described smoking as being 'in itself a species of intoxication occasioned by the fumes of tobacco, [which] undoubtedly, occasions drinking and tippling by those who acquire the habit.'

Guards officers on any sort of duty were forbidden the use of tobacco, and the Guards Club, which was opened in 1810, later had a special 'smoking room', requiring a separate subscription.

Strict orders were issued that there was on no account to be any smoking on the Royal Guards, and Lord Londonderry, Colonel of the 2nd Life Guards, wrote to Lord Combermere, Colonel of the 1st Life Guards, 'What are the Gold Sticks to do with that sink of smoking, the Horse

Guards guard- and mess-room? . . . I have found it worse than any pot-house.'⁵⁷

The Captain of the Guard at St James's Palace was instructed rather more politely to '. . . have the goodness to add to his report that there has been no smoking in the officers' apartments . . . during the twenty four hours he has been on Guard.'⁵⁸

The Crimean War, together with the death of Wellington in 1852, was to lead to a more general acceptance of smoking in the Army, but it was not until 1864 that leave was given for soldiers to smoke in the barrack rooms – and then only from dinner hour until Tattoo. Smoking on Queen's Guard became increasingly prevalent, and the practice was finally accepted officially when Lord Frederick Paulet, Coldstream Guards, declined to sign the required certificate.

Drill parades and reviews were often carried out in Hyde Park, as they had been since the time of James II, and a dramatic incident occurred one day in 1843, when Colonel Robert Ellison, a veteran of Waterloo, who was then commanding the 1st Bn Grenadier Guards, gave his battalion the order 'Present Arms'. He then had a heart attack and fell dead from his horse.

His battalion therefore stood at the 'Present' over his dead body – on a word of command given by him.

Tactical training was also carried out in Hyde Park, which was indeed adequate to prepare soldiers for the type of fighting which had been required at Waterloo, and would also be seen in the Crimean War.

On 19 July 1830, following a parade in Hyde Park, all three regiments of Foot Guards were granted the privilege by William IV of receiving the Sovereign on parade by playing their Regimental March, instead of 'God Save the King'. But today this is continued only by the Coldstream Guards, and with the approval of the Sovereign.

On 24 June 1831, William IV gave the Third Guards the title of 'Scots Fusilier Guards', which they carried until 1877, when they became 'Scots Guards'.

Until Sir Robert Peel introduced in 1829 the Act which created the Metropolitan Police Force, the Army, and particularly the Guards in London, were responsible for the maintenance of law and order. Indeed it was a major role in peacetime, and troops were called out frequently to disperse crowds, protect property and provide escorts for bullion, prisoners, and important visitors to the country, as well as dealing with riotous occasions.

The period after Waterloo was a troubled one. The country had expected freedom and prosperity, but found poverty and repression. The introduction of machinery, the rundown of wartime trades, and the discharge of 33,000 soldiers led to growing unemployment, hardship and unrest, particularly in London and the Midlands.

One incident, known as the Cato Street Conspiracy, was serious enough to lead the Duke of Wellington as Commander-in-Chief to plan a complete campaign for the defence of London. The occasion was a plot to assassinate several Cabinet Ministers while they were dining with Lord Harrowby at his house in Grosvenor Square. The plans were fortunately discovered just in time, and on 19 March 1820, the ten conspirators were surrounded in their hideout at a house in Cato Street, just off the Edgware Road.

A party from 2nd Bn Coldstream Guards, with two peace officers, closed in and captured nine of the ten men. The detachment was commanded by Captain Fitzclarence, and included Sergeant James Graham of Hougoumont fame, who distinguished himself again by saving the life of his officer.

The tenth member of the gang, who was in fact the leader, Arthur Thistlewood, was captured soon after, and all the conspirators were then escorted in handcuffs to the Tower of London by The Life Guards – the last occasion on which the Household Cavalry were to carry out this duty. All the accused were found guilty, and were either executed or transported.

To complete the tale, a detachment of Grenadier Guards was sent to Newgate Gaol on the day of the execution, which involved beheading after hanging. The officers were invited to breakfast with the Governor, but their appetite was somewhat spoiled, when a servant came in and hurried out with the Governor's largest carving knife, which was apparently needed urgently by the executioner to finish off the job.

Another difficult occasion was the funeral procession on 14 August 1821 of Queen Caroline, George IV's deserted and humiliated consort. She died at Hammersmith, but wanted to be buried in her native Germany. Her coffin was therefore escorted across London to the docks by the Household Cavalry.

To avoid publicity and trouble, the authorities had routed it through the suburbs, but the people of London had always shown sympathy for the unfortunate woman, and they were determined to see that her coffin travelled now through the heart of the city of which she had been Queen.

The Blues, leading the Escort, found the Kensington Gate blocked by an angry crowd, and both they and The Life Guards were soon involved in a free-for-all which continued until the magistrates agreed to allow the procession along Knightsbridge.

All along the route the Escort found mobs manning barricades which achieved their purpose of forcing the procession to move not through the suburbs, but down Oxford Street and into the City. There the dead Queen was received with due ceremony and respect, and a decidedly eventful State duty had been completed.

Under considerable provocation, The Life Guards had at one stage eventually opened fire and killed two rioters. An unsympathetic coroner's jury returned a verdict of 'Manslaughter, against the Officers and Soldiers of the First Regiment of Life Guards.' The Regiment now found themselves given the title of 'The Piccadilly Butchers' but some rather more sympathetic citizens raised a subscription for them (which they passed on to the Duke of York's School for the sons of soldiers.)

In addition to their responsibilities for maintaining law and order, the Guards in London were called upon to provide armed escorts on most occasions when Royalty travelled abroad in the capital. It was no light task at a time when the Monarchy was far from being universally respected.

Escorts were required for social as well as ceremonial occasions, and the Household Cavalry even rode with the King to the theatre, a practice which continued for gala performances until 1914, when on 11 May the King and Queen were escorted to Covent Garden by The Blues.

The Foot Guards were also used on occasion to provide protection for the theatres themselves, a custom dating back to Stuart times. In 1755, the actor-manager, David Garrick, suffered from such rowdyism during one production at Drury Lane that after six nights he 'sent for the military'. The Guards came to his aid, and thereafter a Foot Guards picquet was mounted there and at Covent Garden regularly until the twentieth century. Indeed there is still a small room at Drury Lane known as 'The Barracks'.

The duties of the Army even included fire-fighting, and the Guards were commended by the Home Secretary for their part in trying to cope with the fire which destroyed the Houses of Parliament in October 1834. Two years later, troops saved the Foreign Office from a similar fate, and in 1841, the Scots Fusilier Guards helped to rescue the Regalia during a serious fire at the Tower of London.

Routine duties were heavy too, and the Household troops had, until the

(*Overleaf*) Guard Mounting at St. James's Palace. The Guard is formed by the Grenadier Guards. The coatee is still being worn, rather than the present style tunic, which was adopted soon after the Crimean War.

police were formed, to find guards for as many as thirty public buildings in London, including the Bank of England, British Museum, Royal Mint, Royal Academy and the Savoy Prison.

Conditions for the Army were not good early in the nineteenth century, but they improved steadily, as the standard of living rose throughout the country. The Guards took a particular interest in the welfare of their men, and indeed took the lead in instituting several new amenities in their Regiments, for which the officers sometimes paid out of their own pockets.

The Blues, for example, established a Regimental hospital in Windsor in 1804, and the Coldstream followed suit in London ten years later, still some years before the first Army hospitals were opened.

Regimental schools were instituted in 1811, a Sergeant schoolmaster being appointed with a special allowance of £10 a year.

A particularly significant amenity initiated by the Guards was the provision of married quarters for the men. The wives and children of Guardsmen had to date lived in the barrack rooms, as was the custom throughout the Army when in England. When a battalion went abroad, four or six wives per company were chosen by lot to accompany their husbands.

The only possible privacy under these conditions was often a blanket or curtain stretched across the room, which was utterly inadequate – though it was said that the arrangement had a very moderating effect on the behaviour and language of the single men.

This unsatisfactory position was improved oddly enough as a result of an outbreak of cholera in 1832. The overcrowded barrack rooms were obviously a health threat, and also some families were billeted out in cholera-infected areas. Separate married quarters were therefore organised inside barracks as a temporary measure to meet the emergency.

The Household Division led the way in setting up more permanent married quarters, when a group of officers in 1852 raised £9,000 privately and used it to build a hostel for fifty-six families in Francis Street, just off the Vauxhall Bridge Road. They were bought out a few years later by the War Department, who pointed out that it was illegal for soldiers to pay rent to officers for their accommodation, even though it was only the equivalent of twelve new pence a week.

But the practice of providing married quarters then became official policy, and was extended throughout the Army, a feature of the Great Exhibition of 1851 being a display of this new military accommodation. Some of the first official married quarters in London were built in 1860 as part of the new Chelsea Barracks then being constructed.

Meanwhile the Committee of Guards officers that had organised the married quarters project now devoted the money to a club in the Westminster area, but this was not a success, and was sold. The proceeds were then used to improve the interior of the Guards Chapel which had been built in Wellington Barracks in 1838, and has remained the place of worship for the Household Division in London ever since.

Another innovation was the setting up in 1863 of a Guards Home at Maida Vale to look after the daughters of serving Guardsmen. It was initially financed by the officers at their own expense, and continued as a Household Division charity until 1943.

Only three infantry barracks were available in London in 1821, and none of them could house a complete battalion. Most men and their families were therefore still billeted out in inns, or on private citizens, and it was not until 1834, when Wellington Barracks were completed, that there was enough barrack accommodation for the five battalions stationed in the capital.

The barracks were then:

Household Cavalry
Regents Park Barracks, London
Hyde Park Barracks, London
Cavalry Barracks, Windsor (now Combermere Barracks)

Foot Guards
Tower of London
Wellington Barracks, London
King's New Barracks (near the National Gallery)
Portman Street (later called St George's Barracks in Granville Place, Portman Sq.)
Knightsbridge Barracks (near St George's Place, Hyde Park Corner)
Infantry Barracks, Windsor (now Victoria Barracks)

Although these districts in London are now all very central, they were at this time on the outskirts of the capital. Donkeys grazed then in what is now Lowndes Square, and Brompton was a suburb; it was unsafe to visit the village of Kensington after dark, because of footpads and ruffians, while Queen's Gate was out in the country, and was known for its farms and market gardens. Hyde Park Barracks with its role of the police station of the day, was kept busy protecting citizens from robbery and violence.

No serious campaigns disturbed the 'long peace' and indeed there were only two calls for service overseas between 1815 and 1853.

The first occasion was when a Guards Brigade (consisting of 1st Bn Grenadier Guards and 1st Bn Scots Fusilier Guards) was sent to Portugal from 1826–28, but saw no fighting.

Then in 1839, another Guards Brigade (made up of 2nd Bn Grenadier Guards and 2nd Bn Coldstream Guards) was sent to Canada to deal with a revolt by the French element of the population. They were not involved in fighting, but were kept there until 1842 pending the settlement of a boundary dispute.

The campaign in Canada is perhaps best known, at least in the Household Division, for the tale of 'Jacob', whose head and neck are preserved in the Guards Museum, hung with an officer's gorget, inscribed, 'Jacob, 2nd Bn Coldstream Guards, Died on Duty'.

Jacob was in fact, a large white goose, who saved the lives of many of the Coldstream Guards by giving the alarm one snowy night when the rebels

Service Abroad

were about to launch a surprise attack against them. He was then taken on as an honoured Regimental pet and brought back to London, where he used to parade up and down alongside the sentry at the barrack gate. He was eventually run down by a van in the Portman Street barracks, but is not forgotten.

By 1853, a new threat of war was growing and when on 30 April 1854, Britain declared war on Russia, the long peace was ended.

Jacob the goose

Chapter 9

Changing Times (1854–1900)

It had become clear early in 1854 that Britain might have to support her ally, Turkey, against aggressive moves threatened by Russia. The Government began therefore to assemble an expeditionary force in Malta, under the command of Lord Raglan, formerly Grenadier Guards.

For the first time for some 800 years, Britain now found herself fighting alongside rather than against the French, though it was not as yet exactly an enthusiastic comradeship in arms.

The Household Cavalry were forbidden by Queen Victoria to leave the country, but a Guards Brigade[59] sailed for Malta in March, and thence to the Crimea in April (See Map 6 on page 125.)

It was a fine force, in that it was made up of regular soldiers of seven to eighteen years service, whose efficiency had been improved by attendance at the new training camp set up the previous year at Chobham. But the Army as a whole was rusty and mismanaged after forty years of peace, and their thinking, organisation and equipment were hopelessly inadequate, as became painfully clear all too soon – at the expense, as always, of the troops.

THE BATTLE OF THE ALMA (20 SEPTEMBER 1854) The main allied objective was to capture the port of Sevastopol. It was too strong to be taken by direct assault from the sea, and the Anglo-French force of 63,000 was therefore landed thirty miles north of Sevastopol, with a view to attacking the fortress from the land.

The Crimean War (1854–6)

(*Overleaf*) Crossing the Alma.

119

The landing on 14 September was successful, but as the Allies moved south, they found the Russians under Prince Menschikoff entrenched on the heights above the line of the river Alma.

A fierce battle took place on 20 September, in which the British Light Division crossed the river and initially drove the enemy back. But they were then themselves forced back by Russian counter-attacks, and the 1st Division were called upon to advance to their support. All three Regiments of 1st Guards Brigade crossed the river, and the Grenadiers and Coldstream then paused to reorganise. Markers were called out, and the lines were carefully dressed, as if on Horse Guards. The Scots Fusilier Guards however, having been delayed during the crossing, did not wait to re-form, but pressed forward up the slope. The other troops in front unfortunately withdrew at this moment, and confusion developed, as the two bodies met.

At a crucial moment, the Colour Party of the Scots Fusilier Guards[60] found themselves in the front of the fighting round the enemy strongpoint, the Great Redoubt. They were for a while almost surrounded, but stood firm, until the battalion could rally round them.

The Queen's Colour was found afterwards to have twenty-three bullet holes in it and the pole was shot through; but both officers were miraculously unhurt, though two of the Escort were killed. Two of the Colour Party were awarded the Victoria Cross, when it was instituted two years later on 29 January 1856. They were the first of forty-four members of the Household Division to win this highest award for gallantry over the next 90 years. (See page 286.)

The Allies now closed in on Sevastopol, planning to attack it from the south, because this would enable them to make use of the harbour of Balaclava. But the Russians thwarted this plan by establishing new defences. They also managed to reinforce the garrison substantially, and Lord Raglan no longer had any great chance of achieving the quick victory he wanted. He therefore settled down to starve the enemy into submission.

THE BATTLE OF INKERMAN (5 NOVEMBER 1854) The Guards were not involved in the Battle of Balaclava on 25 October, though The Royals, took part in the Heavy Cavalry Brigade charge. Two weeks later, the Russians launched a heavy attack on 5 November against the British positions around Inkerman which were held by 1st Guards Brigade.

As day dawned, the battlefield was shrouded in thick mist, which intensified the usual 'fog of war', and enabled some 30,000 Russians to close in and work round the flanks of the 6,000 or so British troops holding the approaches to Balaclava.

It was an area of valleys and ridges, and the fighting soon developed into a confused mêlée, over which the commanders could exercise little control. It has been fairly called 'the soldiers' battle', for all depended on the determination and initiative of scattered bodies of troops acting in isolation.

It was well summed up in the memoirs of Lord Wantage, V.C. (Scots Fusilier Guards): 'Few battles have been fought in which the personal influence of the company officers had so much to do . . . no divisional,

brigade or even regimental order was given. The men, headed by their officers, fought in companies or half-companies.'

The Grenadier and Scots Fusilier Guards were holding forward positions at Kit Spur and Sandbag Battery, where they beat off repeated attacks, although heavily outnumbered.

The Grenadier Guards had their Colours with them in Sandbag Battery, and a desperate struggle took place, in which the Colour Party was surrounded, and the battalion was finally reduced to some 100 men. But led by the Commanding Officer, they fought their way out and reached the British lines after six hours of incessant fighting, in which the Sandbag Battery had changed hands no less than seven times.

The succession of Russian attacks was repulsed, but only with heavy casualties, the Guards losing some 600 all ranks out of 1300.

The battle of Inkerman caused severe losses to the Russians too and might have resulted in a victory for the Allies had the French pursued the enemy more effectively. As it was, it was inconclusive.

It was the last time any Colours of the Brigade of Guards were taken into battle[61] and the Grenadier Guards won three Victoria Crosses in their defence, just as the Scots Fusiliers Guards had won two at the Alma.

Because of the notable part played by the non-commissioned officers of the 3rd Battalion Grenadier Guards at Inkerman, the anniversary of the battle has been a cause for celebration in the Sergeants Mess ever since.

When the 3rd Battalion ceased to exist in 1961, Queen Elizabeth gave the

Roll Call. The Grenadier Guards call the roll after the Battle of Inkerman. (From a painting by Lady Butler.)

123

The burial of Coldstream
Guards officers after the
Battle of Inkerman.

title of the 'Inkerman Company' to the left flank company of the 2nd
Battalion, so that the achievements of the 3rd Battalion in the Crimea should
be kept alive.

Winter was now closing in, which was grim enough, but then on 14
November a terrific storm lashed the Crimean coast. Twenty-one ships
were sunk, and with them disappeared much of the army's food, clothing,
equipment and comforts. Tents were destroyed by the hundred, leaving
the men with almost no shelter. Tunics and bearskins were certainly not
the most suitable dress for such conditions.

As the snow, frost and icy winds swept in, the troops had to endure the
grimmest hardships. Cholera and scurvy killed many, and all suffered in
varying degrees from frost-bite or trench-feet. It was little comfort to be
sent to hospital, for conditions were hardly better there, despite the dedicated
efforts of Florence Nightingale. By the end of February 1855, the Guards
Brigade strength was reduced to 450 fit men out of the original 4,000 –
and that was despite a draft of 500 the previous November.

Conditions improved somewhat during 1855, very largely owing to the
efforts of the first 'war correspondent' Billy Russell.[62] He had gone to the
Crimea to report on the campaign for *The Times*, and he sent back a series
of highly critical despatches – over the new-fangled machine called the
telegraph.

His reports on the gallantry and the hardships of the troops, the incom-
petence of the commanders and staff, and the disgraceful lack of equipment
and supplies, swayed public opinion as could nothing else, and they were
largely responsible for the greatly improved administration in the latter
half of the campaign.

124

The deadly siege of Sevastopol dragged on through 1855 and it was only on 9 September that the fortress was finally occupied. It was not the end of the campaign, though, and the troops had to survive another grim winter before peace was signed at last in March 1856.

On 8 July 1856, the Crimean Guards Brigade paraded at Aldershot and were addressed by Queen Victoria, who, it is recorded, 'quite broke down and burst into tears when she talked of the poor fellows that were not there to receive her thanks'. The Guards had lost 425 killed, and over four times that number from sickness. But they had won thirteen Victoria Crosses,[63] which were presented by Queen Victoria herself, who took a very deep personal interest in all those who had served in the Crimea.

So ended the war that was to spark off some much needed changes in the British Army.

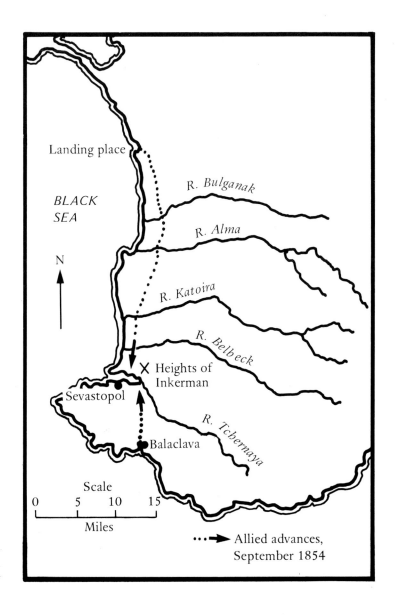

6 Crimea

126

The end of the Crimean War saw some of the most sweeping changes in the Army for a very long time. The initial impetus came from the highly critical reports publicised by Mr Russell, together with the inspiring example, and determined lobbying of Florence Nightingale. Public opinion was stirred as never before, and an era of reform gathered way.

The changes were initiated and carried through largely thanks to two outstanding men, who became responsible for the Army at this time. They were Sidney Herbert, three times Secretary of State for War between 1846 and 1863, and Edward Cardwell, who held that post from 1868 to 1874.

Sadly, the main resistance to change came from the higher levels of the Army itself, many of whom preferred the old ways. Also, any improvements had to be carried out against the usual background of demands for economy, and so changes were slow to mature. But overall the conditions, the status and the efficiency of the Army improved markedly in the second half of the century, though weaknesses were to be exposed by the South African War.

The Wind of Change

(*Opposite*) Coldstream Guards Drummers in the Crimea.

Divine Service outside Sevastopol.

The soldiers' accommodation could clearly be improved, and between 1865 and 1870, new barracks were completed at Chelsea and a new camp set up at Shorncliffe. Both the Cavalry and the Infantry Barracks at Windsor were re-built, and the Foot Guards quarters at St John's Wood, Portman Street, and in Dublin were given up.

In 1870 the Vestry of Chelsea complained that Hyde Park Barracks was 'an evil, a nuisance, a demoralisation, a deterioration of property and a depreciation of rates.' But they received an equally pungent counter-blast in the Household Brigade Magazine, which retorted, 'Let them sweep out their dirty hordes of drunken dissolute Bedouins of the streets before they become public accusers of the best conducted men in the pay of the Crown.'

Hyde Park Barracks were however re-built in 1880, and the first occupants were The Blues, who gave an Opening Ball, attended by the Prince and Princess of Wales, which cost every officer £70. The Life Guards set out to do even better the next year, at even greater cost, but the Regimental rivalry ceased when Queen Victoria expressed her disapproval of such extravagance.

Married Quarters also began to be built as a normal practice, following the example set by the Household troops. (See page 116.)

Education was sadly lacking in the Army, and it was estimated that up to sixty per cent of the men were illiterate. Sidney Herbert had introduced some reforms in 1846, but little developed for another ten years, and even then, men had to be offered rewards to persuade them to study. Nor were most officers particularly enthusiastic about attending the new-fangled Military University set up in 1858 at Camberley (later to become the Staff College).

Discipline was another question which aroused strongly divergent opinions within the Army, partly because of the marked reluctance of many officers to abandon flogging as the standard punishment, although public opinion was fiercely opposed to it. In 1812, the maximum sentence had been limited to 300 lashes, and in 1868, flogging was confined to 'active service' only, but it was not till 1881 that it was finally abolished officially. Deserters were still treated severely, and were branded with a 'D' for Deserter under the arm with a tattooing iron, a specimen of which can be seen in the Guards Museum.

Other major reforms carried out during this period were the introduction of new terms of service and improved pay, together with the abolition of the purchase of commissions, and 'double rank'.

Up till 1847, military service had been 'for life', though men might enlist or be conscripted for shorter periods during a war. The ranks included many jailbirds and tough characters who fought well, but were not easily controlled in peacetime. In that year, the principle of a fixed engagement of twenty-one years was introduced, while the Short Service Act of 1870 led to most men being enlisted for seven years with the Colours and five in the Reserve. The Foot Guards had an addition their own engagement of 'three and nine'.

(*Opposite above*) Foot Guards Uniforms, 1821. A group of Coldstream Guards officers and men on Horse Guards with the Horse Guards building behind to the left. The orders of dress shown are from left to right: a Lieutenant/Captain in marching order, who wears a bearskin with a white plume because he is in the grenadier company; a Sergeant in the light company, as indicated by his green plume; a Colour Sergeant in the grenadier company; a Private in the grenadier company, holding the horse; Captain/Lieutenant Colonel Dan McKinnon, in Court Guard Order, and wearing his Waterloo medal; and a Colour Sergeant in an infantry company. (From a painting by D. Dighton.)

(*Opposite below*) The Battle of the Alma, 1854. The Scots Fusilier Guards Colour Party protecting the Colours in the action that won them two Victoria Crosses. They are, from left to right, Ensign H. J. Lindsay, Sergeant J. McKechnie, and Ensign A. M. Thistlethwayte. (From a painting by Lady Butler.)

(*Overleaf*) The Battle of Monte Piccolo, 1944. 'S' Company of the Scots Guards in a typical infantry battle of the Italian Campaign. (From a painting by Terence Cuneo.)

A group of officers celebrate with a Christmas dinner during the siege of Sevastopol.

The Household Cavalry, however, did not favour short service soldiers, and continued until 1903 to enlist men for twenty-one years with the Colours. They had the support of the Queen for this policy, for when Sir Garnet Wolseley, a strong supporter of a short-service Army, wrote to commend the Household Cavalry for their work in Egypt in 1882, he received the somewhat chilly Royal retort: 'The Queen is glad to hear that Sir Garnet Wolseley entertains such a high opinion of Her Household Cavalry; she would remind him that they are the only Long Service Corps in the Army.'

Pay was improved by the granting of good conduct pay, but it was only a penny a day after three years, and sixpence after twenty-eight years. Basic pay was the traditional 'shilling a day' (5p), plus an extra penny for being in the Foot Guards. But it was subject to such stoppages for cleaning materials, haircuts, laundry and barrack damages that the men saw little of it. It was not till 1890 that the private soldier had officially to receive a minimum of twopence a day in cash, but that was enough for a pint of beer in those days.

A Guardsman could however, supplement those meagre rates in various ways. If he was lucky enough to be on Queen's Guard on a Royal birthday or other Royal occasion, he received an extra day's pay. Ninepence a day could be earned for acting as a 'guinea pig' in a drill squad for Volunteer officers under instruction, while some fatigues at the Royal Army Clothing Depot at Pimlico were paid for.

A rarer duty was to act as an 'extra' at Covent Garden or Drury Lane

(*Opposite above*) The Battle of Inkerman, 1854. Isolated groups of the Grenadier Guards fight in what was called 'the soldiers' battle'.

(*Opposite below*) 6th Guards Tank Brigade, 1944. Churchill tanks advance through the close 'bocage' country of Normandy in their first action at Mont Pincon. (From a painting by Terence Cuneo.)

Theatre, a custom dating back at least to the late eighteenth century when the rate was ninepence per performance and sixpence for rehearsals. It is said that the practice was given Royal assent by Queen Victoria when she noted with disapproval the highly unmilitary bearing of some of the so-called soldiers in the chorus at a Royal Command Performance of *Aïda*. The custom continues still, but the agreed rate is £2·40.

Nor were the officers much better rewarded. An Ensign's pay up till the Crimean War was only four shillings and sixpence, (twenty two new pence) a day, and his Mess expenses alone were probably higher than that. This was not, however, any undue worry to most Guards officers, who generally had ample means of their own.

One officer who indeed took a positive delight in extravagant spending was Colonel Owen Williams, who commanded The Blues from 1884 to 1893. The entertainment that he offered in his riverside villa, near Marlow was grandeur itself, and he might be said to have set the fashion of the 'week-end'.

He missed few opportunities to show off, and would deliberately arrange to miss a train, so that he could, with some ostentation, order a special train. This was before the days of nationalisation and was not unusual; indeed officers stationed at Aldershot used to order their own train at a cost of £5, to get them back from late nights in London.

On the march from London to Windsor, he would plunge in full uniform into the Thames and swim his charger across, emerging soaked, but quite unruffled, and with a large cigar still in his mouth.

He also took immense pride in his Regiment, and his world consisted of The Blues, and 'the rest of the Army', for which he had little use. Indeed, when he became a Major General, he was heard to mutter at a Levée, 'Oh, the degradation of having to wear a *red* coat!'

Sadly he died leaving a mountain of debts.[64]

The firmly established custom of the sale and purchase of commissions, which dated back to the times of Charles II, had by the nineteenth century become subject to particularly blatant abuse, and even a form of 'black market'. The regulation price for command of a company of Foot Guards, for example, was just under £5,000, but the post might change hands for around £9,000, while a Cavalry lieutenant-colonelcy might fetch £14,000, more than double the official rate.

But there were many who sincerely believed in the value of the system, and, as over the flogging issue, the debate was bitter and prolonged. Finally, Cardwell settled it by persuading the Queen to issue a Royal Warrant ending the custom in 1871, just 210 years after it was begun.

Another custom abolished at this time was 'double rank', a privilege that the Household troops had enjoyed for over two centuries. The last holder of a 'double rank' is believed to have been Captain/Lieutenant Colonel Parry Bonham of the Grenadier Guards who died in 1945 at the age of ninety-three.

Apart from changes applicable to the whole Army, the Household Division also carried out its own internal reorganisation. The Foot Guards

began to function more as one body, and on 14 July 1856, the appointment was authorised of a Major General, Commanding the Brigade of Guards, i.e. all Regiments of Foot Guards.[65] He set up his headquarters in the Horse Guards building, and in 1870 also became responsible for Home District (now London District), as well as controlling the interests of the Brigade of Guards.

The first officer to hold the post was Major General Lord Rokeby of the Scots Fusiliers Guards. It is probably just a coincidence that in November of the same year, his Regiment were authorised to have pipers on their establishment despite some unappreciative protests from the other Regiments, and even from the English element of the Scots Fusilier Guards!

An official Guards journal, today called 'The Guards Magazine'[66] was started in 1862, and can boast the remarkable record of having had only three Editors in the 114 years of its life. The first was I. E. A. Dolby (1862–1905), who was succeeded by Captain Sir George Arthur, Bt. (1905–44), and Sir Charles Petrie, Bt., from 1944 to today.

The Household Cavalry leave for Egypt, 1882.

135

The Moonlight Charge,
1882.

137

It was about 1856 that the Household Brigade Cricket Club were given permission to adopt the Royal racing colours of blue, red, blue for their tie. It is now the Guards tie, worn by all ranks, and the colours have been adopted as those of the Household Division.

TRAINING The Crimean War demonstrated the need for a very much more professional approach to soldiering throughout the Army, and in May 1857 a Council of Military Education was set up to study the question.

Officers had not to date been expected to acquire any great scientific knowledge of their profession beyond an understanding of musketry, the drillbook manoeuvres then required for battle, and the elements of administration and organisation. The vital requirements were courage and leadership in battle, and these qualities they seldom failed to show.

Training at battalion level was left very much to the Adjutant and the non-commissioned officers, and it was a normal occurrence for most officers to arrive in Hyde Park in their own cabs for parades and exercises. This was changed by an Army Order of 1883, which made every officer responsible for the training of the troops under his command.

The threat from Prussia, as demonstrated by the war of 1870, stirred the Government to treat training more seriously. Manoeuvres involving a degree of realism were begun in 1871, and all available units, including a Guards Brigade, went to Aldershot for seven weeks, usually during August and September. But after only two years, large-scale exercises were abandoned on the grounds that they were too expensive, and they were not re-instituted until 1892.

Tactics in the whole Army were still based largely on the rigid barrack-square drills of the Crimea, and it required the South African War of 1899–1902 to show the higher command, by bitter experience, just how out-of-date their thinking still was.

Training for the men continued to be based on drill, musketry, marching, and now a new idea called 'gymnastic training'. The Brigade of Guards had in fact started gymnastics on their own initiative as early as 1843, but they must have offended Victorian prudery, for instructions were received from the Duke of Wellington that 'no gymnastic exercises should take place in any situation exposed to public view.'

About this time, horse-drawn transport was provided at battalion level for the first time, and selected officers and men were sent off to Woolwich to be trained as drivers.

Signalling also began to be taught, involving instruction in semaphore and the heliograph, for Mr Bell and Signor Marconi had not as yet adapted their inventions for military use.

In 1890, the Army was equipped with the new magazine rifle, the Lee Enfield, which was a vast improvement on the rifles and muskets, which had served the soldier well for two centuries.

The Guards expanded their training organisation by moving the Guards Depot in 1877 from Warley to its renowned site at Caterham, where it was to remain for the next 82 years. The barracks, with their grim, austere

buildings and grounds were situated next door to a lunatic asylum, whose inmates were reported by successive generations of Guardsmen to have looked over the wall, and remarked to the sweating recruits next door, 'You'd be much better off in here, boys.'

Five years later a site in Pirbright, near Woking in Surrey, was taken on as a training and musketry area, and the Guards have used the area ever since.

The Heavy Camel Regiment. The Household Cavalry Camel Regiment, wearing the new-style khaki uniforms and pith helmets.

Imperial Policing

The second half of the nineteenth century brought no major war for Britain, but the Army was kept occupied with a series of minor campaigns and 'imperial policing' operations worldwide.

The Guards took part in many active operations overseas, including the periodic posting of a battalion to Ireland to deal with the insoluble troubles

Lt.Col. F. A. Graves-Sawle   Capt. E. M. S. Crabbe

Lt. The Hon. H. Amherst   Lt. Count Gleighen   Lt. D. E. R. Dawson   Lt.Col. C. R. Rowley

Lt.Col. The Hon.
E. T. Boscawen

Lt. L. G. H. D'Aquilar   Lt. H. G. Wolrige Gordon   Lt.Col. Mildway Willson

Capt. A. C. Pearson, R.M.

Lt. C. Crutchley   Capt. V. J. Dawson   Lt.Col. Sir W. G. Gordon
(Adjutant)   Cumming, Bt.   Lt. A. S. Drummond

Lt. Col.
I. J. C. Herbert

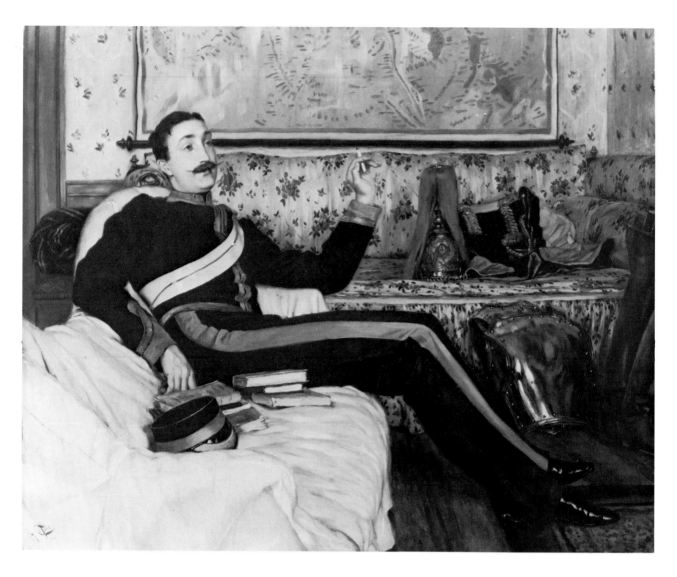

Colonel Fred Burnaby.

(*Previous pages*) The Guards
Camel Regiment.

there. They were not stationed in India, however, because they had their permanent peacetime commitment to carry out duties in London. They therefore normally served overseas on active service only, not for peace-time garrison duties, as did Regiments of the Line.

A Guards Brigade, commanded by Major General Lord Paulet (Cold-stream Guards) and consisting of 1st Bn Grenadier Guards and 2nd Bn Scots Fusilier Guards, was sent to Canada in 1861 to protect the frontier during the American Civil War. They saw no fighting and the main feature of the expedition for the troops was that the journey from England took no less than forty-four days, including eleven days spent travelling on open sledges.

EGYPT 1882 Real active service materialised in 1882 when trouble developed in Egypt, and an expeditionary force was formed.

In 1875, shares in the Suez Canal Company were bought for Britain by Disraeli for £4,080,000, with the help of a £4 million loan from Baron Lionel de Rothschild. Since then, the preservation of peace in Egypt has been a major interest of the two joint shareholders, Britain and France. But

142

on 11 June 1882, the news arrived in London that the Egyptians under a Colonel Arabi were actually demanding 'Egypt for the Egyptians' and had massacred 150 Europeans.

The British Government reacted with strong indignation to such an outrage, and the Royal Navy were ordered to bombard Alexandria. At the same time, an expeditionary force was assembled under General Sir Garnet Wolseley to deal with the rebels, and also to ensure continuing control of the Suez Canal.

The force included a cavalry division consisting of one British and one Indian cavalry brigade, and in the former was a Household Cavalry Composite Regiment. This was a precedent, caused by the determination of the Household Cavalry not to be left out of the fighting again, having been forced to stay at home on State duties ever since Waterloo.

One squadron was finally selected from each of the three regiments (First and Second Life Guards, and The Blues) and the force sailed on 1 August. The Prince of Wales had asked to be allowed to serve in Egypt with the Household Cavalry, of whom he was Colonel-in-Chief. But he was told by the Secretary of State: 'It is clearly undesirable that His Royal Highness should go. This is one of the penalties which attach to his high position.'

On 28 August, the Cavalry Brigade[67] was summoned to go to the aid of the British camp at el Kassassin where a force of 2,000 infantry had been surrounded and attacked all day by a superior Egyptian army under Colonel Arabi.

The cavalry arrived at dusk, and moved round a flank under a brilliant full moon. The guns which they had in support opened up effectively, whereupon the Household Cavalry formed line, and swept forward in the famous 'Moonlight Charge', which drove the attackers back to their camp.

The expeditionary force also contained the 1st Division which included a Guards Brigade[68] commanded by Major General The Duke of Connaught, son of Queen Victoria. Their first action was the Battle of Tel-el-Kebir on 13 September.

The plan was an ambitious one, involving an eight-mile advance by night, followed by a dawn attack against the main enemy position held by twice their own strength. In the event, all worked perfectly, and it was a 'drill-book operation', lasting thirty-five minutes. The Egyptian Army were routed, and the Cavalry Division pursued them to Cairo, which they occupied on 14 September, closely followed by the Scots Guards, who marched in, with pipes playing.

This short, sharp and highly successful colonial campaign caught the public imagination, and the Guards Regiments involved received an enthusiastic welcome on their return to London.

SUDAN (1884) Peace in the Middle East was short-lived however. As far back as 1881, one Mahomet Ahmed had declared himself to be 'the Mahdi', the pre-destined leader of the Moslem world. He soon attracted a substantial following, particularly in the Sudan, and in October 1883, his forces defeated and annihilated a colonial force of Egyptians, under Hicks Pasha.

The threat in the Sudan increased, and early the next year, General Gordon was sent to Khartoum to arrange its evacuation. He spent his last night in England in Hyde Park Barracks with The Blues. He had arrived at a London station, with nowhere to go, and was taken by a friend to the Household Cavalry Mess. He had no suitable clothes to wear for dinner, and so ate in the ante-room off a tray.

About the same time, another colonial force of 4,000 Egyptians in the Sudan was also surrounded by the Mahdi and virtually destroyed. Soon General Gordon was cut off in Khartoum and besieged by the Mahdi's forces.

Drastic action was clearly called for, and the country naturally turned again to Sir Garnet Wolseley, confident that he would soon dispose of the Mahdi, as he had of Arabi Pasha.

His first task was to relieve Gordon in Khartoum, and for this he had two plans. The first was to send a force as far as possible up the river Nile in some of the tourist steamers belonging to that enterprising travel agent, Mr Thomas Cook. The second was to send a highly mobile force, mounted mainly on camels, to move cross-country direct to Khartoum.

Both ideas, not surprisingly perhaps, met with marked opposition from the authorities at home, and the Duke of Cambridge, who was then Commander-in-Chief, condemned the idea of camels in particular, as being 'unsound, and distasteful to regiments, officers and men'.

Nevertheless, both plans were eventually agreed, and thus was initiated one of the stranger incidents in the story of the Household Division, for the Guards, both Horse and Foot, were about to become part of a 'Camelry Corps' (see illustration on page 139).

The Household Cavalry were called upon to contribute to a Heavy Camel Regiment, which formed at Aldershot (less camels) in September 1884. The First and Second Life Guards, The Blues and also The Royals each contributed a detachment of two officers and forty men to the Regiment, as did seven other cavalry regiments. The Regimental Commander was Colonel the Hon. R. Talbot of the First Life Guards.

The Foot Guards, offered a chance to match the cavalry at their own game, formed a rival Guards Camel Regiment, commanded by Lieutenant Colonel the Hon. E. Boscawen (Coldstream Guards), and composed of similar detachments from each of the three Regiments.

Both bodies arrived in Egypt in December 1884, and travelled initially by steamer up the Nile. They then collected their camels, and set off somewhat unsteadily and uncomfortably into the desert, heading for Khartoum, now 150 miles away.

One compensation was that they had all now abandoned scarlet and blue, and were wearing the new 'khaki' uniform, copied from the Indian Army. Queen Victoria had not been enthusiastic about her Household troops appearing in what she called 'a sort of café-au-lait shade',[69] but had eventually agreed to it.

Almost three weeks later, they reached the wells at Abu Klea, still 100 miles from Khartoum, where some 15,000 Dervishes barred their way, and proceeded to attack them when they formed the usual defensive square.

The enemy were successfully beaten off, but The Blues suffered a sad loss, when Colonel Fred Burnaby, a well-known personality in the Household Cavalry was killed in this encounter. He had joined the Regiment in 1859 at the age of sixteen, the son of a well-to-do sporting parson in honour of whom he called all his chargers by Biblical names. He was exceptionally large and strong (six foot four inches tall with a forty four inch chest – two inches more than Muhammad Ali). One of his party tricks was to bend a Mess poker round the neck of guests – including on one occasion, the Prince of Wales.

He took up ballooning, and on one flight got swept out of control across to France, only to be reprimanded on his return for 'leaving the country without permission'. He travelled widely, wrote, and established a reputation for the unconventional.

Perhaps his most famous exploit occurred when he was at Windsor, and two miniature ponies, sent to Queen Victoria as a gift and due to be presented to her at a parade, were dumped by brother officers in his bedroom. It was a good joke – until the ponies refused to move an inch – and the Queen was waiting below. Burnaby thereupon took one pony under each arm, and carried them downstairs and out into the parade ground.

He had volunteered to join the Camel Corps in Egypt because he could not bear to miss any excitement, and he met his end trying to save some men who had been left outside the safety of the square.

On 28 January 1885, the expedition came within sight of Khartoum, only to learn that it had fallen two days before, and General Gordon was dead.

So ended what the Guards might well have thought was their first and last appearance on camels. But in fact this was not so, for in the 1930s the battalions stationed in Egypt mounted their Intelligence Section on camels.

1885 produced one more Battle Honour for each Regiment when a Guards Brigade, composed of 3rd Bn Grenadier Guards, 1st Bn Coldstream Guards and 2nd Bn Scots Guards, rounded up the remnants of the Mahdi's army near the undistinguished Sudanese village of Suakin.

The occasion is more noteworthy perhaps because a New South Wales battalion was attached to the Guards Brigade, the first time that Australian troops had fought as part of the British Army outside their own country.

A very similar colonial campaign occurred in 1895, when an expeditionary force, which included a composite Guards Company, was sent to Ashanti on the west coast of Africa.

They soon completed their task, which was to depose the local ruler, King Prempeh; his crime was that he had not only offended Victorian principles by carrying on a prosperous slave trade, but, far worse, he had actually dared to raid the neighbouring British colony of the Gold Coast to 'stock his shop window'.

New Guards Battalions

In 1897, the strength of the whole Army was increased, and the Brigade of Guards for their part received the welcome news that the Coldstream and Scots Guards were both to be allowed to raise a 3rd Battalion, which they did in 1899.

The following year saw another major development in the history of the Household Division, when they formed a completely new Regiment, the Irish Guards. On 1 April 1900, Army Order No. 77 stated that 'Her Majesty the Queen, having deemed it desirable to commemorate the bravery shown by the Irish Regiments during the operations in South Africa in the years 1899–1900 has been graciously pleased that an Irish Regiment of Foot Guards be formed to be designated the "Irish Guards".'[70]

Volunteers came rapidly from the rest of the Brigade, from other Irish Regiments, and direct from Ireland, so that by 20 September, the 1st Bn Irish Guards was officially constituted.

Queen Victoria presents a State Colour to the Scots Guards at Windsor on 15 July 1899.

Chapter 10

Before the Storm (1900–14)

The glorious nineteenth century ended with one colonial campaign that was not quite as easily settled as Suakin and Ashanti. This was the Boer War, which began on 12 October 1899.

The British Government had few doubts that they would soon dispose of these troublesome Dutch farmers in South Africa who dared to defy the impressive might of Queen Victoria's Empire.

In the event, it was the Boers who taught the British Army many lessons in the course of the three years' war. They were exceptionally skilled as tacticians, marksmen, horsemen and guerillas, and they used these skills to outwit the cumbersome, unimaginative tactics of the British Army, whose last real war had been in tunics and bearskins in the Crimea.

Indeed, the Boer War may be said to have saved Britain in 1914, for it brought home to the Army of 1900 just how ill-prepared they still were for modern warfare, and thus gave them fifteen vital years in which to catch up. Fortunately this was achieved, thanks to a brilliant Secretary of State for War, Lord Haldane.

In 1899, however, the campaign began disastrously. The Boers seized the initiative from the start, and using their mobility to the full, soon had the small British garrisons in South Africa effectively besieged in Kimberley, Mafeking and Ladysmith. (See Map 7 on page 150.)

Reinforcements were hurried out to the scene, and included two Guards formations. A Household Cavalry Composite Regiment was formed,

The Boer War (1899–1902)

(*Overleaf*) Training, 1899
On the verge of the Boer War, training is still more suited to the Crimea.

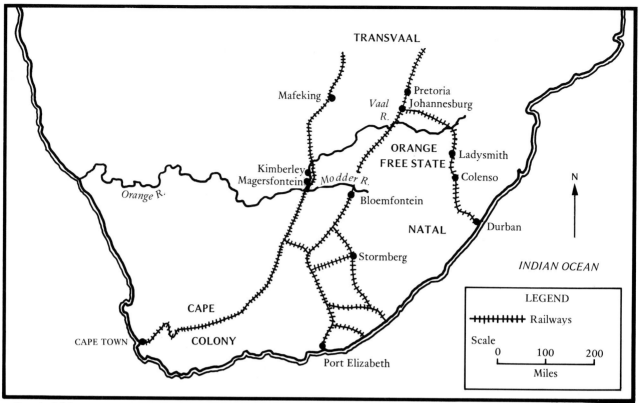

7 South Africa

which joined 2nd Cavalry Division, while 1st Guards Brigade[71] was also mobilised, and joined the 1st Division commanded by Lord Methuen (Scots Guards).

The first two months saw one setback after another, culminating in the three defeats of the so-called 'Black Week', 10–16 December 1899: Stormberg (10th), Magersfontein (11th) and Colenso (15th).

Early next year, the situation improved somewhat when Lord Roberts took over as Commander-in-Chief, and set about relieving Kimberley which had now been besieged for four months. His plan was for a bold advance from the Modder River by a complete cavalry division, and at 0300 hours, 11 February, 4,000 horsemen, including the Household Cavalry Composite Regiment, set off.

For once, the Boer commander Cronje was outflanked and outmanoeuvred, and the cavalry swept on, ending with a dramatic three-mile gallop under fire.

On the fifteenth, Kimberley was relieved at last, and the generals dined in the Town Hall that night with Cecil Rhodes, who had been among the beleaguered.

Cronje had escaped, but he was forced to surrender soon afterwards at Paardeberg; then Ladysmith was relieved on 28 February, and the string of successes was crowned by the capture of the Boer city of Pretoria.

The situation had swung dramatically against the Boers, but they were far from defeated yet, and the war now entered its second phase – mobile guerilla operations. More troops were required, and two more Guards battalions were sent to South Africa as part of 16th Brigade,[72] making seven Guards units serving in the war.

150

The problem now was to get to grips with the elusive 'commandos', who lived off the land, with no defensive positions, no base camps and no lines of communication, and so were remarkably difficult to pin down and eliminate.

New tactics were clearly needed, too, and during 1901 a series of lines of fortified block houses were built across the country in an attempt to restrict the mobility of the Boers. In order to keep watch between these forts as well as to dominate the surrounding countryside, new mobile units had to be created.

The Household Cavalry had returned home in November 1900, and so the Foot Guards stepped somewhat smugly into the breach and formed two Guards Mounted Infantry Companies.

All Regiments, including the newly-created Irish Guards contributed, and after six weeks' hectic training at Aldershot the 'Aldershot Mounted Foot', as they were unkindly called, set sail for South Africa in November 1901.

The policy was to encircle and so round up the commandos, but it was a slow process, and the campaign became a war of attrition. Finally on 30 May 1902, the Boers capitulated, and the Guards, both mounted and foot, returned home.

Although the campaign had finally ended in success, there was general disquiet at the weaknesses that it had exposed in the efficiency of the Army, and a Royal Commission was set up to study the matter. This in turn led to wide reforms in all aspects of Army life during the next decade, and to the creation of the magnificent professional Army that was to defy the Kaiser in 1914.

Peace and Prosperity

Meanwhile, the end of the war, together with the establishment of the 'Entente Cordiale' with France, marked the beginning of an era of peace and prosperity in Britain, in which King Edward VII set the social pace, matching the country's mood of reaction to many years of austere Royal widowhood. The result was a decade of glittering ceremonial and brilliant

'The Aldershot Mounted Foot'

social gaiety, a second 'Age of Elegance'. Royal occasions included balls, reviews and parades as well as all the pageantry of State functions. Court life was centred on Windsor as well as London, and there were also Royal visits to Edinburgh and Dublin, in which the Scots and Irish Guards were naturally closely involved.

Foreign Monarchs, of whom there were then some fifteen in Europe (compared with only six today), paid State Visits to Great Britain, and were treated to the pomp and circumstance that was expected from the world's greatest Imperial Power.

The King now took part himself in many public ceremonies which Queen Victoria had shunned. He opened Parliament in person, rode on the King's Birthday Parade, and led the Garter Knights in their procession to St George's Chapel at Windsor. Levées at St James's Palace were revived, and numerous glittering parties were held at Buckingham Palace, which had just been renovated and reorganised.

The Guards were closely involved not only in many State duties, but also in the social activities at Court. At State Balls, Guards officers attended in full dress, including swords, though they were allowed to remove them when dancing. What was not permitted was that they should reverse when waltzing, lest their spurs cause grievous bodily harm to other dancers!

But no Royal connections could save the Brigade of Guards from the Treasury axe, and when the new Liberal Government came to power in 1905, they demanded the disbandment of two Guards battalions, as part of extensive cuts in defence expenditure.

3rd Bn Scots Guards, having been created only nine years before, were inevitably one of the victims, and they were disbanded the next year.

3rd Bn Coldstream Guards were destined to meet the same fate, but were saved at the last moment by a call for reinforcements for the garrison in Egypt. The supply of Coldstream recruits was good, and so the battalion were sent off to Cairo, where they remained for the next five years. 'Out of sight' was 'Out of mind', and they survived, anyway for another fifty years.

Also in 1906, campaign medals were issued for the Boer War, and the King noticed when distributing them to the Household Cavalry that those for the men were inscribed with the rank of 'Private'. This rank had held some significance in the seventeenth and eighteenth centuries, when members of The Life Guards were in fact 'Private Gentlemen' and were addressed as 'Mr'. But now it applied to every soldier in the Army, and the King considered that his personal troops should again have a distinctive title. He therefore decreed that men of the Household Cavalry should from that moment be called 'Troopers'.

The medals were somewhat reluctantly re-engraved by the War Office, who also issued the necessary Order approving a title which was to be unique to the Household Cavalry until after the First World War, when it was generally adopted by all cavalry regiments.

In 1901 the Irish Guards, celebrating St Patrick's Day as a Regimental occasion for the first time, attended a church service at Wellington Barracks, wearing in their caps sprigs of shamrock just presented to them by their first Colonel, Field Marshal Lord Roberts, V.C. As they waited to be dismissed, an orderly of The Life Guards appeared with several boxes containing more shamrock, but sent this time as a personal gift from Queen Alexandra.

The Royal shamrock promptly replaced that already being worn, and thus began a tradition that has been maintained ever since. Queen Alexandra donated shamrock to the Regiment every year throughout her lifetime, and the Royal gift has been continued ever since, first by the Princess Royal, and thereafter by Queen Elizabeth the Queen Mother.

The shamrock is grown in Ireland by the O'Keefe family at Rosscarbery, near Cork, and come what may, a sprig reaches every serving Irish Guardsman on St Patrick's Day, wherever he may be. The tale is told of the consignment that reached the 1st Battalion of the Regiment when stationed in Constantinople in 1923, and was found, when opened, to be brown and withered. The Quartermaster reassured the Commanding Officer, as have so many Quartermasters on so many occasions, with those welcome words, 'Leave it to me, Sir'.

Sure enough, come the day, the battalion were presented with sprigs of fine fresh green shamrock. The Commanding Officer naturally enquired how this miracle had come to pass.

'Well, Sir,' came the reply, 'I just gave it some of what you and I like best. I gave it a sup of Irish whiskey.'[73]

The individuality of the Irish was further demonstrated by the acquisition in 1902 of a Regimental mascot, the only one officially approved within the Household Division.[74] He was an Irish wolfhound, selected from eight entrants and presented to the Regiment by the Irish Wolfhound Club. He was given the regimental number 1463, and the name Brian Boru, after the famous King of Ireland, who died in 1014.

Brian Boru, the first of the Irish wolfhound mascots of the Regiment, here seen in the care of a Drummer Boy.

Army Reforms

Peacetime soldiering certainly had its social side in Edwardian days, but it was also a time when the Army set out with marked success to remedy its weaknesses and to bring itself up-to-date.

Many dramatic reforms were achieved, thanks largely to the initiative and skill of Lord Haldane, who was Secretary of State for War from 1905 to 1912. Under his imaginative leadership, the Army was revitalised at every level, and became professional as never before.

At the top, Haldane created the Army Council, and built up a trained staff to serve it. He then reorganised the Regular Army, so that an Expeditionary Force of a cavalry division and six infantry divisions was always in existence, and ready for war.

The Militia became the Special Reserve with the role of providing reinforcements for the Regular units to which they were attached. The Yeomanry and Volunteers were completely reorganised into the Territorial Force, which was prepared for active service.

The Guards contributed two Brigades to the Expeditionary Force.

1st Guards Brigade was at Aldershot, and 4th Guards Brigade was composed of battalions in London and Windsor. The Household Cavalry were committed to provide a Composite Regiment for the cavalry division.

As well as reorganising the structure of the Army, Haldane infused into it a new spirit which affected and influenced every rank. For the first time for centuries, the soldier began to be treated far more as an individual, who could be trusted to think and act for himself. Education was encouraged, and living conditions were modernised. Married Quarters were built for all barracks, and the accommodation was immeasurably improved by the provision of mess-rooms, reading rooms, better washing facilities, lighting and heating.

As a result, better men enlisted, and the standards of training improved. The regular soldier began to regard himself as a professional and to be prouder of his skills and his responsibilities.

Training followed a planned pattern throughout the year, working up from individual training to six weeks of large scale manoeuvres each summer in August and September. 'Tactical Exercises without Troops', otherwise known as 'TEWTs', were introduced, and promotion examinations became matters to be treated with new respect.

The Guards, even when stationed in London, trained on the same basis as the remainder of the Army, and took part in the summer manoeuvres. Camouflage, however, does not seem to have been considered a necessary military skill then, for the Foot Guards still trained in white jackets until 1910, while the Household Cavalry were wearing scarlet and blue as late as 1912.

It was while watching the manoeuvres in the summer of 1913 that King George V noticed that the Household Cavalry, wearing khaki for the first time, had no badges for their new khaki caps. He therefore offered his own Royal Cypher as the design, and it was adopted. On the forage caps, the Garter motto 'Honi Soit Qui Mal y Pense', is used as the border, whereas on the khaki service dress caps, the Regimental title is used.

The skills required of a soldier in those days were few compared with today. The only weapons in a battalion were rifles (the new short Lee Enfield was just coming into use), pistols and perhaps a machine gun. What little transport existed was still horse-drawn, wirelesses were unknown and communications were by field telephone.

Fighting efficiency in the case of the infantry depended primarily on skill at arms and marching ability. Very high standards were attained in both, as was to be proved when war came. Above all, the small professional Army consisted of men who were individuals, each ready to play his own part, and to think for himself as seldom before. Discipline now came much more from within, not through fear of the lash. The motivation was patriotism and duty, strengthened by a deep spirit of comradeship and regimental pride.

Those who spoke of an Army unequalled since the time of Cromwell were not exaggerating. The dedication and the spirit of the 'contemptible little Army' of 1914 had much in common with that of the New Model Army. It was soon to be put to the test. The storm clouds were gathering, and the

The Sergeants' Mess.

The tailors, with boys to help.

Life in the Guards 1904

Meat Inspection, a duty carried out by the Picquet Officer until the Second World War.

Meals were eaten in the barrack rooms.

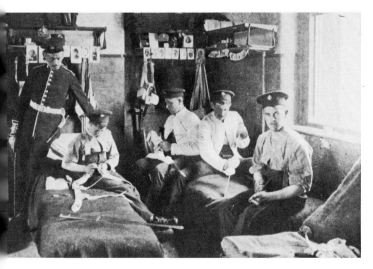

'Shining Parade'. The men are wearing the Brodrick Cap, which was issued for a few years only, before being discarded as impracticable.

The Battalion cobblers

Foot Guards Uniforms,
1902 (Irish Guards).
From left to right, Colour
Sergeant and a Private in
Guard Order; Officer in a
frock coat, Officer in
Guard Order; Field Officer,
mounted, wearing Butcher
boots; Private in undress
uniform; and Drummer
in Review Order.

German staff were even now putting the finishing touches to their 'Schlieffen Plan', which they never doubted would crush France, together with the insignificant forces that Britain was expected to send to her support.

'The lamps are going out all over Europe.' declared the Foreign Secretary,[75] on 3 August 1914. 'We shall not see them lit again in our lifetime.'

Chapter 11

The Great War (1914–18)

On August Bank Holiday 1914, Great Britain declared war on Germany. Immediately there was an outburst of patriotic fervour, and a rush of volunteers to get to France, in order not to 'miss' the war that everyone thought would be over by Christmas.

The Household Cavalry duly formed their Composite Regiment, composed of one squadron from each Regiment. It sailed for France on 15 August 1914 with its horses, and joined the 4th Cavalry Brigade[76] commanded by Major General The Hon Cecil Bingham of The Life Guards.

The Commanding Officer of the Composite Regiment was Lt Colonel E. B. Cook, First Life Guards, who refused to allow any of his officers to be medically examined, because he knew that he himself would be rejected as unfit.

The Foot Guards quickly absorbed their reservists and formed 1st and 4th Guards Brigades,[77] which moved straight to France the same month, and joined 1st and 2nd Divisions respectively.

The German blueprint for the defeat of France envisaged a great enveloping movement across neutral Belgium and Northern France by a special force of 600,000 men, which would then swing west of Paris and cut off the allied troops defending the capital (See Map 1.)

According to plan, the Germans forced open a seventy-mile wide gap in the allied defences, extending from Le Cateau to the Channel. The French suffered 300,000 casualties in August alone, and could not halt the relentless advance.

British Expeditionary Force

(*Opposite*) Part of the Household Cavalry during the Retreat from Mons in 1914.

In the path of the German thrust stood the British Expeditionary Force of 120,000 men. The Germans derisively called it a 'Contemptible Little Army',[78] and had no fears that it could possibly hold up the advance of their triumphant force.

Indeed, the Germans continued to sweep all before them, and on 23 August, the BEF began the great Retreat from Mons. In the next eight days, they marched steadily and grimly back, at times fighting fiercely on the way, but more often just stumbling in utter exhaustion back towards Paris, baffled and bitter, but unbeaten.

It was the greatest retreat by British troops since Corunna, and it was perhaps with memories of their forebears on that occasion that the Guardsmen made history repeat itself – this time at Landrecies.

On 30 August, 4th Guards Brigade passed another brigade of 2nd Division who were resting by the roadside. Without orders the exhausted grimy Guardsmen sloped arms, marched to attention and to the beat of their respective regimental marches on mouth-organs, they swung past 'as if they were on Guard Mounting'. Thus are traditions born and re-born.

On 1 September, the same brigade found itself acting as rear-guard to 1st Corps, and fought a fierce battle against the pursuing Germans at Villers-Cotterets, forty miles north-east of Paris. Some fifty men of the Grenadier Guards were cut off in this battle and ceased firing only when every one was a casualty. This encounter helped to check the German advance, and was almost the end of the retreat, which had covered some 200 miles in seventeen days.

But the enemy was now equally exhausted, and on 6 September the British Expeditionary Force turned and fought back. More than that, they advanced 60 miles to the line of the river Aisne.

Guard Mounting, September 1914. The King's Guard, wearing khaki Service Dress, march back into Wellington Barracks. The Guard is from the Grenadier Guards, and the Ensign carrying the Colour is the Prince of Wales (later King Edward VIII).

During September 1914, five more Guards units were mobilised, and formed into 7th Cavalry Brigade and 20th Infantry Brigade[79] both of which were sent to Zeebrugge in October, in a vain attempt to save Antwerp.

They were then hurried to France for the First Battle of Ypres, one of the most crucial and costly engagements in the war. The British Army was under intense pressure and was stretched to the limit, with companies doing the work of battalions. Thanks to the incredible staunchness of the British soldier, utter disaster was averted, but only at the cost of losing the cream of the pre-war Regular Army.

All the Guards units in France were involved, and The Blues set the pace with an exploit known as the 'Mad Gallop'. The incident occurred when they were ordered to make a diversionary attack on 26 October to relieve the pressure on 20th Infantry Brigade, who were next to them, near Kruiseecke.

While one dismounted squadron gave covering fire, the remainder of the Regiment galloped straight across the front of the enemy lines. Fortunately the Germans were too astonished for accurate fire, and the exploit achieved its object, with few casualties.

Four days later on 30 October, perhaps the most critical day of the First

First Battle of Ypres (19 October–22 November 1914)

Battle of Ypres, the Household Cavalry fought as infantry in one of the finest engagements in their history.

They were entrenched on the Zandvoorde Ridge near Gheluvelt, in the centre of three weak British cavalry divisions, who were all fighting as infantry, and had the task of covering a nine-mile front against strong German forces.

A major attack was imminent, and the German High Command had declared, 'We will finish with the British, Indians, Moroccans and other trash, feeble adversaries who surrender in great numbers if they are attacked with vigour.' Furthermore, it was said that the Kaiser himself was expected to come and watch the defeat of the British Household Cavalry who had often escorted his carriage down the Mall.

On 30 October, 7th Cavalry Brigade were attacked by a complete infantry division and three light battalions. The odds were overwhelming and two complete squadrons of The Life Guards, together with the Machine Gun Section of The Blues, were wiped out before the positions were finally overrun.

Among them was C Squadron of The 1st Life Guards, and as a tribute to those who died in this battle, the squadron was never re-formed during the war.

The Household Cavalry War Memorial was later set up on Zandvoorde Ridge and stands there still today. It was unveiled by Field Marshal Earl Haig as Colonel of The Blues on 4 May 1924.

All three Guards Brigades were heavily involved in the struggle at Ypres, and all suffered grievous casualties. On 29 October at Gheluvelt, 1st Bn Coldstream Guards had no officers left and only 80 men; they were reinforced, but four days later again had no officers left at all and only 120 men. The Irish Guards lost almost 1,000 men in two weeks. By 12 November, 1st Guards Brigade was reduced to five officers and 468 men, out of a total of 4,500 all ranks in August.

The Household Cavalry Composite Regiment, who had fought throughout, often as infantry, were by now reduced from 350 to a mere 63 all ranks, and so were disbanded.

Somehow the Expeditionary Force held on, and the German attack was halted, but only at a cost of 58,000 casualties, bringing the total since August to 92,000.

Defeat had been averted, but the future held only four grim years of crude trench warfare, well described as being 'almost medieval in its savagery and wholesale butchery'.

The winter was grim indeed, but on 1 February 1915, Lance Corporal O'Leary of the Irish Guards[80] won the Regiment's first Victoria Cross. He personally shot down five Germans behind their barricade, and then killed three more who were training a machine gun on his comrades. For good measure, he finally captured two prisoners.

It was Ireland's first VC, too in this war, and he promptly became a national hero. 11 July 1915 was declared 'O'Leary Day' as a boost to recruiting, and the Irish Guards were known for a while as 'O'Leary's Lads'.

The spring of 1915 saw a renewal of the bitter fighting in the trenches, with the Germans on the offensive. All the Guards Brigades were involved, and once more suffered heavy casualties. The Household Cavalry fought again as infantry, and on one occasion in May, a squadron of The Blues reached its objective with only two men unwounded.

Among the casualties was Captain Lord Leveson-Gower, who was hit in the thigh, and was to be seen, smoking a huge cigar, and sitting literally on top of a small unwounded German to keep himself dry and out of the mud. He was carried back, as he delighted to relate afterwards, by two corporals called Coffin and Churchyard.

The year 1915 saw two important events in the history of the Household Division. The first was the creation of the Welsh Guards, and the second was the formation of the Guards Division.

It was on 6 February 1915 that the Major General, Sir Francis Lloyd discussed with the Secretary of State for War, Lord Kitchener, the King's wish that a Regiment of Welsh Guards should be formed.

'When do you wish them to be ready?' he asked Kitchener.

'Immediately.'

'Very well sir,' he replied, 'they shall go on Guard on St David's Day.'

The Royal Warrant forming the Regiment was signed on 26 February 1915, and on 1 March 1915, the King's Guard was mounted for the first time by the Welsh Guards. The Captain of the Guard was the Commanding Officer, Lieutenant Colonel Murray-Threipland (formerly Grenadier Guards),[81] and Lord Kitchener dined with him that evening at St James's.

On 19 March the leading company of the 1st Battalion was given the title of 'Prince of Wales Company', and in August the Regiment received its first Colours from King George V. Two weeks later, it went to France to join the Guards Division.

It was Lord Kitchener who initiated the concept of a Guards Division, that is a division composed entirely of Household Division troops, except for supporting arms. He envisaged it as a permanent formation in the Regular Army and believed that it would serve as an example to the whole Army, and be of great benefit.

But the wisdom of concentrating almost all the Guards into one élite formation in wartime was not accepted everywhere, and the proposal was discussed fiercely and at length (as on the creation of the Guards Armoured Division twenty-six years later).

Kitchener evidently foresaw the arguments that would arise, for he planned with great secrecy. He consulted the King and the Major General, but not the War Cabinet or the Commander-in-Chief in France, until it was a *fait accompli*.

The division was formed in France during August 1915, and was ready for action by mid-September. Command was given to Major General The Earl of Cavan, Grenadier Guards, great grandson of the 7th Earl, who had commanded the Guards Brigade at Aboukir Bay in 1801.

The Divisional Commander carried out an inspection of the division in September, and significantly he concentrated on their drill as much as on their field training, seeking, in his own words, 'That high standard most proper for all Guardsmen under all and every condition.'

His insistence on this standard is exemplified by the comment in his report: 'I was particularly impressed with Brigadier General Ponsonby's word of command – and with the exact timing of the motions of the 'Present' and 'Slope' throughout both Brigades.'

The Guards Division consisted of 1st, 2nd and 3rd Guards Brigades, each of four battalions of Foot Guards[82] together with the usual Divisional Troops. These included a Pioneer Battalion, formed from 4th Bn Coldstream Guards, and a Cyclist Company, manned by the Household Cavalry, who also provided rather more appropriately a Divisional Cavalry Squadron.

The divisional sign was the 'Ever Open Eye', first used as the distinguishing sign for the vehicles of the Division, and then adopted for the whole formation.

The division early received a distinguished visitor in the shape of Major Winston Churchill, who was appointed to 2nd Bn Grenadier Guards for 'an attachment under instruction' in 1915, before he went on to command a battalion of the Royal Scots Fusiliers.

Loos (25 September – 27 October 1915)

The first battle in which the Guards Division were engaged was at Loos in September 1915. The initial attack was made by other troops on 25 September and it failed with heavy casualties. The Guards Division were then brought in on the 27th, not to exploit success as planned, but to capture the original objectives centred on a feature called Hill 70.

Their approach march to the start line meant an advance of two miles in full view of the enemy the whole way and under heavy fire, and it has gone down in history as an inspiring example of Guards discipline in battle.

It is probably best described in the dramatic account in *The Times* of 8 November 1915:

The men on reaching the ridge were met by a tornado of shrapnel fire. Nevertheless the Brigade advanced with the steadiness of men on parade, and men in other battalions have spoken again and again of that wonderful advance as being one of the most glorious and impressive sights of the war, and of how they were thrilled to see those large silhouettes pressing silently and inescapably forward against the skyline.

Had the same war correspondent been at the Battle of Fontenoy in 1745, he might have described it in the very same words (except that the 'shrapnel'

would have been 'grapeshot').

The comparison with Fontenoy can be taken further, for the actual assault at Loos meant covering a long, open uphill slope under intense fire from the front and from both flanks.

The plan had been that the attack would not be launched unless a neighbouring feature was in our hands. It was not in fact taken, but 3rd Guards Brigade were ordered to put in their attack nevertheless – and an order cancelling it arrived just too late to be implemented.

Hill 70 was captured and held for two days, but casualties were so heavy that the whole division was then withdrawn. It had been a grim initiation, particularly for the Welsh Guards, being their first battle.

The Duke of Connaught talks to Major General Feilding, commanding the Guards Division. The staff officer to the left is wearing the Divisional sign of the 'ever-open eye'.

The Somme
(1 July–
15 November
1916)

1915 was a depressing year generally for the Allies, who failed to break through the formidable German defences and suffered crippling losses for little return.

Now from February to June 1916, the Germans launched massive attacks against the key French fortress of Verdun, and in its defence, the French lost the frightful total of 460,000 men.

It therefore fell to the British under Sir Douglas Haig, to bear the brunt of mounting the allied counter-offensive in July. It began on 1 July 1916, and after a bombardment which had lasted seven days, fourteen British and five French divisions advanced for the first bloody encounter of the five-month Battle of the Somme. By that evening, the British had suffered no less than 60,000 casualties. It was 'the greatest loss and slaughter in a single day in the whole history of the British Army'.[83]

Throughout July and August, the bitter struggle continued, and in mid-September, the Guards Division were called on to launch an attack at a spot called Ginchy.

The Affair
at Ginchy
(15–17
September
1916)

The battle was planned as a Corps attack against some of the strongest German positions yet met. But the British High Command pinned its hopes on the new 'tank', its latest secret weapon, which was to be used for the first time. Ten tanks were allotted to the Guards Division, who were in the centre of the Corps line. Objectives were selected up to a depth of two miles into the German defences, and the Cavalry Corps stood by, mounted, ready to exploit the breakthrough.

The force involved was massive, but so was the task. As the Guards Division Commander, Major General Sir Geoffrey Feilding, (Coldstream Guards) remarked in his pre-battle message: 'This is perhaps the greatest battle that has ever been fought. The Guards Division has been specially selected for the operation – the eyes of the whole of England will be watching us and I have absolute confidence that we shall live up to our reputation . . .'

So, at 0620 hours, 15 September 1916, the Guards Division attack began. For the first time in history, three Coldstream battalions advanced together in line. Behind them, in the second waves, were both battalions of the Irish Guards, also in action together for the first time.

Steadily, the leading troops pressed forward, taking their first two objectives. But the divisions on both their flanks failed to keep pace, and the Guards were soon in serious trouble, particularly from an uncaptured strongpoint called the Quadrilateral to their right flank. The tanks had not arrived on time, and indeed did little to help during the battle. The infantry were on their own, and casualties mounted fast.

Several times, men rallied to the sound of a hunting horn, blown by Lieutenant Colonel John Campbell of 3rd Bn Coldstream Guards, who inspired his own and other regiments by his outstanding leadership, and won the Victoria Cross for his action – and also the nickname of 'Tally Ho Campbell'.

164

An attack on the Somme, 1916.

Eventually the third objective was captured, but the survivors were now totally unsupported, and ahead of any other troops. No reinforcements were available, and they were forced to pull back again to the second line, where they dug in, and faced twenty-four hours of constant attack and bombardment, before they were relieved on the night of 16 September.

The cost to the division was 4,964 casualties in two days, and the Prince of Wales Company of the Welsh Guards, for example, was led back into reserve by a Lance Corporal.

Trench Warfare

The winter of 1916–17 was exceptionally cold, and conditions in the trenches were grim indeed. It was a life that is hard to envisage today. It meant hardship, suffering, sacrifice and endurance that was rarely called for in the Second World War.

The enemy were often no more than forty yards distant. Death was never far away and nerves were always taut. The noise of artillery and mortar concentrations was the din of hell, with the guns ranged onto each trench to within a matter of feet.

165

Conditions were appalling, for everywhere was mud, so deep that wounded men drowned in it. Fit men would be stuck fast up to the waist and might not be dug out for several hours. There was no escape from it, and a Brigade Order was issued prohibiting men from standing in water for more than twelve hours at a time.

There was no escape either from tension and strain, the incessant din, the hiding of fear, and the gathering of courage to face the next step. There was the all-pervading smell of death, the constant loss of friends, and above all, the endlessness of the slaughter. The average expectation of survival for a subaltern was estimated at about three weeks.

Discipline and regimental pride became two bastions to which men could turn, as something that was bigger than themselves, to which they could cling when nothing else seemed to make sense. They bound men together, so that, where as individuals they might not have survived, they could, and did carry on as a body.

So the regimental spirit carried men through the Great War as it had done before, and has done since, and will do in the future. Rudyard Kipling summed it up: 'A man may join for the sake of King and Country, but he goes over the top for the honour of his own platoon, company and battalion.'[84]

An incident that exemplifies this is the story of Company Sergeant Major Bradbury of the King's Company, 1st Battalion Grenadier Guards, who on 5 February 1917 had both legs blown off by a shell. He asked to speak to the Adjutant, and Captain Pearson-Gregory hurried to him, expecting a farewell message to the dying man's family.

'You won't forget, Sir,' were the Sergeant Major's last words, 'the battalion has to find a fatigue party of a hundred men tomorrow early.'

Grimly, the troops endured that miserable winter, looking forward to the warmth of spring, even though it was bound to bring more costly offensives aimed at breaking the deadlock on the Western Front.

1917

1917 began with two momentous events. The Russian Revolution in March meant that the Allies could no longer rely on Russia to continue to man the Eastern Front effectively. But this blow was offset to some extent by the news on 6 April, that the United States had joined the war.

A further surprise was the unexpected German withdrawal of fifty miles, back to the Hindenburg Line.

The Allies closed up to the new German defences, and in April, launched the unsuccessful Nivelle Offensive, which brought the French Army near to mutiny.

In order to help his ally, Haig again attacked on his front, and this led to some of the bloodiest fighting of the war at the Third Battle of Ypres, otherwise known as Passchendale.

(*Previous pages*) A typical front-line trench, near Loos in 1915. The officer in the foreground is the future Field Marshal Lord Alexander, then a Captain in the Irish Guards.

The Guards Division took part in the initial attack on 31 July 1917, and advanced two and a half miles on a front of some 1500 yards – an almost unprecedented achievement then.

It looked like a breakthrough, but then the rain fell for the next four days. The whole battlefield became impassable, and the offensive was literally bogged down for the next two months. When it was resumed in September, the Guards Division were involved at Passchendale, where the battlefield was still a quagmire. Conditions were so bad that the trenches had sometimes to be re-dug at dawn and dusk every day, and 48 hours in the front line was considered the limit that men could endure.

Finally the offensive was abandoned, as the battlefield had become truly impassable owing to the continuing rain. During the Ypres offensive, the Guards Division had advanced 6,000 yards, but at a cost in casualties of 303 officers and 7,898 other ranks. Nor was there long before the next battle – at Cambrai.

The success of this battle depended on achieving surprise, for the plan was to use tanks 'en masse' for the first time, and to break through the Hindenburg Line. It was also essential to consolidate all objectives rapidly before the Germans could bring up reinforcements.

The attack was launched at dawn on 20 November, and to gain surprise the customary preliminary bombardment was omitted. The plan worked, the tanks proved successful this time, and advances were made up to three miles.

But one key position called Bourlon Wood was not captured as intended, and the task was given to 2nd Guards Brigade. It was a formidable undertaking, for the enemy were known to have been reinforcing their positions for the last few days. Moreover, orders for the dawn attack did not reach 2nd Guards Brigade until the afternoon of the 26th, and company commanders were not briefed till midnight for an attack six hours later, over unknown ground against unknown enemy defences. The Divisional Commander had in fact protested that it was an impossible task, but he was over-ruled. His doubts were to prove only too well justified.

At 0620 hours, 27 November, the attack went in. The artillery barrage had not been properly co-ordinated and was soon ahead of the troops. The few tanks allotted in support failed to arrive. And unknown to the planners, the Germans had been preparing their own attack for the same day; they had ample reserves to hand, and it was a case of the three Guards battalions against seven German.

2nd Guards Brigade gained their objectives, and fighting continued all day, with positions being won and lost several times over. But the Germans brought up reinforcements, while none could reach the Guardsmen.

By the end of the day, 3rd Bn Grenadier Guards and 1st Bn Coldstream Guards had lost every officer and most NCOs, while the 2nd Bn Irish Guards had lost 320 all ranks altogether out of 400. There were not even enough

Third Battle of Ypres (31 July– 10 November 1917)

Battle of Cambrai (20 November– 3 December 1917)

169

Guardsmen left to prevent the prisoners from escaping and rejoining the fight. Finally, the remnants of the brigade withdrew.

The Germans had won the battle of Bourlon Wood, and three days later, on 30 November, they launched their powerful counter-offensive. Within a matter of hours, they had advanced three miles, and not only regained most of the ground lost during the previous week, but had also broken through the former British line.

The position was critical, but as the Germans pushed forward, the Guards Division happened to be in their path, resting after the Battle of Cambrai. They had no artillery support, but 1st Guards Brigade checked the German advance by recapturing the village of Gouzeaucourt, while 3rd Guards Brigade regained the Quentin Ridge.

The German offensive now in turn petered out, and both armies prepared for their fourth winter of deadlocked trench warfare.

1918

The year began on a depressing note. It was the fifth year of this terrible war, and the collapse of the Russians in December 1917 had made it possible for the Germans to transfer one and a half million troops to the Western Front for an offensive there.

Support from the United States was not yet making itself felt, and the appalling British casualties of the last two years were beginning to tell. One result was that all divisions were reduced from twelve to nine battalions. This led to the re-forming of 4th Guards Brigade, under Brigadier General Lord Ardee (Irish Guards). It consisted of 4th Bn Grenadier Guards, 3rd Bn Coldstream Guards and 2nd Bn Irish Guards, and was sent to 31st Division.

On 21 March 1918, the Germans launched what Churchill described as 'without exception the greatest onslaught in the history of the world'.[85] On a front of fifty four miles, sixty four German divisions advanced against thirty two British divisions.

The Allies were forced to withdraw over a wide front, and on 11 April 1918, Haig issued his dramatic Order of the Day: 'To All Ranks of the British Army in France . . . With our backs to the wall and believing in the justice of our cause, each one of us must fight to the end . . .'

At this crucial moment, 4th Guards Brigade found themselves called upon to hold positions near Hazebrouck at all costs, for they were at that moment almost the only fighting troops between the Germans and the Channel coast. For two days, they held on against overwhelming odds. It was the end of the brigade as a fighting force, but the Germans did not get through.

Part of this success was due to the amazing gallantry of Captain T. T. Pryce of 4th Battalion Grenadier Guards in a feat which won him a posthumous VC. With a company reduced to less than forty men, he inspired them to hold out for ten hours against at least one enemy battalion, perhaps twenty times their numbers, and supported by three field guns, firing over open sights at a range of only 300 yards. Finally, to quote the citation:

'Captain Pryce had only 17 men left and every round of his ammunition had been fired. Determined that there should be no surrender, he once again led his men forward in a bayonet charge, and was last seen engaged in a fierce, hand-to-hand struggle with overwhelming numbers of the enemy.'

The Commander-in-Chief, Sir Douglas Haig, wrote of the whole brigade action: 'No more brilliant exploit has taken place since the opening of the enemy's offensive, though gallant actions have been without number.'

The German onslaught was renewed in May, and the Allies were pressed back steadily until 18 July, when the French began a carefully-planned counter-attack. It was successful and forced the enemy to withdraw right back to the Hindenburg Line, from which they had first advanced four months before.

On 21 September 1918 the Guards Division had its final challenge, when it was ordered, as part of the attack on the Hindenburg Line, to cross the Canal du Nord. All three Guards Brigades took part, and every objective was gained. It was a copybook battle, but the losses were still almost fifty per cent. In this battle, Lt Colonel Lord Gort, commanding 1st Bn Grenadier Guards added a VC to the MC and DSO with two bars that he had won already.

The final success was the capture of Maubeuge on 9 November, and then at 1100 hours on 11 November, came the Armistice.

One week later, the Guards Division set out to march to the Rhine, nearly 200 miles away, where they were stationed round Cologne as part of the Allied Army of Occupation in Germany until March 1919.

Other Guards Units

The story of the Guards in the Great War is dominated inevitably by the Guards Division, but mention must be made of several other Guards units that fought in France.

The Household Cavalry proved their versatility from the start and at various times acted as cavalry, infantry, cyclists, artillerymen and machine gunners.

7th Cavalry Brigade remained in existence throughout the war, but in addition, the Household Cavalry formed in September 1916 an infantry battalion called the Household Battalion. It had a fine record under the command of Lieutenant Colonel Wyndham Portal of The First Life Guards, and fought from December 1916 to February 1918 when it was disbanded because of the heavy losses suffered.

In March 1918 when the Household Cavalry finally lost their horses, they were converted into 1st, 2nd and 3rd Guards Machine Gun Battalions, each with sixty-four Vickers machine guns. A 4th Battalion was also formed from the Foot Guards, while a 5th Battalion was created as a reserve and training unit. Together they formed what became known as the 6th Regiment of Foot Guards, otherwise called the Guards Machine Gun Regiment. They fought from May to October 1918 in support of various divisions, rejoining their regiments when this unique force was disbanded on 30 April 1920.

Another unusual formation was Brassey's Brigade, created on 4 September 1918. It consisted of 4th Guards Brigade in lorries, the 1st and 3rd Guards Machine Gun Battalions (i.e. The 1st Life Guards and The Blues respectively), a battalion of cyclists and four 18-pounder guns in lorries. Its role was to act as a mobile advance guard during the final advance, and it was thus among the very first mechanised forces.

Just to round off the record, the Household Cavalry manned a battery of tractor-drawn six-inch guns. This unit had the quaint title of the 520th (Household) Siege Battery, and was in action from the summer of 1918 onwards under the command of Major the Hon. J. J. Astor of The 1st Life Guards.[86]

The Imperial Guards

The formation of the Household Battalion in 1916 led to a proposal by Lord Denby, then Secretary of State for War, that 'an "Imperial Guards Brigade" should be formed, consisting of the new Household Battalion to represent the Mother Country, and forming battalions from picked men of the Australian, Canadian and South African troops now in France.'

The idea provoked the interesting comment from Lord Stamfordham, the King's Private Secretary, 'But would it do to take the Household Cavalry Battalion to form the foundation of what must be essentially a Guards Brigade? . . . one is aware of a certain lack of sympathy between the Household Cavalry and Brigade of Guards as evidenced by the former not even being members of the Guards Club.'[87]

A decision was deferred until after the war, when it was considered again. Among the points then discussed were suggestions for a red, white and blue plume for the bearskins, and a motto of 'For Crown and Empire'. But the scheme finally foundered, largely on the question of pay, since rates were so much higher in the Commonwealth countries than in the British Army.

Although this particular concept never materialised, the Household Division have since maintained close links with the Commonwealth, based on bonds of mutual respect in two world wars, and today all Guards Regiments have official links with units of the Canadian, Australian or Pakistan Armies.[88]

Epitaph

It is not easy to sum up the story of the Guards in the Great War. They played their full part, as the horrifying casualties of 14,563 killed and 28,398 wounded show only too clearly. They won twenty-three Victoria Crosses, and they had, in the words of Lord Cavan, shown always 'the steadfast maintenance of our greatest traditions'.

But perhaps their most important contribution was the development and the dissemination of the Guards way of doing things. It was all-embracing; it took for granted leadership of the highest order, discipline, and gallantry at all levels. It also extended to matters such as leaving trenches always better than they were found, smartness whatever the conditions, the maintenance of morale, meticulous administration and a care for one's men that transcended every self-interest.

The results had an impact far beyond the ranks of the Household Division, and led to a general confidence that the Guards could be relied upon to do all that could be done, and to do it well.

'We can sleep tonight. The Guards are in front of us,' was a saying.[89] It was an exacting reputation to maintain, but it had always been done in the past, and Guards training made it clear that things could and would continue to be done that way. The existence of such a reputation served itself to strengthen the resolution of every Guardsman to live up to what was expected of him. In striving always to do so, he created further traditions for future generations to maintain.

It is perhaps fitting to end this chapter with the same words as did the historian of the Guards Division in the Great War:

'Remember, then, whichever way the balance doth decline.

If God is in his Heaven, and the Guards are in the line,

All's Well.'

Chapter 12

Between the Wars (1919–39)

The Guards Division returned from their spell in the Army of Occupation in March 1919, and on 22 March, the complete Household Division marched through the City of London and then past the King at Buckingham Palace, a prelude to the Victory March on 19 July. The Irish Guards had their two wolfhounds on parade, and the Scots Guards paraded two Flanders cows, Bella and Bertha, which had been acquired in 1914. The latter are still commemorated by two silver models belonging to the Officers' Mess of the 2nd Battalion.

The men of the Brigade of Guards had until this time been called 'Privates', but on 22 November 1918 they were given the title of 'Guardsmen' by the King, an honour granted 'as a mark of His Majesty's appreciation and pride of the splendid services rendered by the Brigade of Guards during the war.'

With the war won, the Government began the inevitable post-war reduction in the strength of the Armed Forces. It was a disillusioning period for the Army, for following an ill-managed demobilisation scheme, it now had to watch its treasured regiments being mercilessly pruned in the name of economy. It was not even a question of retaining the pre-1914 Army. The Great War had been 'the war to end wars', so the argument went, and there need therefore be no thought of preparing for another. The Geddes Axe fell upon many famous regiments, and the Household Division bore its share.

The 1st and 2nd Life Guards were in 1922 amalgamated into one regiment called The Life Guards. For a short time they were called The Life Guards

(First and Second)', but soon adopted their current title of 'The Life Guards.'

The many differences between the two Regiments were resolved, as they always can be, and the previous existence of two Regiments was perpetuated by the fact that from 1925 to 1953 The Life Guards retained two Sovereign's Standards.[90] They and The Blues were also allowed to continue the unique privilege of being the only cavalry regiments to retain Squadron Standards.

There was talk at one stage of reducing the Household Cavalry to one regiment, and The Blues were earmarked for disbandment. But they just escaped, and were to survive as an independent regiment for another forty-seven years.

The wartime battalions of Foot Guards were soon disbanded, but unfortunately it did not stop there. In 1920, there was a totally unexpected proposal to reduce the Brigade of Guards still further, by abolishing the Irish and Welsh Guards completely.

The plan was to make the Irish Guards (who had lost their 2nd Battalion in 1919) into a third battalion of the Scots Guards, while the Welsh Guards were to be reduced to one company, which was to be incorporated into the Grenadiers. This to the planner's tidy mind, made a neat organisation of three Guards Regiments, each of three battalions.

The reaction was instant and furious. The arguments raged in messes, clubs, Whitehall, the Press and Parliament, and formidable support was soon ranged behind these two national regiments.

Within eleven days of the news breaking, the Army Council had been forced to think again, and on 15 June 1920, Mr Winston Churchill announced in the House of Commons: 'There is no intention of disbanding the Irish or Welsh Guards so long as they are able to maintain their recruiting in such a manner as to preserve the national character of the Regiment.'[91]

That was enough, and both Regiments have flourished ever since.

Peacetime Soldiering

The Household Division now settled down to the routine of peacetime soldiering. The Household Cavalry were stationed at Windsor and in London. The Brigade of Guards usually had eight of its ten battalions at home, with two overseas.

Those at home found themselves in an atmosphere of growing disillusionment and discontent. The 'world fit for heroes to live in' had turned out to be an unhappy life of unemployment, strikes, bitterness and poverty. There were over two million unemployed.

In April 1921, the Guardsmen were involved in aid to the Civil Powers during the six month Coal Strike, and Reservists were actually recalled to bring battalions up to strength. The Guards protected various installations and stood by in case of real trouble. Similar duties faced them during the General Strike of 1926, and again in 1931, when the Hunger Marchers threatened to advance on London.

State duties and Royal occasions continued nevertheless. In 1919 the Prince of Wales became the first Colonel of the Welsh Guards and took a keen interest in the Regiment and its activities. Shortly before a King's Birthday Parade, he was discovered gardening at Fort Belvedere, wearing his bearskin to get used to it – a wise precaution!

In July 1921, King George V presented new Colours on Horse Guards to all battalions of the Brigade of Guards, except the Irish and Welsh Guards, and on 16 October 1926 the Guards Memorial on Horse Guards was unveiled by the Duke of Connaught.

Commitments overseas were few, but the Brigade of Guards did become involved in a number of operations.

Constantinople

In April 1922, 1st Bn Irish Guards sailed for Constantinople (now Istanbul) to join the international force stationed there. (See Map 1.)

The situation in the Near East after the end of the war was confused and explosive. Turkey, having sided with the Germans in the war, had been subjected to harsh peace terms, which provided for the occupation of parts of the country by the Allies, who included Turkey's traditional enemy, Greece.

One of the Turkish generals, Kemal Ataturk, refused to accept these terms,

'The Guardsman who dropped it', the famous cartoon by H. M. Bateman.

and organised a highly successful nationalist insurgent movement to fight for independence for Turkey and also to drive out the hated Greeks.

The main concern of the Allies was that the Dardanelles must be kept open for all shipping, and they therefore stationed a force of eleven battalions (four British, six French and one Italian) in and around Constantinople to achieve this. They were supported by warships of the Royal Navy.

The British contingent was called the 'Army of the Black Sea', and the Irish Guards, when they joined it, became part of the garrison of Constantinople.

In September, the situation became highly explosive, when Kemal Ataturk drove the Greek Army of Occupation in Anatolia back into Smyrna (now Izmir) and sacked the town. He then threatened to advance north and cross the Dardanelles into Thrace, so as to drive the Greeks completely out of Turkey.

This was clearly a direct challenge to the Allies, and to their policy of retaining control of the Dardanelles. Reinforcements were called for, and seven extra battalions were sent out from England, including 2nd Bn Grenadier Guards and 3rd Bn Coldstream Guards. They arrived in Constantinople on 10 October, and joined the Irish Guards, to form 1st Guards Brigade under Colonel J. McC. Steele (Coldstream Guards).

Foot Guards Uniforms, 1925. From left to right, a Guardsman in Fighting Order, a Field Officer in Drill Order; a Subaltern in Marching Order; and a Sergeant in Drill order.

177

But the crisis had by then blown over and the problem was finally resolved by the Settlement of Mundania signed on 11 October 1922, whereby the Dardanelles were handed back to Turkish control.

Life reverted to normal peacetime activities for 1st Guards Brigade, and when on 2 October 1923, Turkey was granted her independence, the Allied force, including the Guards, returned home.

China

The next trouble in which the Household Division was involved was in the Far East, when two Guards battalions were sent to China in 1927, thus disproving the popular theory that 'the Guards never go east of Suez', a myth which arose because the Household Division were almost the only regiments never to serve in India.

The Chinese Civil War had by 1926 brought the fighting to the Yangtse valley and the resulting increase in nationalist feeling led to growing hostility

8 Far East

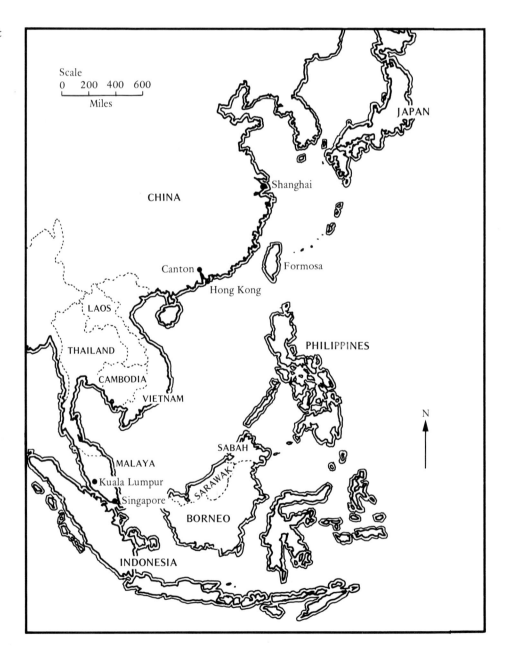

to the special rights of the British and other European powers in the Treaty Ports of Shanghai and elsewhere.

In January 1927, the British Concession area at Hankow was attacked and overrun by a Chinese mob, and the British Government decided to send more troops to protect British interests.

2nd Bn Coldstream Guards arrived in Shanghai early in March 1927, followed by 2nd Bn Scots Guards, who were stationed in Hong Kong. Both battalions formed part of 1st Infantry Brigade, commanded by Colonel B. W. Sergison-Brooke (Grenadier Guards).

A crisis developed in Shanghai at the end of March, but it was settled after a few days, and the Coldstream Guards were not involved. Some Chinese pamphlets were found within the battalion inciting the Guardsmen to 'place the upstart, frog-minded officers at the receiving end of their rifles', but this happily did not evoke any response. No further trouble followed, and the Coldstream returned home in February 1928.

The Scots Guards were also stationed at Lo Wu, inland from Hong Kong, and before they left, they constructed in the hills above their camp, a large white Scots Guards star, surrounded by the words '2nd Battalion Scots Guards', as proof positive of their presence east of Suez. The star is still there today and was tidied up by the Irish Guards when stationed there in 1973.

Egypt

In 1928, the 1st Bn Welsh Guards moved into Kasr-el-Nil barracks in Cairo. These bug-ridden odoriferous buildings had long since been condemned as unfit for human habitation, but they had to be occupied nevertheless. Each successive battalion, having battled with flies, lice, shite-hawks, heat and hopeless hygiene, tried to leave the crumbling place slightly better than they found it – not that any Quartermaster taking over ever admitted this.

Cairo and Alexandria became regular overseas stations for two Foot Guards battalions at a time from 1928 to 1939, and all regiments spent several two-year tours there.

Palestine

A somewhat more operational posting was Palestine which had been a troubled land ever since the Balfour Declaration of 1917. That controversial document gave the Jews a hope, whether intended or not, of one day acquiring what they regarded as their 'Promised Land'.

Unfortunately, the Arabs had also been led to believe, whether intended or not, that Palestine, where they had always lived, was to be theirs in return for their services to the Allied cause in the Great War.

It was an insoluble dilemma, involving many highly emotional human issues, and it led to a conflict between Arab and Jew that is sadly still with us today. Unfortunately for Britain, the responsibility for trying to solve it rested at that time with the British Government, because they had been given a Mandate by the League of Nations for the administration of Palestine.

In 1936, it was the Arabs who were causing the trouble, in protest against the growing number of Jews being allowed into Palestine, and in September, 3rd Bn Coldstream Guards and 2nd Bn Scots Guards then at home, were ordered to Jerusalem. Their role was to keep the peace between the two sides, following the Peel Commission which had been instructed by the League of Nations to study the immigration problem. The fighting had died down, however, as a result of the Commission's presence, and the battalions were thus able to enjoy three months sightseeing before returning home soon after Christmas.

The peace did not last long, however, and the next year two Guards battalions (3rd Bn Coldstream Guards and 1st Bn Irish Guards), were again sent to Palestine, this time from Egypt. It was, as the Irish Guards described it 'an exhilarating little war against an energetic and skilful enemy'.

There was active patrolling and ambushing by both sides, while the Arabs also began mining roads and railways. This was countered by the simple expedient of placing several Arabs in the leading vehicles of any convoy or in the first compartment of any train.

The Coldstream had the tricky task on 19 October of reoccupying the Old City of Jerusalem. No fire support was permitted and the Holy Places were out of bounds. To achieve secrecy, the battalion was referred to as 'Monck's Regiment' (see page 25), and the operation (carried out in gym shoes) was successfully completed with no casualties.

As a foretaste of the ironies of peace-keeping, the battalion found itself on one occasion protecting the Arabs from the Jews in one part of Jerusalem, and the Jews from the Arabs in another part.

Nor was it all one-sided fighting, for the two battalions saw enough action to earn between them four Military Crosses and seven Military Medals, before they returned to Egypt. But it was not the last that the Household Division was to see of Palestine.

(*Opposite above*) Horse-Drawn Transport, 1938. Just a year before the outbreak of the Second World War, battalion transport was still partly horse-drawn, and only just being converted to motor. (*below*) Motor Transport, 1938.

Soldiering at Home

Active service overseas was welcomed by most members of the Household Division, for soldiering at home was frustrating in the extreme for the period between the wars.

Economy dominated every activity, with the result that there was a depressing lack of equipment, ammunition and transport. Indeed motor transport was almost non-existent, and even Expeditionary Force units did not change from horse to motor transport till 1936.

This period has been described with some bitterness and justification as 'the era of the green and white Flag', for that was how anti-tank guns were represented on training, while tanks were simulated by trucks marked with a large 'T', or by cardboard shapes mounted on bicycles. Much of the equipment was still as in 1918. Wooden police rattles were used instead of machine guns, and there was not enough live ammunition for adequate range firing, let alone blanks for exercises.

All equipment, and transport in particular, was so short that exercises

had sometimes to be staggered, so that different formations could use the same vehicles. Training followed a programme which progressed from platoon and company training to the annual army manoeuvres in the autumn. But it was all discouragingly unrealistic and inadequate, and gave the Army little scope to prepare for the real thing.

The cry of the politicians was the famous statement: 'The British Empire will not be engaged in any great war during the next ten years'; first pronounced reasonably enough in 1919 but then advanced year by year as an excuse for spending the minimum money on defence.

This ostrich-like attitude inevitably had a frustrating effect on the Army, particularly when they saw their potential enemy building up highly efficient, fully-trained, 'blitzkreig' forces, equipped with an abundance of guns, tanks, aeroplanes and weapons of all sorts.

Only in 1936 did the threat from Nazi Germany begin to register and by then there was a formidable backlog to be overcome. But during the next three years belated efforts were made to bring the Services somewhat nearer to the level of efficiency and effectiveness that was needed. While Britain sought, still without great urgency, to make up for lost time in building up her defences, Hitler marched arrogantly across Europe. In March 1938, he occupied Austria and then threatened to annex the Sudetenland, long part of Czechloslovakia.

Britain, still following a course of appeasement, offered to send a military force, called 'C Force' to supervise a plebiscite in the area. It was to be commanded by Brigadier A. F. A. N. Thorne (Grenadier Guards), and was formed from the Coldstream and Scots Guards. But the Germans not unnaturally refused to allow such a body to have access to Czechoslovakia, and in October 1938 it was stood down.

So the year 1939 began with the storm clouds gathering and Britain striving desperately to make up for the wasted years.

On 1 September, Britain and France mobilised, and two days later, the Second World War began.

Chapter 13

Adversity (1939–41)

When Neville Chamberlain announced the outbreak of the Second World War on Sunday, 3 September 1939, the mobilisation of the Household Division was remarkably similar to that of 1914.

Mobilisation

The Household Cavalry again formed a Composite Regiment, which was not only still horsed, but was equipped with Hotchkiss machine guns, as used in 1918. The Regiment moved in February 1940 to Palestine, where they joined The Royals and several other regiments in 1st Cavalry Division. For the first time the squadrons consisted of men from both The Life Guards and The Blues, instead of from one Regiment only.

The Brigade of Guards moved swiftly onto a wartime footing. Five battalions were formed into 1st and 7th Guards Brigades, which, as in 1914, joined the British Expeditionary Force in France within a few weeks. Two regular battalions, 3rd Bn Coldstream Guards and 2nd Bn Scots Guards, were already in Egypt, the Welsh Guards were in Gibraltar, and three battalions were at home.

Reservists and volunteers poured into each Regiment, and the training organisation was rapidly expanded to cope. Each Regiment set up its own Training Battalion[92] and within the next twelve months, a further eight Guards battalions were created, which made it possible to form five more Guards Brigades.[93]

In addition, the Grenadier, Coldstream and Scots Guards all formed their

183

A Household Cavalry
Patrol in Palestine, 1940.

own Holding Battalions which acted as depots for the Regiment, and also carried out Royal Guards and wartime duties in London. This system continued until November 1943 when the three Holding Battalions amalgamated and became the Westminster Garrison Battalion at Wellington Barracks, which also contained a company each from the Irish and Welsh Guards.

The King's Life Guard no longer rode to Whitehall from Hyde Park Barracks, but drove there in a hired furniture van, and mounted 'on site', in khaki and wearing steel helmets. The same order of dress was adopted for the King's Guard at Buckingham Palace, but the Foot Guards marched to and from their duties. These arrangements continued throughout the war, despite the blitz, flying bombs and V2's.

France (1939–40)

The Allied line of defence in Europe ran along the eastern frontier of France (see Map 2 on page 28) and was protected in the south by the Maginot Line, that 'impregnable' network of fortresses.

The British Expeditionary Force was allotted a sector, with the French Army on both flanks. They were separated from the Germans by the neutral territory of Belgium, so there was no direct contact with the enemy.

There were two alternatives open to the Allies in the event of a German attack through Belgium. The first was to hold the line of the River Escaut, some five miles inside Belgium, which required little change of position, but did mean giving up the whole of Belgium to the enemy without a fight.

The second possibility, was to advance sixty miles across Belgium to the

184

line of the River Dyle nearer the German frontier. This was a shorter line of defence and a better one, in that part of it could be flooded. But it did involve abandoning prepared positions for unprepared ones, and there was also the risk of being caught between the two. But this was the course agreed on, and it had the overriding advantage that it might prevent Belgium being overrun.

Meanwhile, the British Expeditionary Force, including 1st and 7th Guards Brigades,[94] spent the winter training and digging defences called the Gort Line; there was little scope for any realism, except when 1st Guards Brigade spent a month in positions in front of the Maginot Line.

So the winter passed, and in April the war opened up in Norway. Still nothing seemed to be happening in France.

But the 'phoney war' was to become the real thing all too soon.

Finland (February–March 1940)

Meanwhile, a bitter campaign had been continuing throughout the winter far away to the east in Finland, where this tiny but proud nation fought for survival against the overwhelming strength of Russia, at that time Germany's ally. The gallant struggle of this small country against impossible odds stirred Britain to try to help her, and at the same time to strike a blow indirectly against Germany. (See Map 9 overleaf.)

So in January 1940 it was decided to form a Ski Battalion to fight in Finland. It was commanded by a Coldstreamer, Colonel Jimmie Coats, and was officially called the 5th Battalion Scots Guards; unofficially they were known as 'the Snowballers'.

Volunteers were called for from the whole British Army, and about 1,000 responded, including many from the Household Division. Six hundred of them were officers, and 163 agreed to serve as NCOs or Guardsmen, a supreme example of improvisation at its best – or worst.

They assembled on 6 February 1940, and were given 23 days in which to be ready for operations.

A week was spent training at Chamonix, and on 14 March, the Battalion embarked for Finland. But sadly, the Finns surrendered that very day, and this unique force was disbanded a week later.

Norway (April–June 1940)

The war began in earnest on 9 April 1940, when German forces invaded Norway and rapidly moved northwards. Britain had in fact been planning to occupy certain key ports in northern Norway herself, in order to forestall just such a move by the Germans, but now it was too late.

24th Guards Brigade, commanded by Brigadier The Hon W. Fraser (Grenadier Guards), had been warned for active service on 1 April, and they were now despatched to Norway in great haste as part of the British force under General Mackesy, sailing from Greenock on 11 April. The Brigade consisted of 1st Bn Irish Guards, 1st Bn Scots Guards and 1st Bn South Wales Borderers.

The principle of loading units together with their equipment had not yet been learned, and the Irish Guards found that their maps were on another ship, while the Scots Guards landed with push bikes as their only transport, and smoke bombs only for their 2 inch mortars.

The plan had been to land at the key port of Narvik and to occupy it; but the Germans had got there first, and 24th Guards Brigade therefore landed instead at Harstadt, thirty-five miles to the north. (See Map 9.)

9 Norway and Finland

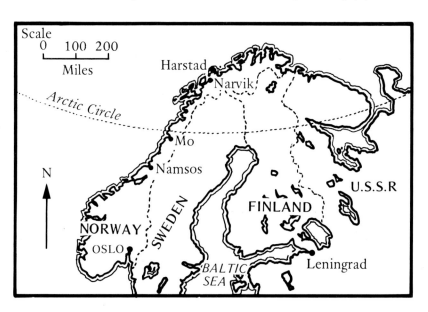

On 30 April, the brigade commander was wounded, and Lieutenant Colonel Trappes-Lomax, commanding 1st Bn Scots Guards, took over.

Other British forces which had landed in southern Norway had been forced to withdraw on 3 May, leaving the Germans free to concentrate against General Mackesy's forces in the north. The plan therefore was to block the enemy advance northwards, a task which was allotted to 24th Guards Brigade.

On 10 May, came the news of the invasion of Holland and Belgium, and the next day the Scots Guards, now called 'Scissorforce', sailed out of Harstadt towards Mo, 150 miles south of Narvik, with orders to hold it 'at all costs'.

The Irish Guards should have joined them, but their ship was bombed and had to return to Harstadt. The South Wales Borderers' ship, which contained the only three tanks available to the brigade, ran aground and sank.

So the task of halting the German advance, intended for a complete brigade, devolved on 1st Bn Scots Guards, commanded by their Second-in-Command. Before recording how they faced this challenge, it is worth telling in more detail the story of the Irish Guards' ill-fated voyage.

Just after midnight on 14/15 May, three Heinkel bombers attacked their ship, HMT *Chobry*, as it sailed through Arctic twilight, and it was set on fire. Ammunition began exploding and it was found that none of the lifeboats could be lowered. Men could survive only a few minutes in the Arctic waters, so there was little that could be done, except wait and hope for rescue.

The raging fire had by now divided the ship into two parts, with the officers, many of whom had been killed, all one end, while most of the men were on the other.

But as the Guardsmen filed up on deck they immediately heard the familiar voice of Regimental Sergeant Major Stack:

'Get on parade, Face that way.'

The sentries on deck were posted as markers, and the battalion was soon formed up in mass, with its weapons and equipment.

As they waited, the padré, Father Cavanagh, started to recite the Rosary, and 'with bared heads on a burning ship in the Arctic Circle, men said the prayers that they had learnt long ago in the quiet churches and farmhouses of Ireland.'[95]

The bombers were still attacking, but two escort vessels came alongside, and began taking men off. The Captain of one of them, Commander Craske, RN, of HMS *Wolverine*, has described the scene:

We closed on their burning and sinking ship. I never before realised what the discipline of the Guards was. We got a gangway shipped forward and the men were ordered to file off on to us. There was no confusion, no hurry and no sign of haste or flurry. I knew that there might be only a matter of minutes in which to get them off. I had four ropes fixed so as to hurry up the transfer. They continued to file steadily off in one line. I cursed and swore at them, but they had orders to file, and they filed. I saw someone who seemed to be a young officer and in no measured terms I told him to get them off by all four ropes. In a second they conformed to this order by one of their own officers, still steadily and without fuss or confusion. Their conduct in the most trying circumstances, in the absence of senior officers, on a burning and sinking ship, open at any moment to a new attack, was as fine as, or finer than the conduct in the old days of the soldiers on the *Birkenhead*. It may interest you to know that 694 men were got on board in sixteen minutes.[95]

The battalion had lost its Commanding Officer and virtually all its senior officers, but it was back in action five days later.

Meanwhile, the Scots Guards had been fighting a series of fierce delaying actions under hopeless conditions. They faced incessant air attacks, for there was virtually no darkness and the Germans had complete air superiority. They were constantly outflanked by German troops trained and equipped for mountain warfare, and there was little time for rest or sleep. They marched 100 miles in a week, fighting the whole way, and with no support until the Irish Guards joined in on 20 May.

But the general position was grim, and both battalions were withdrawn back to Harstadt by 31st May. Every available soldier was now needed to defend Britain against invasion, and it had been decided to end the Norwegian campaign. On 7 June, King Haakon left Norway, and three days later 24th Guards Brigade was back home.

The road to Dunkirk

Despite seeing Denmark and Norway overrun by the Germans in April–May 1940, Holland and Belgium still maintained their neutrality, in the faint hope that they might thus prevent Hitler from attacking them. They were soon disillusioned.

On 10 May 1940, at 0530 hours, the 'sitzkrieg' ended and the 'blitzkrieg' began, with fierce air attacks on airfields and key towns in Holland, whose armed forces could do little against an overwhelming German armoured and airborne assault.

In accordance with Plan D, the British Expeditionary Force, including both 1st and 7th Guards Brigades, immediately moved forward to the line of the River Dyle, and began to take up their new defensive positions round Louvain, fortunately with little interference from the Germans.

On the morning of the 11th, while the British Expeditionary Force was moving forward across Belgium, and the Germans were rapidly overrunning Holland, the newly-formed 20th Guards Brigade,[96] back in England, were returning to camp from a night exercise.

They arrived back to find themselves ordered to move at once. Only 2nd Bn Irish Guards were immediately available, but they, with one company of Welsh Guards under command, sailed for Holland the next day.

They were called 'Harpoon Force' and their task was to 'safeguard the Dutch Government and restore the situation in the capital'. At dawn on the 13th, they arrived at the Hook to find clouds of smoke rising from Rotterdam, while the Hook was also subjected to frequent air attacks.

They disembarked, wondering slightly where to start on 'restoring the situation', when at 1130 hours, the unmistakable figure of Queen Wilhelmina of the Netherlands stepped out of a car and approached. Her wish was that the Royal Navy would take her to one of the Dutch islands, so that she could continue the struggle from there. But no one had any charts of the local minefields, and so she was reluctantly persuaded to board a British destroyer for England, followed by her Government.

The next day, Holland surrendered, and the Irish and Welsh Guards returned home – only to be called on again a week later for a rather sterner task at Boulogne.

The triumphant German Panzer forces, having conquered Holland, now swept across Belgium, overwhelming the British Expeditionary Force who were forced back into France. On 20 May, the Germans reached the Channel coast at Abbeville.

The BEF was now cut off, not only from the rest of the French Army to the south, but also from their own supplies coming from Cherbourg and the Atlantic ports. Worst of all, there was the danger that a German thrust northwards from Abbeville would capture the Channel ports and so isolate the British forces in France from England. To prevent this last threat and to cover the withdrawal of Britain's only army, troops were rushed from England to hold the vital Channel ports – a Greenjacket Brigade to Calais and 20th Guards Brigade to Boulogne.

Once again, the Guards Brigade was on an exercise when it was ordered on 21 May to move to France the same afternoon. This time both Guards battalions were prepared, and within thirty-six hours, they were facing the tanks of the German 2nd Panzer Division on the outskirts of Boulogne.

For three days, the two battalions held out, and the German Corps Commander recorded in his War Diary 'the enemy is fighting tenaciously for every inch of ground'. But the pressure against them grew daily and they were forced back steadily into an ever-decreasing perimeter, until by 24 May, they were hanging on grimly to nothing but a tight area round the docks.

In the final stages, as the Germans closed in on the quay area, the two battalions received impressive support from the Royal Navy, whose sailors fought ashore alongside the Guardsmen, and whose ships' guns fired point blank from open decks against the German tanks.

On the evening of the 24th, their task was completed and they were ordered to withdraw at once. But the Germans now dominated the quay itself, and the Welsh Guards lost most of two companies who could not be evacuated. But even then, the Welshmen left behind fought on for two more days before being captured. They were commanded by Major Windsor-Lewis who was wounded and captured, but made a remarkable escape six months later.

It was at this moment that a Captain in a Line Regiment recalls watching a party of Guardsmen being marched onto the quay by a Drill Sergeant, who halted them, and despite some shellfire, inspected their weapons. He then marched up to the Captain, saluted smartly, and asked permission to carry on and embark.

By a strange coincidence, while the 2nd Battalion of the Welsh Guards was making a last-ditch stand in Boulogne, their 1st Battalion[97] was doing much the same at Arras, where the Commanding Officer, Lieutenant Colonel Copland-Griffiths, had been appointed Garrison Commander.

With his own battalion, three Line battalions and various other groups, he held the town from 17 to 24 May, despite fierce attacks by the Germans, including Rommel's 7th Armoured Division.

Lord Gort reported in his Despatches:

'the defence of Arras . . . had been carried out by a small garrison, hastily assembled, but well commanded and determined to fight. It had imposed a valuable delay on a greatly superior enemy force against which it had blocked a vital road centre'.

Meanwhile, 1st and 7th Guards Brigades on the River Dyle were involved in the grim withdrawal back through Belgium to Dunkirk. For almost two weeks, they marched and fought, occupying and abandoning one rearguard position after another, attacked by air, and hampered by streams of refugees. At one moment 1st Guards Brigade were marching on the right of a road, while 2nd Infantry Brigade marched on the left, and the vehicles of 1st Division drove down the centre. There was some sharp fighting, and two Victoria Crosses were won[98] before the last battles were fought round Dunkirk.

7th Guards Brigade's last action was at Furnes, before they were evacuated on 1 June.

1st Guards Brigade held the perimeter round Hondschoote, and also withdrew on 1 June, except for 2nd Bn Coldstream Guards, who were ordered to form a final rearguard for the British Expeditionary Force. They did not finally leave Dunkirk until about 2100 hours, 2 June, aboard HMS *Sabre*.

It was a disastrous retreat, very similar to those at Corunna and Mons. But as in 1809 and 1914, so in 1940, there were incidents that proved that the Guards' traditions continue unchanged.

3rd Bn Grenadier Guards, for example, were seen marching into Dunkirk, at Attention, with arms sloped, and 'looking like Guardsmen', just as the Grenadiers had swung into Corunna 131 years before. It was perhaps of particular significance to them, because all three battalions of the Regiment were involved, and it was also the scene of their Regiment's first battle, 282 years before.

A Quartermaster of the Welsh Guards, was seen standing waist deep in the sea, dishing out tea to his men from a dixie held by two Guardsmen 'above sea-level'.

Somehow, over 330,000 men of the British Expeditionary Force were brought back to England in the 'miracle of Dunkirk', and they included most of the six battalions of Foot Guards who had been in the Expeditionary Force – each with their complement of personal weapons intact. 'Nor is it a legend that their trousers were pressed', wrote Field Marshal Lord Alexander in his *Memoirs*.

At Bay (June– December 1940)

The Guards returned to a Britain standing at bay, threatened daily with invasion, but defiant still, as the whole country rallied to the inspiring leadership of Winston Churchill. Pikes were issued to the Home Guard as in 1803, the same Martello Towers were manned, the same beaches were watched and the same strategy planned for a fighting withdrawal.

The Reserve Regiment of the Household Cavalry made barricades for the defence of Hyde Park by wrapping barbed wire round the riding school jumps. They reconnoitred battle positions known as the 'Acton Line', and drove there in motor coaches – provided that it was during union hours, as the civilian drivers went home at night and over weekends.

From Windsor they guarded nearby reservoirs where it was thought the enemy might land in sea-planes and they also carried out anti-parachutist patrols in the Great Park mounted on bicycles.

The Holding Battalions of the Foot Guards protected vulnerable points in and around London, fought fires in the blitz, patrolled the London parks, and carried on mounting the Royal Guards.

Three special Guards were also mounted which deserve mention.

The first was a detachment of Life Guards armoured cars which was detailed to escort the King when he travelled in dangerous areas – a revival of the historic role for which they had been formed in 1658.

The second force was the Coats Mission, formed in June 1940 to safeguard the Royal Family in the event of invasion. It was provided by the Holding Battalion of the Coldstream Guards and was commanded initially by Major Jimmie Coats, who had formed the Ski Battalion in February that year. Plans were made to escort the Royal Family to selected private houses in various parts of the country, and to guard them there. Fortunately there was never any need to put these plans into effect, and the force was finally disbanded in January 1943.

The final special force was a company, again provided by the Coldstream Guards, to guard the Prime Minister at his country base of Chequers, from September 1940 to July 1943.

An unexpected duty for the Scots Guards Holding Battalion, stationed at the Tower of London, was to guard Rudolph Hess, when he was held at the Tower after landing in Britain by parachute on 10 May 1941 in a dramatic attempt to arrange peace terms. He was transferred the next week to Mytchett, where he became the responsibility of the Training Battalions at Pirbright.

The Scots Guards also had the task on 14 August 1941 of shooting in the miniature range of the Tower, Josef Jakobs, the first German spy to be executed in Britain during the war.

Most of the Household Division was soon in action again.

The Household Cavalry already had 1st Household Cavalry Regiment in the Middle East and were about to form the 2nd Regiment as the reconnaissance element of the Guards Armoured Division.

From June 1940 onwards, the Brigade of Guards had up to nine battalions engaged in the campaigns in North Africa (1940–3) and in Italy (1943–5). In May 1941 they also formed the Guards Armoured Division, which absorbed a further eight Foot Guards Battalions.

In addition, the Household Division made a contribution to several specialist forces. 1st British (Airborne) Division, which fought at Arnhem in October 1944, contained officers and men from both the Household Cavalry and the Foot Guards. A Guards Commando (Number 8) was formed on the same basis, and carried out operations in North Africa.

The Household Division also formed their own Patrol in the Long Range Desert Group, while many individuals operated in various clandestine and irregular organisations. The story of these irregular units is told more fully in the next few chapters.

Chapter 14

North Africa

(1939–43)

The outbreak of war in September 1939 found two Guards battalions (3rd Bn Coldstream Guards and 2nd Bn Scots Guards) stationed in Egypt where they had been since 1937. There they remained, and when on 10 June 1940, Mussolini threw in his lot with Hitler in Africa, the Coldstream soon moved out into the Western Desert, as part of the 7th Armoured Division, the famous 'Desert Rats'. With them they patrolled the frontier between Egypt and the Italian territory of Cyrenaica, until they were forced back to Mersa Matruh in September 1940. (See Map 1.)

On 8 December, General Sir Archibald Wavell, the Commander-in-Chief in the Middle East, launched his brilliant counter-attack against the Axis, and with a puny force, known as 'Wavell's Thirty Thousand' thrust eighty miles westwards to Sidi Barrani, capturing no less than 180,000 prisoners in the process.

The Coldstream, who were the only Guards unit in this campaign, signalled back at one moment that they could not count the number of prisoners they held, but that 'there were about five acres of officers, and two hundred acres of other ranks'.[99]

When the Coldstream returned to Egypt in January 1941, they joined with 2nd Bn Scots Guards and 1st Bn Durham Light Infantry to form 22nd Guards Brigade, commanded by Brigadier I. D. Erskine (Scots Guards).

But now a new enemy had appeared in North Africa in the person of General Rommel, who, together with his renowned Afrika Korps, formed perhaps the finest fighting force produced by Germany in the war.

On 31 March 1941, Rommel attacked Wavell's depleted forces and drove them back to the frontier.

For the next nine months, 22nd Guards Brigade fought with 7th Armoured Division and 1st South African Division[100] in the to-and-fro desert warfare of that period, until the position stabilised in January 1942 round Gazala and Tobruk – both of which were later to be the scenes of worthy battle honours for the Guards Brigade.

North Africa (1939–43)

In the Western Desert, 1940.

'Knightsbridge Box'

The defensive position known as the 'Gazala Line' consisted of a series of strong-points or 'boxes', protected by minefields, each of which was provisioned as for a siege. One of the most vital of these was the 'Knightsbridge Box', which dominated the main axis of advance for any German attack eastwards. Rommel could achieve no strategic success so long as it remained in our hands, while from the Allied point of view, it was not only an essential pivot for any armoured operations, but it also controlled all supply routes to the Gazala Line.

It was some two miles square, with the infantry round the perimeter, artillery in the centre and anti-tank guns sited in depth.

The defence of this key position was entrusted to 22nd Guards Brigade, now re-named as 201st Guards Brigade.[101] Into the Knightsbridge Box went 3rd Bn Coldstream Guards, 2nd Regiment, Royal Horse Artillery, one Scots Guards company, and some of their 2-pounder anti-tank guns. To the north of Knightsbridge were the remainder of the 2nd Bn Scots Guards on the Rigel Ridge, while to the south the Free French Brigade held the equally important Bir Hacheim Box.

On 27 May, Rommel attacked, and as expected, he by-passed all strong-points and penetrated deep into the Eighth Army positions. But he still had to eliminate these boxes, and despite fierce attacks, the garrison held out.

These tactics by both sides were remarkably similar to the French cavalry charges against the British squares at Waterloo, except that on this occasion the artillery were within the square.

On 4 June, the Eighth Army launched a counter-attack, which developed into the fierce armoured battle known as the 'Cauldron'; Rommel emerged the winner, and the Allies sustained severe losses. Only six days later, the Free French at Bir Hacheim to the south were overrun after a most gallant defence, and Rommel was now free to turn against Knightsbridge.

He attacked fiercely, and at 0100 hours 12 June, the garrison was ordered to withdraw. But it was considered too late to do so that night, and they had to hold on for one more day.

It was a grim day too, particularly for the Scots Guards. They were heavily attacked on the Rigel Ridge, but received magnificent support from the eight 25-pounder guns of the 6th South African Field Battery, who fired over open sights at the German tanks, and fought their guns to the last.

But no armoured support was available, and the enemy tanks could not be kept at bay much longer. Throughout a day of hand-to-hand fighting against the bulk of the 21st Panzer Division, the Rigel Ridge was held, but only after a most bitter and costly struggle.

At dusk, both battalions were finally ordered to withdraw. Somehow, the few remaining tanks of 22nd Armoured Brigade managed to hold open a corridor, through which the weary Guardsmen marched back, having held their key positions for seventeen days.

It was after the battle of Gazala that Rommel made his famous comment, that the Guards Brigade was 'almost a living embodiment of the virtues and faults of the British soldier – tremendous courage and tenacity, combined with a rigid lack of mobility.[102]

A dramatic description of the scene of the battle of Rigel Ridge comes from Captain N. B. Hanmer, then in the Royal Sussex Regiment, who visited the battlefield some six months later, after the Battle of Alamein:

It was an amazing fact that none of these positions had been salvaged by the Germans . . . not one of our men had been buried . . . . The sand appeared to have some sort of preserving quality and the bodies were hardly decomposed.

A position which impressed me greatly was the 6-pounder anti-tank positions manned by the Scots Guards. They must have fired their guns until the German tanks were right on top of them. Almost every gun had the body of a Scots Guardsman drooped across the shoulder piece or slumped over the breech.

Several men were still crouching in slit trenches with rifles, as if they had continued engaging the enemy with .303 when their guns had been put out of action. There was an officer lying on his face, his finger round the trigger of a Bren gun . . .

It made me feel rather moved to look at those guns, and see the dead men by their guns, which they seemed to serve even in death.

Tobruk

The remnants of the Scots Guards now returned to Egypt, while the remainder of 201st Guards Brigade pulled back into Tobruk, which it was planned to hold as a base for future operations. This had been successfully achieved for nine months from April to December 1941, but the position was very different now.

Last time, the thirty mile perimeter had been held as part of a detailed plan, based on charted minefields and with a rehearsed counter-attack by troops who knew the ground and the minefields thoroughly. Now the garrison consisted of weary troops, rushed into strange positions, which were themselves suffering from six months of neglect. Above all, there was general confusion, for there was little time for the newly appointed commander to organise into a coherent force the variety of units suddenly flung into the garrison.

201st Guards Brigade, with some seventy tanks from 4th Bn, the Royal Tank Regiment reached Tobruk on 14 June, and were placed in reserve with a counter-attack role. The brigade was now commanded by Brigadier George Johnson (Scots Guards), who took over on the day they moved into Tobruk. It consisted of 3rd Bn Coldstream Guards, 1st Bn Worcestershire Regiment, and 1st Bn Sherwood Foresters.

There seemed little immediate danger, for Rommel was apparently fully occupied with his thrust towards Egypt, which had penetrated almost to the frontier. Then suddenly, Rommel turned in his tracks, and at dawn on 20 June struck fiercely and unexpectedly at Tobruk. On a front of only 600 yards, Stuka dive bombers literally blasted a gap through the minefields, into which streamed two infantry and two armoured divisions. It was an irresistible assault, and they broke through.

At 0900 hours, the Coldstream Guards were ordered to counter-attack. But of the forty tanks that should have supported them only five now remained. No orders or information could be obtained from any source, and confusion grew hourly, as German tanks thrust deep into the town, and the dive-bombers attacked with impunity.

During the day, the pressure increased steadily, as enemy tanks and armoured cars closed in on the infantry positions. That evening Brigade Headquarters was overrun, and the Brigadier and his staff were taken prisoner, together with the Commanding Officer of the Coldstream Guards.

There now occurred a fine example of leadership. Major Tim Sainthill of 3rd Bn Coldstream Guards found himself in command of the battalion, reduced to only about two hundred men. More German forces were closing in, and the forward platoons had been overrun. It was impossible to contact any higher headquarters, and it seemed hopeless to continue.

But Major Sainthill did not accept defeat. Instead, he rallied whatever troops he could find, organised a hasty defensive position and prepared to fight on.

The night was one of growing confusion, and it became increasingly obvious that no other proper defence was being organised. Next morning no orders came at all, only reports that Tobruk had surrendered, that all vehicles were to be destroyed and all troops were to wait in their positions for the enemy.

Major Sainthill's reaction is said to have been to the effect that surrender was a manoeuvre that he had never been taught in the Coldstream, and so he did not intend to try it now for the first time.

His force was unquestionably surrounded and all signs of resistance by the garrison had disappeared. Indeed, they could be seen and heard destroying their weapons and equipment.

Major Sainthill decided not to follow suit, but to put his men into transport and try to escape in a body by daylight, relying on boldness, bluff, and the general confusion to get them through.

'Head roughly due south', were his orders. 'Drive hard, shoot hard and go right through in a confusion of dust and bullets'.

By luck a South African gunner officer appeared who knew a way through the minefields. A rendezvous was fixed in the desert. And at 0900 hours, 21 June, they set off.

As they approached the perimeter, each driver put his foot hard down and and roared into the dust of the truck ahead. The firing grew every second, some trucks 'brewed up', some got lost and some were captured. But somehow sixty vehicles got through and found their way back to the British lines, with seventeen officers and 183 ranks from the Coldstream, and some 200 from other units. It was a fine exploit, for which Major Sainthill was awarded a well-earned Distinguished Service Order.

But there was no respite. Rommel still threatened Cairo, where civilians were being evacuated and secret documents burned. Every man was needed for its defence, and at the end of June the survivors of the Coldstream and Scots Guards were combined into a composite Guards Battalion which continued until 201st Guards Brigade was re-formed in September 1942 and sent to Syria. It now consisted of 6th Bn Grenadier Guards (from the UK), 3rd Bn Coldstream Guards and 2nd Bn Scots Guards.

(*Opposite*) Major Michael Crichton-Stuart (Scots Guards), who was the first commander of 'G' Patrol of the Long Range Desert Group.

196

No Foot Guards units fought at the Battle of el Alamein in October 1942, but the Guards were represented there by 1st Household Cavalry Regiment.[103] They had spent the first year and a half of the war sitting in frustrated inactivity in Palestine, until in May 1941, Rashid Ali, the pro-Axis leader of Iraq, laid siege to the RAF base at Habbaniya just west of Baghdad; an extremely *ad hoc* mobile column, which included the Household Cavalry, was then formed to restore the situation.

In a strange assortment of commandeered transport, led by the Commanding Officer in a yellow taxi, they dashed 500 miles across the desert at the head of 'Habforce', as it was called, relieved Habbaniya and occupied Baghdad. A month later they hurried back westwards to capture the Palmyra Oasis in Syria just ahead of the Vichy French.

In September 1941, having crossed the desert for the third time, they occupied Teheran, this time just ahead of Britain's new allies, the Russians, who were entering the city from the east.

Then at last, in February 1942, they were equipped as an armoured car regiment, and moved via Cyprus, to Egypt, where they played an active part in the Battle of Alamein. Soon after this however they were withdrawn from the Eighth Army, and sent to Syria to man the frontier with Turkey, where they remained for the next fifteen months.

1st Household Cavalry Regiment

This did not mean that there were now no Guardsmen fighting in North Africa, for operating deep in the desert was a band of scruffy-looking, bearded figures, who called themselves 'G' (Foot Guards) Patrol of the Long Range Desert Group. (or LRDG.)

'G' Patrol had been set up in December 1940 with volunteers from the Coldstream and Scots Guards then in Egypt, and they were soon waging skilled guerilla warfare behind the enemy lines, carrying out surprise attacks on the rear areas of the Afrika Korps, as well as passing back a stream of valuable information.

The patrol's first exploit was a raid on an enemy post, 1,100 miles out into the desert of South West Libya. They returned to Egypt, via the Sudan, covering no less than 4,300 miles in 45 days. Even this remarkable record was broken by 'G' Patrol's last operation, in which they travelled 3,500 miles in thirty-seven days.

Less spectacular, but just as valuable, was the 'Road Watch' kept by the Patrol and others, which provided a detailed daily tally of much of the traffic behind the enemy lines. The Patrol was disbanded in May 1943, when the North African campaign ended.

Some were surprised that the Guards excelled at such a game, which obviously called for the greatest initiative, self-reliance and independence. But in fact, operations of this type demanded just the self-discipline and self-confidence to which all Guardsmen are trained.

'It was no accident', wrote Michael Crichton-Stuart, 'that the man whose gun was always ready for action, despite the desert dust, the driver whose

Long Range Desert Group

truck tyres were always at the right pressure, the reliable guard on solitary
night watch, was, in barracks among "the smartest on the square".'[104]

The Special Air Service

The Long Range Desert Group worked closely in North Africa with another
organisation, called the Special Air Service (SAS) which not only contained
a high proportion of Guardsmen, but had in fact been formed by a Guards
officer.

Second Lieutenant David Stirling had transferred in mid-1940 from the
Scots Guards to No. 8 Commando, formed and commanded by Brigadier
Bob Laycock of The Blues. It consisted largely of Guardsmen from all
Regiments and formed part of 'Layforce', which was intended to capture
and occupy the island of Rhodes. This operation never materialised, but the
commando moved to the Middle East in March 1941 and took part in the
raid on Bardia in April.

In June, however, orders came for Number 8 Commando to be disbanded.
But David Stirling had other ideas. He was convinced that small groups of
determined men operating behind the enemy lines could achieve results
out of all proportion to their numbers. As part of his thinking, he experi-
mented with parachuting, but ended up in hospital with an injured back.

198

Still on crutches, he decided that the only way to get his ideas across was to start at the top, i.e. the Commander-in-Chief. He managed to get inside Headquarters, Middle East Command, but not unseen; and with a sentry in pursuit, he dived into the nearest room. It was unluckily occupied by a Major in his own Regiment, who remembered him chiefly for going to sleep during his lectures. The meeting was unhelpful, except that it had shaken off the sentry.

Risking all, he now marched boldly into the office of a very much more senior officer, General Neil Ritchie, Deputy Chief of the General Staff. Greatly to his credit, the general not only listened as the young officer explained his strange purpose, but then, impressed by what he heard, he arranged a prompt meeting with the Commander-in-Chief, General Auchinleck.

The outcome was that Stirling obtained permission to recruit a force of seven officers and fifty-nine other ranks for his scheme, and so the SAS was born. This interview is 'held by many to be Stirling's greatest achievement'.[105]

The first recruits included 'Jock' Lewes, an Australian in the Welsh Guards, and Tom Langton of the Irish Guards. The former had rowed for Oxford and the latter for Cambridge, and it was in honour of this that a light and dark blue background was chosen for the SAS badge of a winged dagger.

The SAS worked closely with the LRDG, but whereas the latter specialised in desert reconnaissance and observation, the SAS were primarily demolition experts, who arrived at their objective by land, sea or air as appropriate. Both groups worked on the same rule of leadership, a basis also of Guards discipline, that one never expects others to do what one is not prepared to do first oneself.

Nor were they alone in such activities. Other Guardsmen were indulging in many similar exploits throughout the war.

Among them was Brigadier Arthur Nicholls of the Coldstream Guards, who was awarded a posthumous George Cross for inspiring courage and leadership while organising guerilla warfare in Albania in 1943; Major David Smiley (The Blues) and Lord Jellicoe (Coldstream Guards) also operated in Albania and elsewhere with the SAS; and Captains Stanley Moss (Coldstream Guards) and Leigh-Fermor (Irish Guards), carried out the dramatic kidnapping in his own garrison area in Crete of General Kreipe, commander of the German Sevastopol Division.[106]

(*Opposite*)
Officers and men of the Coldstream and Scots Guards who formed 'G' Patrol. The figures in the centre of the front row are genuine Bedouin.

First Army

November 1942 saw dramatic changes in the North African campaign. The Eighth Army victory at El Alamein on 4 November forced the Germans to retreat westwards again, abandoning Tobruk. Meanwhile, on 8 November, the first Allied assault landing of the war, Operation 'Torch', was carried out under General Eisenhower at Algiers and Casablanca at the other end

Colonel David Stirling,
founder of the Special Air
Service, standing by a patrol
of the Long Range Desert
Group.

of North Africa, as part of a strategic pincer movement against the Afrika Korps. (See Map 1.)

850 ships put ashore the British First Army and the United States 2nd Corps with virtually no opposition, and the Allies swept rapidly eastwards in an effort to capture Tunis and Bizerta before the enemy could recover.

But the Germans were able to fly in reinforcements from Europe very rapidly. They managed not only to halt the Allied advance some fifteen miles short of Tunis, but also to hit back strongly.

Included in the First Army was 1st Guards Brigade, who had been in the UK since Dunkirk. The brigade consisted of 3rd Bn Grenadier Guards, 2nd Bn Coldstream Guards, and 2nd Bn Hampshire Regiment, and was commanded by Brigadier F. A. V. Copland-Griffith (Welsh Guards). They landed on 22 November, and four days later, the Hampshire Regiment were detached and rushed into action at Tebourba. From that battle, they emerged with only three officers and 170 men, having shown outstanding courage; six Welsh Guards officers attached to them at the time were all killed.

Longstop Hill (December 1942 – January 1943)

Knightsbridge and Tobruk were already well-known names. Now the Guardsmen of First Army were about to win recognition on two craggy desert features called Longstop Hill and The Bou.

One of the three gateways to the coastal plain of Tunis was barred by these formidable features. To the north of the road was Djebel Ahmera known to the world as 'Longstop Hill'. Five miles to the east was Djebel Bou Ouden, or 'The Bou'. 1st Guards Brigade was to see much of both of them over the next six months.

On 22 December, 2nd Bn Coldstream Guards were ordered to capture Longstop, in order to open the way for 6th Armoured Division to break out and capture Tunis. The attack was successful, and the positions were handed over the same night to an American unit.

It had not been realised, however, that Longstop was dominated from behind by another feature, Djebel el Rhara. This was still in German hands, and from there, the enemy mounted fierce attacks which drove the Americans back.

So, within six hours of marching back to their concentration area, the weary Coldstream Guards were ordered to turn about, plod back over twelve muddy miles and re-capture Longstop. They did so, and then held it, with the help of American and French troops, all under command of the Coldstream Guards Commanding Officer.

But the Germans were also aware of the importance of Longstop, and on Christmas Day they attacked again, this time with heavy armoured cars, and re-captured it for the second time. The Coldstream lost 210 all ranks, and the Americans with them, who fought with great courage, lost 300.

There was no chance now of capturing Tunis by a swift coup, and with the onset of winter, a period of static warfare set in. Fighting was fierce, for the Germans kept up heavy pressure against the First Army and the Americans, in the hope of defeating them before the advancing Eighth Army closed in from the east.

A reorganised 1st Guards Brigade, with 3rd Bn Welsh Guards who had joined in February 1943 in the place of the Hampshire Regiment, was now in Army reserve. This involved constant moves from one area to another to deal with the persistent enemy attacks, and indeed, they were called upon so often to plug holes that they became known as the 'Plumbers', a title earned also by their fathers in the Guards Division in the Great War.

In March, 24th Guards Brigade also joined the First Army from the UK, while in the same month, 201st Guards Brigade rejoined the Eighth Army, after a 2,000 mile drive from Syria. There were thus nine Guards battalions in three Guards Brigades fighting in North Africa.[107] The 1st Household Cavalry Regiment were still with the Eighth Army, and 'G' Patrol of the Long Range Desert Group was also active.

The Deputy Supreme Commander was General Alexander (Irish Guards), with under him, as Commander of XXX Corps, Lieutenant General Oliver Leese (Coldstream Guards), who had previously commanded the Guards Armoured Division. So the Household Division was well represented on the North African front.

The next two months saw the crushing of the Axis forces in North Africa through a series of attacks by the First and Eighth Armies, co-ordinated by General Alexander.

Eighth Army drew first blood on 6 March, when 201st Guards Brigade were involved in a highly successful defensive battle at Tadjera Kbir near Medenine, in which 2nd Bn Scots Guards particularly distinguished themselves, knocking out no less than 52 German tanks.

Rommel now withdrew to the Mareth Line, about three miles in front of which was a 600-foot feature known as the Horseshoe, covering the approaches to the main positions. It was reported to be 'lightly held', and 201st Guards Brigade were given the supposedly simple task of capturing it, as the prelude to a major assault against the Mareth Line itself.

The attack was carried out by 6th Bn Grenadier Guards and 3rd Bn Coldstream Guards on 16 March 1943.

In the event, it was a disaster. The 'outpost', which was reported to be so thinly held that the defenders had not even been able to lay a minefield, turned out to be a prepared position defended by the greater part of the 90th Light Division, reinforced by a battalion of Panzer Grenadiers. In addition, the position was so heavily mined, in three thick belts, that no supporting weapons could be got forward to support the infantry. Finally, the enemy had discovered from prisoners the exact plan of attack, and they therefore directed their artillery and machine gun fire onto the likely approaches with deadly accuracy.

The attack went in, despite the unexpected minefields and heavy mortar fire, and both battalions gained their objectives; but the forward companies had suffered up to 75 per cent casualties.

Then the Germans began to infiltrate behind them, cutting them off from each other and from the reserve companies; no supporting vehicles or weapons could be got forward, and casualties mounted steadily. Clearly the position could not be held once daylight came, and so the order was given to withdraw. But it did not reach all the forward platoons and of those who did receive it, many could not get back.

The Grenadiers lost twenty-four officers and 255 men, no less than fourteen officers being killed – a tragic blow for the Battalion in its first battle. The Coldstream casualties were ten and 126.

But the ring was now tightening around Tunis and on 7 April 1943 it was finally closed.

The Horseshoe (16 March 1943)

With the stage now set for the final assault, General Alexander was given command of all the Allied forces in Tunisia.

His plan for the final round was simple. The Americans on the left of the Allied front and the Eighth Army on the right were to apply pressure on the Germans to pin them down on each flank. He would then launch the most powerful assault possible against the German centre. This was not only the shortest route to Tunis, but would split the German forces into two.

The Bou (27 April 1943)

The axis for the final thrust was north–east from Medjez-el-Bab. The two features of Longstop Hill and the Bou, which controlled this approach, had therefore to be regained from the Germans, who had held them since Christmas.

The capture of Longstop was allotted to 78th Division, and the Bou to 1st Division, who in turn gave the task to 24th Guards Brigade. It was a formidable undertaking.

Starting on 23 April (Good Friday and also St George's Day) the brigade fought its way forward for seven miles to get within striking distance of the two great hills ahead.

That done, the main attack was planned for 1830 hours, 27 April. But at noon it was put forward to 1600 hours, with the result that everything had to be done in a great rush, and platoon commanders ended up by giving out their orders on the move.

The 4,000 yard advance was across flat open ground, overlooked all the way by the enemy on the Bou – and it was now to be carried out in broad daylight.

The objectives of the attack were two ridges running parallel to the line of advance. Point 171 on the left was allocated to the 5th Bn Grenadier Guards, while Points 212 and 214 on the right were given to the 1st Bn Irish Guards. A thousand yards behind them loomed the Bou itself, due to be captured by 1st Bn Scots Guards in Phase Two of the operation.

As the two battalions crossed the start line, they immediately came under the anticipated intense and accurate fire. All over the cornfields through which they were advancing appeared a forest of rifle butts, marking where the wounded lay. But still the thin lines of Guardsmen strode forward, as they had done at Blenheim, Fontenoy, Alma and Loos.

'We could not believe it,' commented a German prisoner afterwards, 'We thought no one could cross that plain.'

Down in that plain, an Irish Guardsman is recorded as remarking 'Thank God for drill. It keeps you going.'

The Grenadier Guards gained their objectives, but with heavy casualties. The final objective was taken and held throughout that night by a subaltern and twelve men, who also captured sixty prisoners and four guns.

The Irish Guards on the right reached Point 212, but by then had only 173 men left in the battalion; three of the four companies had only one officer left, and were completely cut off.

No supporting arms could reach them, and for the next two days, they held grimly to their bare rocky hill-top against a series of heavy German attacks by tanks, guns and infantry which came not only from the Bou ahead, but also from their open right flank, and even from the rear.

It was close-quarter fighting, with the Guardsmen reduced at one point to throwing rocks at the Germans, having run out of grenades.

Lance Corporal Kenneally won a VC for 'extraordinary gallantry in attacking single-handed a massed body of the enemy and breaking up an attack on two occasions – an achievement that can seldom have been equalled.' In fact it was remarkably similar to the feat of Lance Corporal

O'Leary VC of the Irish Guards in 1915, and it is intriguing to wonder whether this was just a coincidence or whether one inspired the other.

The attack on the Bou itself was carried out as the next phase by 1st Bn Scots Guards and they reached the peak, Point 226. Captain Lord Lyell won a posthumous VC for his gallantry in leading his company, and attacking a German gun position single-handed.

Tragically communications were so bad that the troops on the objective could not get through on the wireless to report their success. But they could receive messages, and they were ordered to withdraw – an error, based on false information that they had failed to reach their objectives.

They obeyed the order and returned – only to be told a few hours later, when the truth was realised, that they must go back and repeat the operation.

But it was too late. The Germans had occupied the Bou in strength. One officer and one Guardsman only of the Scots Guards reached the summit the second time.

Then the weary and depleted battalion was attacked by tanks and was in danger of being cut off completely. They were therefore again ordered to withdraw to positions behind the Grenadiers.

For a further six days, 24th Guards Brigade held their exposed positions against constant attacks. By 1 May, the Irish Guards were reduced to a mere eighty men, and were relieved.

The remaining two battalions were still there, when on the 6th, the Duke of Wellington's Regiment came through and captured the Bou.

It had been a gruelling battle, but it had contributed greatly to the breakout which now took place.

The Divisional Commander wrote that 'while it is impossible to differentiate between the battalions . . . the story of the Irish Guards on Hill 212 will always stand in red letters on the pages of that glorious Regiment's history'.

A great white cross stands today on Hill 212 to commemorate that story.

The end in North Africa (May 1943)

While the Battle of the Bou was being fought, General Alexander had assembled his striking force for the final drive through to Tunis. On 3 May he secretly transferred from the Eighth to the First Army front, one armoured division and one infantry division, together with 201st Guards Brigade, who were now put into 6th Armoured Division alongside 1st Guards Brigade. All three Guards Brigades were thus 'in at the kill'.

On 6 May, two infantry and two armoured divisions[108] swept forward on a narrow front from Medjez-el-Bab, and the next day both Tunis and Bizerta were captured. 6th Armoured Division was then loosed to clear the Bon Peninsula, and 1st Guards Brigade, together with an armoured regiment, cleared the key town of Hammam Lif, east of Tunis, after a brisk action.

It was the end, and General Alexander was able to signal to Winston Churchill: 'Sir, it is my duty to report that the Tunisian campaign is over. All enemy resistance has ceased. We are masters of the North Africa shores.'

It was complete victory indeed. Only 638 out of the 340,000 Axis troops in Tunisia escaped. An enemy had been eliminated.

There were many reunions among the nine Guards battalions now in Tunisia, and at Nabeul on 14 May, 212 officers dined together, after a display by the massed pipes of the Scots and Irish Guards.

On 19 May, there was a Victory March in Tunis, and later, visits by Churchill and the King. Then for the next four months, the three brigades were able to enjoy a welcome period of relaxation and reorganisation before starting their next campaign – Italy.

Chapter 15

Italy
(1943–45)

First Foot-
holds in
Europe
(1943)

The campaign in Italy, fought largely by the troops who had achieved victory in North Africa, was a thankless, relentless struggle with no flanks to be turned except from the sea, and so no choice but to attack one natural defensive position after another, under conditions which strongly favoured the enemy. It led to some of the hardest and most unpleasant fighting of the war, with few spectacular results, only a steady slog, ridge by ridge, river by river, up the length of Italy. (See Map 10, p. 208.)

The first Guards unit involved was 3rd Bn Coldstream Guards, who were sent to garrison the newly occupied island of Pantelleria on 23 June 1943, prior to the invasion of Sicily on 10 July.

Meanwhile one company of 2nd Bn Coldstream Guards were sent off with a naval task force to obtain the surrender of the island of Lampedusa, eighty miles away. The company was just ninety-five strong, and the Italian garrison totalled 4,600, but, following a naval and air bombardment, white flags appeared.

Major Bill Harris, the Company Commander, landed first, accompanied only by Drill Sergeant Knight, and boldly demanded the surrender of the garrison. After some anxious moments and much animated argument, the official document was signed by the Governor, an Italian Admiral, using the butt of the Drill Sergeant's rifle to write on.

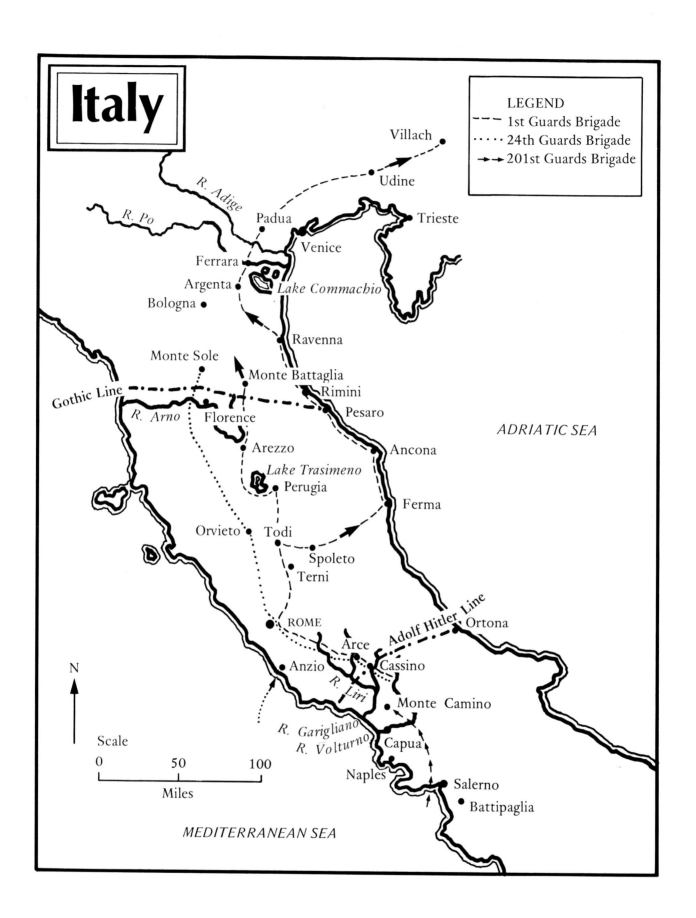

Italy

LEGEND
- – – – 1st Guards Brigade
- · · · · 24th Guards Brigade
- →—→ 201st Guards Brigade

R. Adige

R. Po

Villach

Udine

Padua

Trieste

Venice

Ferrara

Argenta

Bologna

Lake Commachio

Ravenna

Monte Sole

Monte Battaglia

Gothic Line

Rimini

Pesaro

R. Arno

Florence

ADRIATIC SEA

Arezzo

Ancona

Lake Trasimeno

Perugia

Ferma

Orvieto

Todi

Spoleto

Terni

ROME

Arce

Adolf Hitler Line

Ortona

Anzio

Cassino

R. Liri

Monte Camino

N

Scale

R. Garigliano

R. Volturno

Capua

0   50   100

Miles

Naples

Salerno

Battipaglia

MEDITERRANEAN SEA

The following month 201st Guards Brigade, having converted reluctantly from being motorised, joined 56th Division as infantry, and landed with them on the beaches of Salerno on 9 September.

The Eighth Army under General Montgomery had already landed on the foot of Italy on 3 September, but the main assault was to be the landing of six divisions of the Allied Fifth Army under the American General Mark Clark at Salerno.

It was not an ideal site, as the coastal strip was nowhere more than five miles wide, and it was overlooked by mountains. But it was within reach of Allied fighter cover from Sicily, and it offered ten miles of very suitable beaches. Also it was hoped that the surrender by Italy, which was planned to coincide with the landing, would disorganise the Germans to such an extent that the Fifth Army would be able to land and seize Naples swiftly with little or no opposition.

As the invasion fleet sailed past the isle of Capri into Salerno Bay on the evening of 8 September, the ship's loudspeakers announced the Italian surrender. Hopes of an unopposed landing rose. But the Germans reacted swiftly, and when the leading troops landed at 0400 hours on the 9th, they were soon in action.

201st Guards Brigade was in Divisional reserve, and landed amid heavy fighting – the first Guards units to set foot on the mainland of Europe since Dunkirk.

The battle was not going well, and early next morning, they were called on, together with the other two brigades, to capture the original divisional objectives, which were still in enemy hands. The features involved (the Tobacco factory, the Monte Corvino airfield and the village of Battipaglia) were vital to the security of the bridgehead and were to be the scene of bitter fighting.

Both 6th Bn Grenadier Guards and 2nd Bn Scots Guards were held up short of their objectives by strong German infantry and tank defences, but even then the brigade found itself well ahead of the rest of the division, and in a dangerous salient, overlooked by the Germans in the hills. For forty-eight hours, they held on under increasing pressure. Any hopes of a quick break-out to Naples had vanished, and it was now more a question of survival, for elsewhere on the bridgehead, the Germans were within a mile of the beaches.

On 12 September therefore the line was shortened; it was just in time, for Field Marshal Kesselring, commanding the German forces in Italy, now counter-attacked, and on the 12th he drove the Americans to within 1,000 yards of the beaches.

The next day was the critical moment for the Salerno landing, and 201st Guards Brigade came under heavy pressure but held their positions. Both the Royal Navy and the Allied air forces produced impressive support for the troops ashore, and by the 14th, the crisis was past. But it had been another 'close-run thing'.

On 17 September, the Eighth Army, including 24th Guards Brigade, joined up with the bridgehead, and the two Armies turned north.

Salerno (9–17 September 1943)

Monte Camino (5–14 November 1943)

The Allies now came up against the main German 'Winter Line'. Barring any further advance on the west, stood a massive 3,000-foot mountain called Monte Camino, and the task of capturing it was allotted to 201st Guards Brigade.

Monte Camino was reported to be 'lightly held', but those who remembered the Horseshoe wondered (see page 203). At 0200 hours on 7 November, 6th Bn Grenadier Guards climbed slowly up the rugged mountainside widely known as 'Barearse Ridge' (though carefully pronounced 'Bare Archie' by the BBC). At dawn they reached their objective, Point 819, which was taken with the bayonet.

But the real battle was just beginning, for 1,000 yards ahead was another feature, Monastery Hill; this was not only strongly held, but it also dominated both Point 819 and the approaches to it.

So for the next four days, the Grenadiers, together with F Company, 2nd Bn Scots Guards, who had joined them on 7 November, hung on under continuous machine gun, mortar and artillery fire and increasing attacks. They were cut off and faced appalling weather conditions; there was no hot food, and the men had only their emergency rations, together with those taken from the dead. The wounded could not always be evacuated at once, and the cold was so intense that some died of exposure.

When it did become possible to recover casualties, the journey took five hours, with eight men to each stretcher. Rain and hail soaked everyone, and many developed frostbite. The final blow was a small earthquake on the third day.

By the fourth day, ammunition was running low and the enemy launched six or seven attacks. The order to withdraw was given, but it required an attack by two companies of Scots Guards and another battalion to clear a passage for the Grenadiers to return.

The Coldstream and Scots Guards took over for the next three days, and on the 14th, the mountain was evacuated completely. It was finally captured, 3–10 December as a result of a corps attack, which included 201st Guards Brigade.

Monte Camino epitomised the grimness of winter warfare among the mountains of Italy, and the hardship involved. It was slow, dour fighting that tested a man's courage and endurance to the limit.

An interesting postscript to the battle came when some Moroccan Goums, training at Monte Camino some months later, found the bodies of several Guardsmen still on the peak. Being mountain troops, they appreciated what the Guardsmen had achieved and they carved a plaque on the rock of Point 819 which read:

AUX COMBATTANTS BRITANNIQUES
TOMBÉS GLORIEUSEMENT AU MONTE CAMINO
NOVEMBRE DECEMBRE 1943
LES GOUMS MAROCAINS

December 1943 saw some significant changes in the Allied high command in Italy. General Eisenhower left to become Supreme Commander of the forces for the invasion of North West Europe, and was replaced by General Sir Henry Wilson. At the same time, General Leese succeeded General Montgomery as Commander of the Eighth Army.

Anzio (22 January– 5 April 1944)

By the end of 1943, a new impetus needed to be given to the Allied advance up Italy, and it was decided to carry out an assault landing at Anzio. This would not only by-pass the formidable German defences, cutting off the German forces there, but also offered the chance of a bold advance to seize Rome, with all that such a success meant.

The date of Anzio was set for 22 January so that the landing craft could return to the UK after it in time for the Normandy landings in June.

The plan was to land two divisions in the first wave, and 24th Guards Brigade, consisting of 5th Bn Grenadier Guards, 1st Bn Irish and 1st Bn Scots Guards, landed on the left with 1st Division on the morning of 22 January 1944.

Complete surprise was achieved, and a bridgehead eighteen miles long and nine deep was established. Amazingly there was virtually no opposition for thirty-six hours, but the invasion force did not push forward as expected.

Anzio is considered by many to be one of history's great 'missed opportunities'. A bold thrust out of the bridgehead when the landing was unopposed might have achieved far-reaching successes, for there were virtually no Germans between the Allies and Rome. But with memories of anxious moments at Salerno, the American Commander, General Lucas, decided that he must secure his base before risking any advance.

So seventy-two precious hours were spent in consolidating the bridgehead, and when General Lucas finally felt ready, it was too late. The Germans had by now cordoned off the invasion area with eight divisions and more were on the way.

In the seven weeks of fighting that ensued, the three battalions of 24th Guards Brigade, who had taken part in the initial landing, were to lose 80 per cent of their strength, while 1st Bn Irish Guards were to cease to exist as a fighting force.

The Guards Brigade sector was centred on the only road from Anzio to Rome, which was naturally of importance to both sides. Along it were several points which were to be the scenes of some of the fiercest fighting in the bridgehead. They were from north to south, Campolene, Dung Farm, Carroceto, the Factory, the Embankment, the Gully, and the Flyover – names remembered well by those who survived.

On 25 January, the Irish and Scots Guards were beaten back in an attempt to reach Campolene, but they held on in a narrow salient round Dung Farm. Here they were surrounded and badly mauled by a massive attack on 3 February.

Battalion Headquarters of the Irish Guards was overrun and everyone captured, but, as they were being marched off, they turned on their guards and attacked them with whatever weapons they could lay their hands on –

a rifle, a spade, and even a petrol tin. Twenty Germans were killed and nine taken prisoner.

Early on 8 February came another fierce German attack down the road. The forward troops of both the Grenadiers and Scots Guards were overrun and a company of the Irish Guards was also lost. Major W. P. Sidney[109] of the Grenadiers won a VC for holding off the Germans single-handed at the only crossing over the Gully, and so preventing a serious break-through.

The next night there was yet another attack on 24th Guards Brigade, and they suffered so severely that they were withdrawn into reserve in the area of the Flyover. They had suffered grievous losses, but had inflicted far heavier ones on the enemy, and the bridgehead was still intact, though contracting daily, as the Germans launched one attack after another.

On 16 February came the biggest attack yet, mounted by four divisions supported by 450 guns. It was clearly aimed at driving the Allies back into the sea, but they just held on, and finally it was the Germans who withdrew.

24th Guards Brigade were in reserve at this stage, but the Irish Guards had one final grim spell in the line on 21–25 February, which reduced one of their companies to seventeen men. The brigade had by now suffered so heavily that it was withdrawn in March, and sent to Naples to reorganise.

The battalions in 201st Guards Brigade had meanwhile also had severe losses in hard and prolonged fighting along the Garigliano, and in April, the two brigades were amalgamated.

Three battalions (6th Bn Grenadier Guards, 2nd Bn Scots Guards and 1st Bn Irish Guards) returned home with 201st Guards Brigade, leaving in Italy a re-constituted 24th Guards Brigade. With them now was 1st Guards Brigade[110] who had landed at Naples on 5 February, and been sent to hold the line of the Garigliano River until April, when they moved into the rubble of the town of Cassino, which was still held by the enemy.

It was a sinister, unnerving existence, fighting amid the silence and the stench of a ruined ghost town. The enemy were often within 100 yards, with snipers watching always for victims. By day all was still, but with darkness, the ruins came to life. Battalion porters hurried along the 'Mad Mile', accurately registered by enemy artillery mortars and machine guns, to bring rations, mail and ammunition; these were then distributed, patrols sent out and defences improved.

The three battalion headquarters were all underground, two in the crypt of a ruined church and one in the town gaol. The enemy intercepted every wireless message, and to disguise their identity, the Welsh Guards made free use of their native tongue – whereupon their positions were showered with German propaganda leaflets – written in Urdu. But the lighter moments were rare, and it was overall an unpleasant life, which had few compensations.

On 12 April 1944, the Household Division presence in Italy was strengthened by the arrival of 1st Household Cavalry Regiment, who had spent the last fifteen months watching the Turkish frontier with Syria.

Now they operated as an armoured car regiment, much of the time with the Polish Corps under General Anders, who later awarded the Regiment

the exceptional honour of wearing his corps badge of the Mermaid of Warsaw, in recognition of their services with the Polish forces.

On 11 May the great Allied offensive in the Liri Valley opened with the thunder of 700 guns. Cassino itself was not attacked this time, but was by-passed on both sides. The plan succeeded, and on 18 May the Germans with-drew from the Monastery, which had defied the Allies for four and a half months, despite three massive assaults against it. Five days later, as the Canadians broke through the Winter Line, the British and American troops broke out of the Anzio bridgehead.

The Advance up Italy (May–September 1944)

Now the way was open at last for a major advance, and for this phase covering May–September, both Guards Brigades acted as lorried infantry in two different armoured divisions in Eighth Army. In this role, they were to follow roughly parallel routes up central Italy, operating under separate corps, but rarely more than thirty miles apart.

On 19 May, 1st Guards Brigade rejoined 6th (British) Armoured Division with whom they had fought in North Africa, and with whom they now battled their way up the eastern axis that took them through Perugia and Arezzo.

24th Guards Brigade joined 6th (South African) Armoured Division, a most successful and happy association in which they advanced from Rome to Florence, or as one officer put it 'from Orvieto vineyards to the Chianti country'.

On 4 June 1944, Rome fell, the first European capital liberated by the Allies. Two days later, came news of the Normandy landings, while in the East, the Russians were sweeping forward on a 300-mile front. The end seemed nearer, and spirits were high.

The advance up Italy continued, and on 20 June, 1st Guards Brigade reached Perugia, to be met with scenes that were to be repeated soon in France, Belgium and Holland;

> They stopped to stare for a few seconds and then rushed towards us, cheering and flinging out their arms . . . [wrote an officer] a great crowd welled into the street . . . thousands of laughing faces . . . I have never seen such looks of wonder and genuine happiness . . . and we sent back by wireless, a little self-consciously, the message that Perugia ·was indeed liberated.

But these were occasional moments of exhilaration in a grim campaign that was still a hard, punishing slogging match. Progress was slow, for the Germans fought all the way, retreating slowly, shelling, mining, holding and counter-attacking. There were few large-scale battles, but constant encounters at battalion, company and platoon level by day and by night. And inevitably, there was a constant drain of casualties.

It was a great test of leadership, particularly for officers and NCOs, and it was a test too for discipline, not so much from above as from within.

Men needed the strength to be found in regimental pride, self-discipline and courage, if they were to survive the constant strain and to keep going through a series of thankless, unspectacular battles.

An action which took place on 27–29 May was perhaps typical of the gruelling fighting that faced the troops in Italy throughout most of the campaign. It occurred when 1st Guards Brigade's advance was held up by German paratroops established in positions on Monte Grande and Monte Piccolo, just south of Arce, which was on the axis of advance. (See page 130.)

Both features were captured on the night of the 27th, but Monte Grande was lost next day to strong counter-attacks. 2nd Bn Coldstream Guards, with S Company of the Scots Guards who were attached to them, held on however to Monte Piccolo. Captain Neilson, commanding S Company, was wounded early in the battle, but carried on all day till he collapsed; he was later awarded a DSO for his leadership.

By mid-afternoon, S Company had lost all its officers, so Company Sergeant Major Brown took over and led a charge, which drove the enemy back. He then held the position until reinforcements arrived. He was awarded the Distinguished Conduct Medal.

It was hand-to-hand fighting, and at one moment, Lance Sergeant Jones seized the barrel of a Spandau machine gun being pointed at him, turned it on the German crew and killed them. Sergeant Bailey attacked and captured a pill-box from the enemy side, getting three bullet holes through his clothing in the process. That night the Germans withdrew to their next position.

Steadily the Allied advance pushed on up Italy. On 5 August 24th Guards Brigade reached the River Arno at Florence, but despite a series of attacks, it was not until 24 August that the Germans withdrew from the town.

While the battle went on for Florence, Field Marshal Alexander[111] had secretly concentrated a powerful force against the very eastern end of the Gothic Line, on the Adriatic coast. On 25 August he attacked and broke through the defences which the Germans had boasted no Allied soldiers would ever cross.

By early September the Fifth Army, which included both Guards Brigades, had closed up to the Gothic Line in Central Italy, where they prepared for what was expected to be some heavy fighting.

But to everyone's surprise, patrols found it abandoned. A wave of optimism swept over the troops at finding the most formidable defensive line in Italy given up without a shot. In North West Europe, Montgomery was sweeping across Belgium and Holland while the Russians closed in on Germany from the east. It seemed as if the end was in sight.

Winter (1944-5)

But in fact, there still lay ahead some of the hardest fighting yet, and one of the severest winters. It soon transpired that the Germans had only withdrawn to yet another defensive line, based on the chain of peaks that marked the Apennines. Here both Guards Brigades were to spend the next five months.

1st Guards Brigade pushed forward through the Gothic Line, and on 2 October they occupied Monte Battaglia, where they remained till 2 February, manning, in the words of the Welsh Guards Regimental History, 'what must surely be one of the most fantastic winter lines ever designed for the discomfort of the troops.'[112]

The defences were 2,600 feet up at the end of a narrow track which took six hours to climb. That autumn was the wettest in living memory, and men were permanently soaked as well as lashed by biting winds. The position was overlooked on three sides and under constant fire, the only protection being trenches which were usually full of water. Dead bodies and filth littered the area. Mules, Guardsmen, and Indian muleteers sank knee-deep in mud as they brought up supplies each night, and it took three and a half hours to get a casualty down the mountain, using relays of stretcher bearers. It was an improvement when the rain turned to snow and frost.

There were some compensations, though not many. Winter clothing had been issued, and the men were that much more comfortable than the year before. The enemy, after one unsuccessful attack on 11 October when an officer and seventy-five men were captured, made no serious attempts to recapture the peak (perhaps reckoning that the Guardsmen were welcome to it for the winter!). Above all, there were brief periods out of the line, when the comforts and hospitality of Florence could be enjoyed.

In November, the brigade also occupied Monte Verro which was given to the 3rd Bn Grenadier Guards and 2nd Bn Coldstream Guards (with S Company Scots Guards still under command) to look after. It was just about as unpleasant a winter station as Battaglia, and the troops withdrew thankfully in February 1945.

24th Guards Brigade spent their winter in the Sette Valley, having found that any attempt to push forward up Route 6620 towards Bologna was blocked by the feature Monte Sole, barring the way. Plans were made to capture it, but a series of postponements occurred, the last one mercifully cancelling an attack arranged, as at Longstop, for Christmas Day. Two days later, the operation was finally abandoned, to sighs of relief all round.

Reorganisation (February 1945)

In mid-February 1945, both Guards Brigades were pulled out of the line to Spoleto for a complete reorganisation which included the introduction of a Line battalion into each Guards Brigade.

24th Guards Brigade lost 5th Bn Grenadier Guards and 3rd Bn Coldstream Guards, who both returned to the UK; they were replaced by 2nd Bn Coldstream from 1st Guards Brigade and 1st Bn The Buffs. 1st Guards Brigade received 1st Bn The Welch Regiment in place of the Coldstream.[113]

The reorganisation meant two very sad partings. S Company, 1st Bn Scots Guards under Major Richard Coke DSO, MC, rejoined their own Regiment after ten months with 2nd Bn Coldstream Guards, whose respect they had won for their exceptional fighting record – proved by the fifteen decorations which they had gained in that period.[114]

The other separation was that 24th Guards Brigade now left 6th (South African) Armoured Division, with whom they had fought since Cassino. Links with the Springboks and the Rhodesians had grown very close, and it had become a happy and effective partnership indeed.

The Pretoria Regiment (an armoured unit) were perhaps particularly closely associated, and they still wear today a winged blue-red-blue flash of the Household Division behind their own cap badge. The origin of the wings is that on several occasions the South Africans had managed to get their tanks supporting the Guardsmen into such apparently inaccessible spots on mountainsides that it was remarked 'they must have flown there'.

PRETORIA REGIMENT 1944

With spring in the air, Field Marshal Alexander now prepared the final blow, aimed at destroying rather than just defeating the thirty German divisions still holding out south of the Po Valley.

It was a formidable task, even with the air superiority that the Allies enjoyed. Field Marshal Kesselring held a strong line in the mountains of central Italy, while in the plains to the east he could fight delaying actions based on a series of river lines stretching all the way to Austria.

But Field Marshal Alexander intended to prevent this by encircling the German armies where they stood, and so destroying them. The plan was for the Eighth Army to attack up the Adriatic Coast to Ferrara, while the Fifth Army debouched from the Apennines and struck at Bologna. If all went well, the main German forces south of the Po would thus be cut off with the rivers behind them.

The re-grouped 24th Guards Brigade had become an infantry brigade again, and had rejoined 56th Division, with whom they now forced the narrow, flooded Argenta Gap, west of Lake Commacchio, and so enabled the armoured forces to debouch into the plains beyond, led by 1st Guards Brigade as part of 6th Armoured Division.

After some initial opposition, they swept forward, and by-passing Ferrara, linked up on 22 April with the Fifth Army at Finale (an appropriate rendezvous). The encirclement was complete.

Two days later, 3rd Bn Grenadier Guards boldly crossed the quarter-mile-wide River Po by moonlight, taking the Germans by surprise before they could organise any proper defence. 3rd Bn Welsh Guards now took over the lead, and on 27 April reached the Adige.

Once across the river, it was simply a question of rounding up demoralised prisoners. Brigade Headquarters organised 'Exercise Ferreting', announcing that 'the battalion sending in the biggest bag . . . will be adjudged the most successful. Entries close 2400 hours, April the 29th.' The Grenadiers won by two points.

On 2 May the German Command in Italy surrendered, adding 230,000 prisoners of war to the thousands already rounded up. The Italian Campaign was over.

Three days later orders came for 24th Brigade to move to Venezia Giulia, near Trieste, where they came under the command of 91st US Division. There they were to stay for the next six months, reluctantly involved in national rivalries and ideological conflict, as Communism and democracy fought to win the area over to their own side of the Iron Curtain.

On 8 May, VE Day, 1st Guards Brigade crossed the Italian-Austrian frontier and moved to the Austrian village of Villach, which was to be their happy home for a while.

The End in Italy

Chapter 16

Guardsmen in Armour (1941–45)

The Guards Armoured Division

In May 1941 a historic decision was taken, equal in significance to the formation of the Guards Division in the Great War. It was decided to form a Guards Armoured Division.

This meant putting the Foot Guards, some of the finest, and certainly the largest infantry in the world, into tanks, with a role for which many thought they were neither mentally nor physically suited. Not surprisingly, the proposal aroused qualms and controversy in many quarters.

The Household Brigade themselves welcomed the idea, believing that armour rather than infantry was the predominant arm of the future, and that they should therefore meet the new challenge. Moreover, there was an urgent need at that time for more armoured divisions in Home Forces to meet the still-present threat of invasion, and the Guards were for several reasons particularly well placed to form a new one.

They had their own training organisation and were confident that the Guardsmen had the necessary qualities to learn their new role quickly. The various regiments were used to working in close co-operation, and it was also an advantage that the Guards Brigades then in existence were all independent brigades, and so could be reorganised without disrupting existing divisions.

So, on 19 June 1941 Divisional Headquarters was set up under Major General Sir Oliver Leese, (Coldstream Guards) and the division assembled on Salisbury Plain in September.

It consisted at this time of:
    2nd Household Cavalry Regiment (Reconnaissance Regiment)
    5th Guards Armoured Brigade
    6th Guards Armoured Brigade (who left the division in October 1942).

For his divisional sign, General Leese adopted a slightly modified version of the 'ever-open eye' used by the Guards Division in the First World War. The new version was designed by the artist, Rex Whistler,[115] then serving in the Welsh Guards, who painted a selection, ranging from a wink to a 'glad eye', on a dozen vehicles, from which the General and his staff made their final choice.

The division was given only six months in which to become operational, but it was achieved. General Leese, however, left in September 1942 to take over a corps in North Africa, and the new commander was Major General Allan Adair (Grenadier Guards).

There were inevitably several changes of organisation as well, but by the end of 1943, the organisation was settled[116] and the division had been welded into a closely-integrated family. The supporting units from other arms and corps were very much a part of the family, and this was to contribute immeasurably to the spirit and success of the division.

Now everyone wanted above all to have the chance to prove themselves, and it came in July 1944, when the division landed in Normandy and concentrated round Bayeux, eighteen miles west of Caen. (See Map 1.)

The Ever-Open Eye.

Normandy (July 1944)

The Division's first battle on 18–22 July 1944 was in many ways an unsatisfactory opening. Operation 'Goodwood' was an attack east of Caen, by three armoured divisions (7th, 11th and Guards) under VIII Corps, commanded by Lieutenant General Sir Richard O'Connor. The aim was to draw the German armour off the Americans onto the British sector, and so enable the Americans to break out on their front further west.

The attack went in at dawn on 18 July, behind a massive pulverising raid by over 2,000 planes. But although the Germans in the front line were demoralised, they had established a powerful screen of tanks and anti-tank guns behind the bombed area, and all three British armoured divisions were soon held up.

One tank lost was that of Lieutenant J. R. Gorman of 2nd Bn Irish Guards who suddenly found himself facing four heavy German tanks at a range of 200 yards. He directed his gunner onto the nearest, which happened to be a Royal Tiger, the heaviest of the German tanks, and the first of the species seen on the Western Front.

The following conversation then took place:
'Gunner: Fire!.'
'Gun's jammed, Sir.'
'Oh, Christmas! Why?' No answer.
'Driver: Ram.'

Lance Corporal Baron let in the clutch, and the Sherman careered forward straight at the Tiger, which it hit with a resounding crash, a split second before the Germans could open fire. Both tanks were immobilised, both crews hurriedly baled out, and being unarmed, both ran in opposite directions.

Undeterred, Lieutenant Gorman then found another tank, with a heavier gun, manned it and opened fire on the four enemy tanks, damaging two. He was awarded a Military Cross, the first won by the Guards Armoured Division, while Lance Corporal Baron received the Military Medal.

The battle may have seemed no great triumph to those taking part, but it had achieved its strategic aim, in that there were now seven German panzer divisions, plus four heavy tank battalions, facing the British, but only two panzer divisions opposite the Americans. It had also inflicted heavy losses on the Germans (including 100 tanks and 2,500 prisoners), which they could ill afford at this stage of the war.

The Bocage

The next phase of the campaign was a remarkable change, being a two and a half week period of fierce, close-quarter fighting in the 'bocage' of Normandy. In contrast to the open plains round Caen, this was much more like the English West Country, with narrow lanes, thick hedges between small grass fields, and above all, high banks capped with trees and bushes. The numerous small villages and farmhouses all made good strongpoints; in general, the country was in every way ideal for defence and highly unsuitable for an armoured advance. Again, the task was to pin down the German armoured forces with a view to enabling the Americans to make a breakthrough to the west.

The first into action were the 40 ton Churchill tanks of 6th Guards Tank Brigade.[117] The brigade had been formed in 1941 as part of the Guards Armoured Division, but had been detached in October 1942 to become a heavy tank brigade for close support of the infantry.

In July 1943 and in March 1944 the brigade had been close to being disbanded, in order to provide reinforcements for units in North Africa; each time, it was reprieved, thanks to the ultimate intervention of the Prime Minister. Now on 30 July 1944 came their first chance to prove themselves.

They were to support 227 (Highland) Brigade of 15th Scottish Division in an attack aimed at capturing some vital high ground, Hill 309, which was part of the Mont Pincon feature. It was a key position to the Germans, for it formed the hinge of their front in Normandy, and on its retention depended their orderly withdrawal eastwards.

The tanks of 4th Bn Coldstream and 3rd Bn Scots Guards moved off at 0800 hours with the two leading battalions of infantry; but very soon, heavy mortar and artillery fire prevented the infantry from keeping up with them.

Normal procedure now would be for the tanks to wait for the infantry to close up to them. But on this occasion the Churchills, including some equipped with flamethrowers, pushed on regardless, and by that afternoon both tank battalions had reached their objectives.

They were now far ahead of any infantry support, which meant that in such close country they were particularly vulnerable to enemy tanks, anti-tank guns and bazookas. Indeed S Squadron of the Scots Guards commanded by Major William Whitelaw[118] at one stage had eight of it's tanks knocked out by German Jagd Panthers in a few minutes.

Wireless messages describing the enemy armour made it sound like an escaped menagerie, with references to 'Tigers' and 'Panthers' to north, south east and west. 'We gave up counting the brutes,' commented one officer.

But the surviving tanks stayed alone on the vital high ground all night till the infantry came up early next day. They then remained to support them all that day as well, helping to beat off several counter-attacks, until, late in the afternoon, the enemy pulled out.

It had been a most satisfying success. The Guardsmen had proved themselves in their new role, and the Churchill tanks also justified every confidence placed in them. The Corps Commander wrote: 'No tank unit has ever been handled with greater dash and determination,' and so everyone was satisfied.

The Commander of Second Army, Lieutenant General Miles Dempsey wrote later:

The entry of 6th Guards Tank Brigade into the Battle of Normandy was dramatic; it was entrusted with an operation of the highest importance at a decisive moment. Few of its men had been in action before, and a lot depended upon their success. They achieved it completely. Never before has the value of training been so clearly exemplified. The victory of Caumont was their first and finest battle . . . by which they will be for ever remembered.

The next day, 31 July, it was the turn of 2nd Household Cavalry Regiment, who were acting as the Reconnaissance Regiment to VIII Corps. They achieved a fine coup by discovering an undefended and unmined track, which proved to be the boundary between two German divisions, each of which thought the other was responsible for it.

Boldly, they moved up it and captured a bridge over the River Soulevre, six miles behind the enemy lines. So far so good, but it then had to be held by only five men for two hours before other troops could take over. It was a vitally important capture, which may well have influenced the course of the whole 'bocage' battle.

The Guards Armoured Division had meanwhile moved 45 miles from Caen, and now started on two weeks of fierce fighting in the 'bocage', in which at one moment, both the Household Cavalry and the Divisional Engineers were used in an infantry role. 32nd Guards Brigade had some particularly grim fighting round Le Busq and the Le Perrier ridge, and 5th Bn Coldstream Guards, for example, lost three Commanding Officers wounded in two weeks.

The Irish Guards particularly mourned the death of Lieutenant Hugh Dormer. He had already won a DSO for his exploits when he was twice dropped by parachute into Occupied France, blew up important enemy installations and each time escaped back to England. An intensely religious individual, he wrote in his diary just before D Day: 'God grant me the courage not to let the Guardsmen down, knowing as I do how much they count on me.'[119] He was buried by the roadside, and the Guardsmen came with bunches of flowers for his grave.[120]

The Liberation of Brussels (3 September 1944)

On 27 August the Guards Armoured Division transferred from VIII to XXX Corps (Lieutenant General Brian Horrocks), in preparation for what was to be the most spectacular and exciting operation of its history, the liberation of Brussels. (See Map 2, page 28.)

A most welcome development was that 2nd Household Cavalry Regiment now returned to the division in their original role as the Reconnaissance Regiment. This meant that 2nd Bn Welsh Guards could revert to being an armoured battalion, and it thus became possible to form true Regimental Groups, each consisting of an infantry and an armoured battalion from the same Regiment.[121]

This organisation lasted for the rest of the campaign and proved a resounding success. It provided for the closest possible confidence and cooperation between infantry and armour within groups, and at the same time, provoked a salutary element of Regimental rivalry between groups.

On 31 August, the Household Cavalry again set the pace, by setting off at 0100 hours and seizing intact three bridges across the Somme which had the code names 'Faith', 'Hope', and 'Charity'. They then held them all night with the help of the local French Resistance, and the Corps Commander wrote of it as a 'most memorable night's work'.

Now the gallop began, and the next day the division crossed the Somme bridges and dashed thirty miles to liberate Arras. General Adair diplomatically directed the Welsh Guards Group there, and they received a great welcome from the inhabitants, who had not forgotten their defenders of June 1940. (See page 189.)

Douai was reached next day, and there General Adair was visited about noon by the Army Commander and the Corps Commander, and told of their grand plan – nothing less than the liberation of Antwerp by 11th Armoured Division and the liberation of Brussels by the Guards Armoured Division – both as soon as possible. Speed was to be of the essence, and airborne landings were planned to seize various key points on the axis of advance.

'I had a feeling of exhilaration,' recalls General Adair, 'that at last the division was to be given a real opportunity to show its paces. My only fear was that the start might be delayed by the airborne drop.'

At dusk on 2 September, a chilly, wet evening, General Adair gave out his orders in a farmhouse near Douai.

'My intention is to advance and liberate Brussels,' he declared, adding with a grin 'And that is a grand intention.' It was indeed.

222

The plan that followed is worthy of record. The advance was to be on two Centre Lines; the Left (5th Guards Armoured Brigade) was a twisty, secondary road and was for that reason expected to be less strongly defended. The Right (32nd Guards Brigade) was the better road, but likely therefore to be better defended. Either way, the distance was about 75 miles, and involved crossing the width of six maps.

Behind the division came two infantry brigades specially allotted for the occasion; they were the 1st Belgian Brigade (rushed up from Le Havre to join in the liberation of their capital) and 231 Infantry Brigade Group, commanded by Brigadier Sir Alexander Stanier (Welsh Guards), brought in to provide some infantry support.

H Hour depended on the airborne operation, and it was with great relief, therefore, that everyone heard at midnight that the drops were cancelled, which meant that the division could be away at dawn.

So at 0700 hours, 3 September, on a lovely sunny morning, the Household Cavalry crossed the Belgian frontier, followed an hour later by the Grenadier Group leading on the Left Centre Line and the Welsh Group on the Right.

Pockets of stubborn resistance were met from the start, but were usually brushed aside or by-passed. Pont-à-Marcq and Leuze were both more strongly defended, and this caused delays to both columns.

Prisoners were handed over to the care of the Maquis, the local Resistance forces, who also gave invaluable help clearing snipers, providing information, guarding bridges and repairing roads.

Inevitably the advance developed into a race between the two leading groups, and the General was persuaded to pick a winning post – a road junction just within the outskirts of Brussels.

At 1530 hours, the Welsh Guards were held up at Enghien, and the Grenadiers looked the likely winners. But then the Welsh Group requested and received permission to go at maximum speed. As they had Cromwell tanks, capable of 50 mph, while the Grenadier Group had Shermans which could only manage 25 mph, this gave them a sporting chance again, and the pace grew faster and faster.

At each village, wildly excited crowds cheered deliriously, waved, and threw fruit and drink to the tank crews and the infantry. It hardly seemed real after the grim fighting in the 'bocage'.

The Grenadiers were within ten miles of Brussels, when they were then held up again, whereupon the Welsh Guards put their feet down even further.

Then they too were delayed, at Hal, but pushed boldly on. Just after 2000 hours, it was the Welsh Guards who triumphantly passed the winning post.

The very first vehicle into Brussels was in fact an armoured car of A Squadron, 2nd Household Cavalry Regiment, but they were ordered to halt in the suburbs. The crew were Lance Corporal of Horse I. W. Dewar, and Trooper D. Ayles.

Dewar described the scene: 'The Belgians made one mighty rush at us and we were completely swamped. I tried to get a message over, but the aerials had already been whipped off as souvenirs . . . so had our bedding, all our rations, the cooker and everything else.'

223

The first vehicle to reach the centre of the town was a tank belonging to 2nd Bn Welsh Guards. It was commanded by Lieutenant J. A. W. Dent, and was driven by Guardsman E. J. James. The crew were Lance Corporal E. K. Rees and two brothers, Guardsmen Robert and Ralph Beresford.

It was an unbelievable climax to an unbelievable day, which was also appropriately the fifth anniversary of the declaration of war.

The wild exhilaration of the Belgians was deeply moving.

The crowds were five, ten, twenty deep; [wrote one officer] they cheered and waved and sang endlessly . . . it seemed there had never been so much happiness, nothing like this had ever happened before, or could ever happen again . . . and over all the revels and the singing, the dome of the Palais de Justice, a huge and solitary fire, burnt like a flambeau lighting up the night.[122]

The Welsh Guards in a typical scene on the liberation of Brussels.

One officer reported that he had acquired 'a plantation of flowers, ten boxes of cigars, countless plums, two bottles of champagne, and the name and address of nearly every girl in Brussels chalked on his vehicle.'

Allied prisoners emerged from hiding, German snipers were hunted down, and for the rest of the night, utter joy and utter confusion reigned in Brussels as four years of fear and bitterness were ended.

Units found it difficult to reach their allotted areas, but finally, the four groups were located round Brussels, with Advance Divisional Headquarters encamped in the gardens of the Royal Palace of Laeken. Queen Elizabeth of the Belgians had been among the first to greet them, and she now brought the men tea and food.

One of the Divisional command vehicles caught fire, and all the maps for the next day's advance were burnt, which did not help. The Belgian crowds

(*Above*) The Mannekin Pis. This famous statue in Brussels includes in his wardrobe a uniform of the Welsh Guards, which he wears every year on 3 September to commemorate the liberation of the capital in 1944.

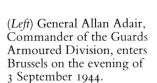

(*Left*) General Allan Adair, Commander of the Guards Armoured Division, enters Brussels on the evening of 3 September 1944.

however were thrilled by 'the great bonfire lit to celebrate the liberation'.

It was not in fact the 'record-breaking' armoured advance[123] that the Press made it, but it was a tremendous satisfaction to the whole division to have been able to prove themselves so dramatically after three years of training followed by the frustrations of Normandy.

The euphoria was short-lived. While Brussels was being ceremonially handed back next day to the Burgomeister and the Belgian Brigade, the Guardsmen became involved in costly fighting across the canals and dykes of Holland, and through villages such as Beeringen and Hechtel, where the Germans now fought stubbornly.

A highlight was the discovery by a troop of the Household Cavalry of a vital bridge across the Escaut Canal, and its capture by a squadron/company

Holland (4–15 September)

225

group of the Irish Guards under Major D. A. Peel, a success which was reckoned to have made it possible to bring forward the advance by several days.

The bridge promptly became known, even at Army level, as 'Joe's Bridge'; in honour not only of Colonel Joe Vandeleur commanding the Irish Group, but also of Captain Joe Hutton of 615 Field Squadron, who removed the demolition charges. The latter had, in fact, 'mislaid' his troop of sappers, but he detailed the four nearest Guardsmen to help him, and they then actually joined him in cutting the wires to the explosives under the bridge.

The Corps Commander, Lieutenant General Horrocks, came up to congratulate the troops involved personally, and at the same time, he asked the Household Cavalry whether they could find out the depth of the German defences beyond the Canal – no easy task, when they were in direct contact with the enemy and could not get round any flank.

Lieutenant Buchanan-Jardine, to whom the task was allotted, decided that the only hope lay in boldness. With two scout cars he crossed the bridge under fire in broad daylight on 11 September and drove eight miles into enemy territory as far as Valkenswaard, where he found the road blocked by a tank. Fortunately he was able to hide his vehicle unseen, and dismount.

After questioning some Dutch civilians, he then returned by the same route, this time at 60 mph. Everything on the outside of the scout cars was punctured by bullets, but incredibly there were no casualties.

For what was described as 'the most daring reconnaissance that was carried out in the last war', he was awarded the Military Cross, while the Royal Netherlands Government gave him the Order of the Bronze Lion for being the first Allied soldier to set foot in Holland.

Arnhem (16 September–6 October 1944)

The Arnhem operation which now follows was a grim reminder that the war was not yet over and that it did not consist of triumphs only.

The Guards Armoured Division were given the task in Operation 'Market Garden' of leading the advance along the 'airborne carpet', laid as part of Field Marshal Montgomery's bold plan to drive deep into the heart of Germany. The operation depended on the swift capture of three major river obstacles as well as many minor bridges; three airborne divisions were to be dropped to do this, and then to hold open a narrow corridor from the Dutch border to Arnhem. (See Map 11.)

101 (US) Airborne Division	Eindhoven, Canal bridges to Grave.
82 (US) Airborne Division	Grave bridge over the Maas. Nijmegen bridge over the Waal. High wooded ground south of Nijmegen.
1st (British) Airborne Division	Arnhem bridge over the Lower Rhine.

It was a gamble, of course, but it was thought to have a good chance of success in the light of the disorganised state of the enemy at that time.

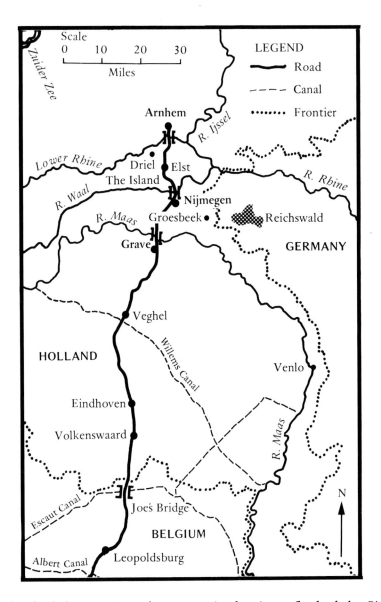

The plan had three major advantages, in that it outflanked the Siegfried Line, it might achieve complete surprise, and the battlefield was within flying range of the UK. The stakes were high, for success could possibly mean that the war might be ended by Christmas.

The hazards included the many obstacles to be crossed without delay; the weather threat to the airborne operations; the administrative problem, and finally, of course, the enemy reaction. In the event, each of these four factors went wrong to some degree, and the accumulative effect prevented final success being achieved.

One officer described it as being 'like threading seven needles with one piece of cotton and we have only to miss one to be in trouble'.[124]

To mention just one of the administrative problems involved, plans had to be made for the situation where the enemy might demolish one or more of the vital bridges along the axis. This possibility alone meant including in the column no less than 9,000 Sappers, with 5,000 vehicles of bridging equipment.

The distance to Arnhem was sixty-four miles, and although the ground forces involved consisted of the equivalent of four divisions, with over

20,000 vehicles, the advance throughout had to be virtually on a one-tank front down one road. This single axis was also exceptionally vulnerable, for to the west of it were a quarter of a million Germans, cut off in Northern Holland, and their only escape route back to Germany lay across that road. 43rd and 50th Infantry Divisions therefore followed up behind the Guards Armoured Division, in order to hold the centre line and to provide badly-needed infantry support.

At noon on Sunday 17 September, the massive airborne assault went in, and at 1435 hours the tank of Lieutenant Keith Heathcote, 2nd Bn Irish Guards, crossed Joe's Bridge and led off down 'the main road to Germany'.

Steadily the tanks rumbled forward behind the barrage, and within minutes were across the Dutch border.

'Advance going well,' reported the Squadron Commander. Then the German anti-tanks guns opened up.

Five minutes later, the Micks had lost nine tanks, and the road was blocked by burning vehicles of all types. A fierce exchange of fire developed, strengthened by the brilliant close support of rocket-firing Typhoons.[125] One by one, the enemy guns were silenced. More tanks pushed on down the road. Before long, the enemy defences were broken and the advance continued.

Eindhoven was reached on the 18th, and the 250-yard long bridge at Grave was crossed early on the 19th. The leading troops were much helped by putting telephone calls through to towns ahead of them and obtaining instant information from Dutch civilians about the defences and movements of the Germans.

By noon that day the Grenadiers, now in the lead, had the pleasure of linking up just south of Nijmegen, with General 'Boy' Browning, also a Grenadier, who was in overall control of the airborne operations as Commander 1st Airborne Corps. But they were behind schedule because of unexpected enemy resistance,[126] and now they learned that the vital Nijmegen bridge had not been captured as planned.

This massive bridge, nearly half a mile long and 100 feet high, was intact, but still held by the Germans. A railway bridge just under a mile to the west was also in enemy hands and equally inaccessible. An attack by a small joint Anglo-American force was hurriedly mounted against both bridges at 1600 hours, in the hope of rushing them, but it was beaten back.

It was vital to get across the river without delay, if Arnhem was to be reached on time. No further British troops could be expected in Nijmegen for at least twenty-four hours, and 32nd Guards Brigade was committed to the defence of the right flank at Groesbeck. All depended on the American paratroopers and the Guardsmen who were already in Nijmegen.

On 20 September, the Grenadier Group, supported by 2nd Bn 505th US Airborne Regiment,[127] fought their way, street by street, through the town, finally clearing the Valkhof, a strongpoint covering the road bridge, by mid-afternoon.

Meanwhile, it had been decided that the 3rd Bn of 504th US Airborne Regiment, commanded by twenty-seven year old Major Julian Cook, should attempt an assault crossing of the 400-yard wide river. They had never carried out a river crossing before, let alone in the flimsy canvas and plywood assault boats which were the only craft available. The opposite bank of the river was strongly held, and the only support available was from the tanks.

At 1500 hours, the first wave of 260 men launched the twenty-eight assault boats about a mile west of the railway bridge. The only form of propulsion was by means of wooden paddles, helped out with rifle butts, and progress was agonisingly slow against the three knot current. The river was lashed by heavy fire, and a smoke screen proved ineffective.

Only thirteen boats returned for a second load, but somehow the sappers of 615 Field Squadron, Royal Engineers made five crossings in all, and a small bridgehead was established on the opposite bank by the American paratroops.

'I have never seen a more gallant operation,' commented General Browning as he watched.

But still no tanks or vehicles were across, and time was getting short. The road bridge was still held and might be blown at any moment.

It was decided to gamble all on trying to rush some tanks across the bridge. An attempt in daylight failed, but just as it became dusk a troop from 2nd Bn Grenadier Guards tried again.

The two leading tanks, commanded by Sergeant Pacey and Sergeant Robinson, raced onto the bridge and, with guns blazing, were lost to sight in the gloom.

Every available German weapon was trained on the totally exposed stretch of road across the bridge. There were even snipers tied onto the girders, and one of them was shot with a pistol by the wireless operator of the leading tank.

Amazingly, the first two tanks got across. Broadside they skidded through a road-block the other end, and roared on into the darkness beyond.

The next two tanks were close behind. Both were hit, but one managed to drive on regardless and all three finally joined up with some of the Americans who had crossed by assault boat.

Next across was Captain Lord Carrington,[128] Second in Command of the Squadron, and he found himself mistakenly attacked in the dark by some Americans. But having hurriedly identified himself, he too survived. It was now 1915 hours.

Behind him in a scout car came Lieutenant Jones of 14 Field Squadron, Royal Engineers, who coolly got out and set about disarming the huge demolition charges, amazingly still unfired.

According to Cornelius Ryan in his book *A Bridge Too Far*, the German commander, General Heinz Harmel, gave the order to blow the charges just as the Grenadier tanks were in the middle of the bridge. The engineer at his side pressed the detonating plunger twice, but nothing happened.

The reason is still a mystery, though there is evidence which indicates that a Dutch Resistance worker might have cut the wires.

The Irish Guards tanks now followed the Grenadiers, and a tiny, precarious bridgehead was formed and held during an anxious night.

The Nijmegen Bridge.

So the Nijmegen bridge was taken and it was, to quote the official Army Group report, 'a magnificent achievement brought about by the actions, so brilliantly co-ordinated and executed, of the Guards Armoured and the 82nd US Airborne Divisions.'

But a vital day had been lost, and the 1st British Airborne Division at Arnhem now urgently needed support, if they were to survive.

The problems in the way of a further advance were however immense. The lines of communication were stretched to the limit, and ammunition was short.

Those last eleven miles across the Island were along one road only, built on a high bare embankment, so that the tanks were silhouetted like targets on a fun fair gallery. Nor was there any chance to leave the road, for the surrounding fields were criss-crossed with deep dykes on both sides. Again, in *A Bridge Too Far*, Prince Bernhard of the Netherlands is quoted as saying, 'We knew tanks simply could not operate along those roads without infantry.'

Virtually no fire support was obtainable from either the artillery[129] or the RAF and, without it, an advance on a one-tank front had little hope, for the Germans, now fully alerted to the threat, were well dug in along the only approach, with a strong screen of tanks and anti-tank guns supported by infantry.

230

The advance was continued nevertheless next morning, with the Irish Guards once more in the lead.

For the first few miles, all was deceptively quiet, then just short of Elst, the four leading tanks were knocked out within minutes by anti-tank guns. The road to Arnhem, now only six miles away, was completely impassable until the guns could be destroyed.

Overhead, some Typhoons circled, waiting for targets to be passed to them. But the one and only wireless link between them and the ground forces had suddenly gone dead.[130]

The few available infantry deployed, but in the open country with little fire support they too were held up. The Welsh Guards' tanks tried another axis, but they could not break through either.

The Corps Commander now accepted that an armoured advance was not feasible, and he ordered 43rd Infantry Division to pass through. But even their infantry could not get beyond Elst, despite a gallant parachute drop by the Poles round Driel.

At first light on the 22nd, two troops of the Household Cavalry managed, under cover of early morning fog, to infiltrate through the German lines and reach the Poles at Driel, with whom they then fought for the rest of the day. They also provided the first direct radio link between the 1st British Airborne Division and XXX Corps.

An attempt by 43rd Division to follow in their tracks that day failed, and so no help had yet reached Arnhem. Now the weather turned worse and prevented supplies and reinforcements for 1st Airborne Division being flown in.

On 22 September, and again on the 24th, the only axis of the Guards Armoured Division was cut twenty miles back near Veghel, and 32nd Brigade had to return and clear it.[131]

5th Guards Armoured Brigade continued fighting north of Nijmegen, in an attempt to break through to Arnhem, but without success. Finally, on the night of 25–6 September, the remnants of the British paratroops were withdrawn. It was a bitter moment for all concerned, and not least for the Guards Armoured Division, who felt it deeply that they had failed to reach Arnhem.

Whatever the verdict of the historians on the 'ifs' and 'buts', it was a tragic ending to the successes and high hopes of the weeks before.

The Final Phase (January to May 1945)

The German offensive in the Ardennes over Christmas 1944 was Hitler's last desperate gamble in the West, and when it failed, the final phase in the crushing of the Third Reich gathered momentum. (See Map 1.)

First, the Germans were driven back across the Rhine in the grim winter fighting in the Reichswald and round Kleve, in which both the Guards Armoured Division and 6th Guards Tank Brigade took part, the latter being the first British tanks to cross the Siegfried Line.

Then on 23 March 1945 British troops crossed the Rhine in strength, and Field Marshal Montgomery ordered an armoured thrust deep into Germany.

Surprisingly, it was 6th Guards Tank Brigade in their 'lumbering' Churchill tanks, who made a most spectacular advance, achieving an impressive, unexpected and very welcome 'gallop' from the Rhine to the Weser, a distance of 140 miles.

On 27 March, the brigade set off, together with 513 US Parachute Regiment. Steady but slow progress was made that day, and as darkness fell, Brigadier Greenacre made the decision to continue the advance by night, with the American paratroopers riding on the tanks. It was an unprecedented technique, risky and bold, but it was to pay off handsomely with impressive distances being covered.

At one stage, Lieutenant Stannard of the Coldstream Guards found a German Panther tank trying to overtake him in the dark. He waved it past and then 'brewed it up' with a neat 'going away shot'.

On 2 April, Munster was captured. The Brigade Group, long accustomed to 'waddling along at 15 mph' had advanced fifty miles in six days, defeating every attempt to stop them. They had taken 2,000 prisoners and opened the road to Hanover and Berlin.

It had also been a most heartening instance of Anglo-American co-operation. The Guardsmen at all levels developed a very real admiration for the American paratroopers of 513 Regiment for their courage and dash, and above all, for their tremendous enthusiasm. It was summed up in their cry, whatever the trouble, 'Come on boys, let's go!'

Meanwhile 4th Bn Grenadier Guards, in partnership with the British 6th Airborne Division, were off on a similar armoured thrust that was to take them finally to the shores of the Baltic. In twelve days, they advanced no less than 240 miles, and on 5 April covered the 42 miles from Osnabruck to Minden in $5\frac{1}{2}$ hours – a record for Churchill tanks. On 7 April, they reached

Guardsmen with American Paratroopers. One of the many instances of close co-operation during the advance into Germany, 1944–5.

232

the outskirts of Bordenau, ten miles north west of Hanover, where they captured not only a vital bridge, but also an airfield complete with Luftwaffe brothel! They were the first troops to reach the Dortmund-Ems canal, and the Weser, and they could claim at one moment to be leading the whole British Army. By 22 April, they were on the banks of the Elbe.

The Guards Armoured Division by contrast had a frustrating finale to the campaign in north-west Europe. After crossing the Rhine on 30 March, they set off with Bremen and Hamburg as their objectives.

It proved to be grim, wearing fighting in the face of endless demolitions, snipers, and stubborn opposition at every village from fanatical paratroopers, supported by a varied assortment of last-ditch defenders of the Fatherland.

On 18 April occurred a coincidence so remarkable that it is worthy of record. Lieutenant John Swinton in 2nd Bn Scots Guards lost his left leg just below the knee, a wound exactly similar to that suffered by his father in the First World War, when serving in the same company of the same battalion, and also within a fortnight of Armistice Day. Swinton père arrived in England on Armistice Day 1918, and his son arrived on VE Day 1945. Both succeeded, despite their disability, in reaching the rank of Brigadier.

On 27 April, 1st Household Cavalry Regiment, having returned from Italy, joined the division as an additional reconnaissance regiment. Thus both the 1st and 2nd Regiments ended the war fighting very appropriately as part of the Guards Armoured Division.

By 5 May when the campaign ended, the division was on the Elbe just west of Hamburg, having advanced 200 miles from the Rhine since 23 March. Two days later, they had the satisfaction of accepting the surrender at Cuxhaven of their formidable foes from the Rhine onwards, the German 7th Parachute Division, who had asked to be allowed to surrender only to the Guards Armoured Division.

2nd Bn Scots Guards found themselves called upon to enforce the formal surrender of Heligoland; the Household Cavalry obtained the surrender of a German destroyer at Cuxhaven, while The Royals occupied Copenhagen.

Farewell to Armour

The tanks of the Guards Armoured Division and of the 6th Guards Armoured Brigade, had completed an advance of 700 miles from Bayeux to the Baltic. Their campaign had included triumphs and frustrations. It had proved beyond question the versatility of the Household Division, and confounded the cynics who said that Guardsmen would be useless in tanks.

But it was generally accepted that it must be as infantry that the Guards could contribute most in the future. So on 9 June 1945, on Rotenburg Airfield, the Guards Armoured Division formed up for the last time, to take part in their Farewell to Armour Parade.

It was an impressive sight, with two lines of tanks at right angles to the saluting base, stretching away for half a mile to a slight ridge. They were shining with battleship grey paint, 'acquired' from the German Navy, and in front of each tank, stood its crew of four.

Farewell To Armour.

'Peace has fair come on us with a vengeance,' remarked one paint-smeared Guardsman.

On either side of the saluting base were two infantry battalions of Foot Guards. In the centre, on the forward slope of the ridge were the armoured cars of the 1st and 2nd Household Cavalry Regiments, with the self-propelled guns of the Leicestershire Yeomanry and 21st Anti-Tank Regiment, who had supported the division so effectively. In front of them between the two lines of tanks were the massed bands of the Scots and Welsh Guards, flown out from England for the occasion.

The salute was to be taken by Field Marshal Montgomery, and he and other VIPs arrived in a total of 36 aircraft.

After a General Salute, there was an inspection from two half-tracks.[132] The bands moved to a flank, and the tank crews mounted.

'Start up,' came the order by Brigadier Norman Gwatkin, and there was the sudden roar of 250 engines.

The four columns of tanks advanced, and counter-marched across the parade ground. Each commander traversed his gun in salute to the Commander-in-Chief, and then turned slowly away towards the ridge.

As the last vehicle disappeared over the ridge, the bands took up 'Auld Lang Syne'. There was silence, and a pause, full of memories. It was four years almost to the day since the Guards Armoured Division had been formed, and much had happened since 1941.

Then over the ridge came the seven armoured battalions, now on foot, and marching like the Foot Guards they were.

When all the columns were formed up, the Divisional Commander gave the order, not heard since 1919:

'Guards Division, Attention.'

'God Save the King.'

Finally, Field Marshal Montgomery called everyone around him and spoke:

I want to say, here and now, that in the sphere of armoured warfare, you have set a standard that it will be difficult for those that come after to reach . . . . The Guards have shown that whatever they are asked to do, whatever they take on, they do well; they maintain always the highest standards and give a lead to all others . . .

Now . . . we need you in the infantry; we need your high standards, your great efficiency in all matters and your old traditions of duty and service . . . .

Then he paid a tribute to General Allan Adair, that was undoubtedly echoed by all present:

I do not know whether [you] realise how much [you] owe to General Allan Adair. From my position as Commander-in-Chief, I do, and can tell you why. . . . he never failed me and he never failed you . . . you owe to him more than you can ever repay, and I will go further; I could say that the Brigade of Guards was lucky to have ready such an officer to handle this armoured warfare for them, as few could have done it so well. In front of you all, I wish to congratulate him on having brought the matter to such a successful conclusion.

Chapter 17

Phoney Peace (1945–56)

The end of the war brought the usual rundown and reorganisation of the Armed Forces, and the Household Division was reduced within two years to its peacetime establishment of three regiments of Household Cavalry and ten battalions of Foot Guards.

The wartime soldiers returned to civilian life, but like their fathers twenty-five years before, many found 'Civvy Street' a disillusioning scene of strife and strikes. The industrial unrest in Britain was matched by political and military unrest worldwide, as Russia cynically changed from the role of a wartime ally to that of an implacable foe in the new 'cold war'.

For the next thirty years, the country was to be theoretically at peace, but was in fact to be involved in a series of counter-insurgency campaigns round the globe that would stretch the Army to the limit. Several factors contributed to the problem.

The first was the 'wind of change' that blew with increasing force throughout the whole of the British Empire. One after another, colonies and other territories jostled to achieve the magic status of 'Independence'. The speed with which they exchanged British guidance and protection for the challenges of self-government led inevitably to internal conflict, fanned and exploited all too often by interested external powers, particularly the Communist nations. The result was that the British Army was constantly called upon to intervene in a role that ranged from 'keeping the peace', as in Cyprus, to fighting a full-scale campaign, as in Malaya or Korea.

237

The second factor was the deliberate 'cold war' initiated by both Russia and China throughout the world, on a battlefield which ranged from East Berlin through Greece to Malaya and Borneo. The Communist technique was, and still is, to foster and support revolutionary movements against the Western Powers wherever they occur, thus fighting in effect 'by proxy' at little cost to themselves, but at considerable cost to the West in terms of money, manpower and effort.

As a result there has been virtually no time since 1945 when British troops have not been campaigning somewhere in the world, and the Guards for their part have been engaged in operations in some sixteen countries. (See page 251.)

It was a considerable challenge for the Household Division to adjust post-war to the three-fold task of active service worldwide, the specialised training required for NATO in Europe, and at the same time the equally specialised skills of ceremonial and other duties at home.

Home Service

The first post-war Trooping the Colour was held in 1947 in khaki. The following year it was to have been in tunics and bearskin caps, but most unhappily it was cancelled because of weather forecasts, which at 0800 hours predicted heavy rain later that morning. In fact by 1100 hours the sun was shining brightly, and many rude comments were being made, not only by disappointed ticket holders, but also by frustrated Guardsmen.

A contrasting responsibility for London District at this time was to provide troops to help run essential services during the strikes that occurred regularly in the docks, power stations, gas works, Smithfield and other places. Indeed, this aspect of public duties became so routine that the staff began work on 'Standing Orders for Strikes.'

A landmark for the Household Division occurred in December 1950 when King George VI directed that the Household Cavalry should come under the command of the Major General, Commanding the Brigade of Guards, and that they and the Foot Guards should together be known as the Household Brigade. The name was changed again in 1968 to 'The Household Division'. (See page 270.)

One act of post-war reconstruction that had to be undertaken was the rebuilding of the Guards Chapel in Wellington Barracks, which had been hit on Sunday 18 June 1944 by a V.1 flying bomb. The disaster occurred during the Morning Service, and 121 people were killed. The entire building was destroyed, except for the apse, which survived almost intact; incredibly, the altar cross remained in position and the altar candles remained burning.

The Chapel was rebuilt to a modern design, except for the original apse which was retained, and the new Guards Chapel was dedicated by the Archbishop of Canterbury in 1963.

Among the many gifts and contributions received was the very generous sum of £5,000 which was subscribed by all ranks of the 6th South African (Armoured) Division, with whom 24th Guards Brigade had fought during much of the Italian Campaign. (See page 216.) The gift was used to pay for the bronze doors in the main entrance to the chapel, and also for the renovation of the mosaics in the apse; the bars on the doors are embossed with the Household Division star, and the flash of the South African Division.

It is of interest today to look again at the Guards Chapel in the context of the plans for the new Wellington Barracks, due to be completed early in the 1980s.

As always after any war, peace brought a need to look anew at old ideas, and the Household Division was no exception. It became the policy now to expect the Guardsmen to think for themselves far more. They could, for example, get up when they thought necessary to be in time for parade, rather than at Reveille, and were expected to maintain their own equipment in

An artist's model of the new Wellington Barracks, due to be built by the 1980s. It retains the existing façade, and is designed to conform to the Guards Chapel built in the 1960s.

good order without constant kit inspections; 'spit and polish' was reduced, and stay-bright buttons were accepted.

Initiative and self-confidence were stressed as essential qualities for every soldier to a greater degree than ever before, for much more was required of the fighting soldier. A Guardsman in the 1950s had to be qualified in over fifty skills, ranging from night patrols to nuclear warfare, from river crossings to radar. It was a far cry from 1939, and it called for a truly professional approach. But that was exactly what was now being achieved, by officers, Non Commissioned Officers and men alike.

A further challenge and change for the Regular Army was the introduction in peacetime of National Service, which began on 1 January 1949 and continued until the last conscripts left at the end of 1962. Service was initially set at twelve months, then increased to eighteen months, and finally, in August 1950, extended to two years with the Colours.

It proved a mixed blessing for the Regular Army, for although it produced much-needed manpower, it threw a heavy strain onto the training organisation, which had to be expanded and adapted to meet the additional commitment.

The Household Division took its share of conscripts, and it was generally agreed that the National Service Guardsman, both officer and other rank, matched the Regular both on parade and on operations. It was a justification among other things of the Guards training system, which was expanded by allocating four Regular units to undertake the training of the additional intake. The Life Guards at Windsor trained all Household Cavalry personnel, and 1st Bn Scots Guards did the same for the Foot Guards. In addition, 3rd Bn Coldstream Guards ran a Junior Leaders Training Battalion for the whole Army in the UK, while 2nd Bn Grenadier Guards carried out the same role for the British troops in Germany.

By 1951, however, it was possible for these units to become operational again, as the whole training commitment was taken over by the Guards Training Battalion at Pirbright. It was a vital task, for the Army was faced with heavy operational commitments from 1945 onwards.

Palestine (1945–8)

The first post-war campaign involving the Household Division was in Palestine, and it developed as early as October 1945, only a month after the end of the war against Japan.

The Palestine problem had remained dormant during the Second World War, when both Arabs and Jews cooperated with the Allies against Germany. Jewish immigration into Palestine was restricted during the war to a total of 75,000 up to May 1944, and there was then to be no more, except with the consent of the Arabs which, of course, meant no more at all.

But now, in 1945, many thousands of homeless Jews sought desperately to flee from Europe, where they had been so cruelly persecuted in concentration camps for six years. Almost all headed for Palestine, the country which they regarded as their National Home, and which they believed, truly or not, had been promised to them under the Balfour Declaration of 1917.

Britain had originally been made responsible for Palestine by the League of Nations, and now she faced the insoluble problem of reconciling the conflicting demands of Arabs and Jews. The choice lay between allowing further immigration and so breaking faith with the Arabs, or curtailing immigration and incurring the bitter wrath of the Jews worldwide. The Government chose the latter, and the Palestine campaign began.

The Jews launched their offensive on 31 October 1945 with a devastating barrage of explosions. The railway line was cut in 153 places, three police launches were sunk, and railway yards and the Haifa oil refinery were damaged.

Ernest Bevin, Britain's Foreign Secretary, issued a White Paper on 13 November, which allowed immigration to continue at a rate of 1,500 per year, but this satisfied neither side.

The Jews had always possessed a well-organised insurgency organisation, supported by the entire Jewish population in Palestine, and now it showed its strength. The largest body was the Hagana, originally accepted as a type of Home Guard. But within this, they had formed a more aggressive, illegal force, called the Palmach, trained before the war by Captain Orde Wingate, founder of the Chindits in the Second World War.

In addition two more extremist groups emerged. The IZL (or Irgum Zwai Leumi) believed in violence, and carried out commando-type attacks against the British, while the Stern Gang were a small group specialising in individual murders.

The Jews were altogether one of the most efficient, dedicated and dangerous enemies that the British Army was to face post-war, and Palestine was an effective initiation to three decades of counter-insurgency campaigning.

The British troops stationed in Palestine to enforce the Mandate were 6th Airborne Division, which included 1st (Guards) Parachute Battalion,[133] and 1st Division, which included 1st Guards Brigade.[134] The latter were responsible for the northern sector of the country, and battalions were stationed around Haifa, with Brigade Headquarters in Nazareth. (See Map 1.) They were fully occupied from the start on internal security duties, which ranged from road checks and patrols to cordons and searches of villages and settlements, aimed at finding arms and terrorists.

Most searches produced little or nothing, and an example of the problems facing the troops was provided by one settlement, where the Coldstream Guards unearthed a large dump of arms, cleverly concealed in such places as under a bull's pen, under hospital floors, in a sewer, in a children's nursery, and under a children's playground—where the supports of the swing acted as ventilation shafts.

An equally difficult and distasteful task was the interception and rounding up of illegal immigrants. Crammed into small unseaworthy ships, they would try to slip ashore by night and disappear into welcoming kibbutzes before the Security Forces could round them up.

More often the ship would be intercepted at sea by the Royal Navy and brought into Haifa harbour. It then fell to the Security Forces to enforce the Government policy, which was that these hundreds of miserable, homeless men, women and children, now within sight of their Promised Land, must either be sent temporarily to detention camps in Cyprus, or perhaps even have to be returned whence they came. Such a task gave no pleasure to the troops, but it had to be done, and was done, with remarkable patience and restraint, even though it probably meant fierce retaliatory attacks by the terrorists in Palestine at the first opportunity.

Reprisals were a very real threat. In June 1946, for example, five Army officers were kidnapped as hostages against the death sentence imposed on a captured terrorist, and two were not released until the sentence was reduced to life imprisonment.

In July, the King David Hotel in Jerusalem was blown up, killing ninety-one, and in December, after a terrorist had been flogged, an officer and three NCOs were captured by the IZL, whipped and left naked and almost dead. No such outrages were carried out against Guardsmen.

In January 1947, 1st Guards Brigade moved to central Palestine, and on 1 March were given the formidable task of organising the cordon and search of Tel Aviv, an area of fifty square miles containing about 300,000 people.

'Operation Elephant' lasted for fifteen days (2–17 March) during which time, martial law was imposed. A curfew was enforced while eight units cordoned off the city, and searched it sector by sector, though with little success.

Reprisals were inevitable, and on 8 March 3rd Bn Coldstream Guards in Citrus House, a large concrete building on the outskirts of Tel Aviv, were attacked and one Guardsman killed. The Colours, hanging in the Officers Mess, came under fire (for the first time since the Crimea!) and had they not been hurriedly removed by the Adjutant the Regimental Colour would have been hit.

Three months later, a tunnel was found being dug under Citrus House from across the road, with a view to blowing up the whole building. What amused or angered the Coldstream, depending on the temperament of each individual, was that an Intelligence Report issued shortly before the incident (but not sent to them) stated: 'Among entertaining rumours is one that a tunnel is being dug under Citrus House.'

Strangely, the tunnel, which was apparently being dug by the IZL or the Stern Gang, was destroyed by the Hagana who, although no lovers of the British, disapproved of such bloodshed. It was a gesture which perhaps prevented another bloodbath like the one at the King David Hotel, and it was certainly appreciated by the Coldstream.

On 26 September 1947, Britain announced that she was giving up the Mandate and handing the whole problem over to the United Nations. The latter duly produced a plan to partition the country, and from that moment the role of the Security Forces changed. They now had to protect themselves against attacks by angry Arabs as well as by the Jews, while at the same time they had the duty of trying to keep the Arabs and Jews from cutting each others' throats.

The tension was heightened in January 1948 when the Arab Liberation Army, under Fawzi Kawukji, who had led the Arab rebellion in 1936, invaded Palestine to assert their rights. The last six months were decidedly hectic, and the Guards were heavily involved.

To take one typical example, fifty-five Irish Guardsmen, with a troop of armoured cars and a handful of Palestine Police, were responsible for maintaining law and order in the town of Safad in north Palestine. There they kept a precarious peace between three to four thousand armed Arab irregulars and, on the other side, some 600 Hagana.

Both organisations were poised to seize this key town the moment the British withdrew, and one Irish Guards officer was offered (but refused) a bribe of £2,000 to disclose to the Jews the exact date of withdrawal, which was for obvious reasons kept a close secret. When the crucial moment came, each Guardsman, who had up to then 'been looking deliberately unconcerned, jumped into his previously allocated place in a vehicle, and the town was cleared in under five minutes. The last they saw of Safad was a mad dash being made by the Arabs and the Jews towards the recently evacuated police station which dominated the town.'[135]

From 6 April 1948, 1st Guards Brigade,[136] with 40 Royal Marine Commando and several other units under command, was responsible for holding an enclave round the port of Haifa, to cover the evacuation which was not due to be completed till 30 July.

There was constant fighting between Arab and Jew, almost invariably won by the latter, who also applied such pressure on the Security Forces, that on 21 April the perimeter was narrowed, to make it easier to hold. Care was taken, however, to ensure that Pross's restaurant remained in British hands, for the satisfaction of British appetites.

The same sort of situation existed in Jerusalem and Southern Palestine and in each of these areas, The Life Guards and their armoured cars were closely involved.

Somehow open warfare was avoided, and on 14 May, the last day of the Mandate, the High Commissioner, Sir Alan Cunningham, left Government House in Jerusalem. Despite the Emergency, he was given the ceremonial honours due to him, and on his final drive from Jerusalem he was escorted by a troop of The Life Guards, while at the airfield the Guard of Honour was provided by the 1st (Guards) Parachute Battalion. When he reached Haifa, 1st Bn Grenadier Guards mounted another Guard of Honour, with the Pipes of the Irish Guards. He then went aboard HMS *Euryalus*, which remained in Haifa Harbour until the British Mandate expired at midnight.

But the job was not yet completed. The Life Guards had to escort some British troops as they withdrew south to Egypt, and en route they passed the Egyptian Army heading in the opposite direction on the first of their series of unsuccessful attempts to conquer Palestine.

1st Guards Brigade, meanwhile, had to hold the Haifa enclave for a further six weeks. The task was duly accomplished, and at 1238 hours, 30 June 1948, the Union Jack was lowered for the last time, signifying the end of thirty thankless years of British responsibility for Palestine.

Malaya (1948–51)

But the very month that the Emergency in Palestine ended, the next campaign began. This time it was in Malaya, where a State of Emergency was declared on 17 June 1948, as a result of growing evidence of a deliberate plot by the Chinese Communists to take over control of the country.

The existing forces in Malaya were not enough to cope with this new threat, and the Brigade of Guards were urgently, and somewhat unexpectedly, called upon to provide reinforcements. The message came through on 13 August, and 2nd Guards Brigade was formed immediately under the command of Brigadier M. D. Erskine (Scots Guards). (See Map 8.)

It consisted of 3rd Bn Grenadier Guards, who had returned only four months before from two and a half years in Palestine; with them were 2nd Bn Coldstream Guards and 2nd Bn Scots Guards. All three battalions had been carrying out State duties in London and Windsor, and so were very much organised for peace rather than war. They were also under strength, and had in their ranks many young soldiers as yet trained only for London duties. But by 5 September they were ready, and set sail for Singapore.

They were greeted on arrival by an American newspaper correspondent with the words: 'Well, Britain's pride of the palaces are just one more bunch of boys in the basha huts of Malaya . . .'.[137] But they were operational by the beginning of November, and took over a sector in Selangor and Pahang.

An equally uncomplimentary welcome came from a bandit newspaper which recorded the arrival of the Grenadiers in their operational area with the paragraph; '600 red-haired pigs have recently arrived at Sungei Bezi . . . they are not used to the heat and tropical storms and a great many have fallen sick of a tropical fever and have been seen daily being carried out for burial. This is owing to their non-acclimatisation and excessive drinking of whisky.'

Nevertheless, that battalion was within the year to kill or capture exactly 100 bandits and destroy fifty-four of their camps, while the Scots Guards inflicted a total of 135 casualties on the Communists – plus one aggressive tigress shot dead with a No. 5 rifle.

It was indeed quite an achievement, for the contrast between Birdcage Walk and the jungle warfare of Malaya could hardly have been greater. Operations in the jungle meant continuous patrols, usually of about ten men with two Iban trackers, and they lasted for anything up to a week. Each party had to be self-sufficient and the men carried loads of not less than 60 lbs. each, including five days rations. In good going, this might enable them to operate within a radius of twenty miles, but under bad conditions progress might be reduced to one mile a day.

This 'ulu bashing', as it was called, was a mental as well as a physical strain, acutely uncomfortable and usually unrewarding. It was estimated at one time that it took 1,800 man-hours spent on patrol for every contact made with a bandit—let alone a kill, which was the justification and eagerly sought reward for the considerable effort involved.

The development of air supply and the evacuation of casualties by helicopter improved the situation considerably, but until this materialised, any wounded had to be carried out by stretcher, an appallingly difficult task involving a change of bearers every four minutes, and agonizingly slow progress.

Jungle warfare called for a very high standard of training, particularly among the junior officers and NCOs, on whom the main burden of leadership fell. Furthermore, the turnover was extremely high because of National Service.

The Scots Guards reckoned that between fifteen and twenty per cent of their officers and men were National Servicemen who could at best be operational for only ten months out of their eighteen months service. There was no regular air-trooping in those days, and the sea voyage meant that two months were lost. Thirty officers went out with the battalion, yet by the end of the two and a quarter year tour eighty had passed through it and fifty-three of them had commanded platoons.

To cope with this problem, Battle Drills for jungle warfare were devised, which proved successful in training men up to standard in three weeks. A Scots Guards officer responsible for training wrote:

> It has sometimes been said that the system of the Brigade of Guards tends to strangle the initiative of young soldiers and junior leaders, and had this been in the slightest degree true, one could have expected to see every sign of it in the platoon and section warfare of Malaya. But it was never true, and never looked like being true, even from the start . . .[138]

Alongside the relentless jungle campaign, the Security Forces and others in Malaya were also engaged in another equally vital struggle—the battle to win the hearts and minds of the people. This significant phrase was coined by General Templer, who, as the High Commissioner in Malaya at this time initiated many imaginative moves as part of this concept, which has since become a commonplace of counter-insurgency operations throughout the world (See page 247.)

One such project was to round up and resettle the half million Chinese and Malay squatters, who were scattered round the edge of the jungle. Such a move not only enabled the Government to protect them from intimidation, but it also deprived the terrorists of a valuable source of food, money and information.

The scheme was eventually adopted throughout the country, but it was first conceived in 1950 by the Commanding Officer of 2nd Bn Coldstream Guards, Lieutenant Colonel R. G. V. Fitz-George-Balfour, who tried it out in his own area. By the end of 1951, some 400,000 squatters had been moved into 500 new 'Kampongs' or 'villages' round Malaya, two of which were named 'Kampong Lang Shui Ho Chuen' and 'Kampong Pui Fah Chuen', which being translated are 'Coldstream Village' and 'Balfour Village'. Coldstream Village was visited again in 1970, and found to be thriving still.

By August 1950, the Grenadier and Coldstream battalions had returned home, and were not replaced, whereupon 2nd Guards Brigade was re-designated 18th Infantry Brigade. The Scots Guards remained as part of it until April 1951 when they too returned home.

The Malayan campaign was a new experience for the Guardsmen, and words written by General Harding, the General Officer Commanding in Malaya, about the Scots Guards when they left the country, could be applied to all three Regiments who fought there (and perhaps to all Guardsmen everywhere): 'They have confounded the critics and proved again, if further proof were needed, that there is nothing Guardsmen cannot achieve when they put their minds and hearts to it.'

Egypt (1945–56)

The third trouble spot during this unsettled decade was Egypt, a land well-known to the Guards since 1882.

As soon as the war ended in 1945, the Egyptian leaders successfully demanded the withdrawal of all British troops. So, at dawn on 28 March 1947, The Life Guards drove out of Cairo's Kasr-el-Nil Barracks, which were then handed back with few regrets to the Egyptians, and the withdrawal had been completed.

Britain was still allowed however to keep 10,000 troops stationed in the Canal Zone to guard not only the waterway, but also the vast dumps of stores stockpiled in Egypt.

But on 8 October 1951, the Egyptian Government abrogated the 1936 Treaty under which this had been agreed, and, to the usual accompaniment of rioting mobs, began to demand complete independence.

Reinforcements were quickly flown in, including 1st Guards Brigade[139] from Tripoli, where they had been stationed since leaving Palestine in 1948. The move proved the value of the recently instituted practice of air-trooping, for the build-up was the swiftest yet achieved by the British Army in peacetime – 6,000 men, 170 tons of stores and 330 vehicles, all by air within ten days.

The violence grew steadily, encouraged by the local Press, with one newspaper offering a reward of £1,000 for the killing of the British military commander, Lt General Sir George Erskine, and £100 for the murder of any British officer.

January 1952 was a particularly lively month. One candidate for the £100 prize was killed as he rushed, pistol in hand, at the Guards Brigade commander, while 3rd Bn Coldstream Guards inflicted twenty seven casualties on a terrorist 'youth commando' for the loss of one sergeant killed.

An uneasy peace ensued for the next four years, with the Canal Zone being kept under firm military control. 32nd Guards Brigade[140] arrived from Cyprus in February 1952, and there were thus two Guards Brigades as well as 1st Guards Parachute Company[141] in the Canal Zone, which was to be the main overseas station for the Household Division for the next four years.

It was not an exciting life, for it was confined to very limited training and endless guards, particularly on the vast Tel-el-Kebir dump. The seventeen-mile perimeter had constantly to be protected against persistent and highly professional pilferers, whose techniques included carrying out their raids

'Hearts and Minds'.

virtually naked, with their bodies covered with grease, which made capture difficult.

It was not easy to keep up the interest and morale of the 70,000 troops in the Canal Zone, especially as so-called 'temporary' units (which included both Guards Brigades), were not allowed to have their families with them in Egypt.

In October 1954 Britain agreed to evacuate the Canal Zone completely by 1956, and 32nd Guards Brigade returned home, leaving 1st Guards

Brigade to cover the final withdrawal, as they had done in Palestine.

The last fighting troops to leave were 2nd Bn Grenadier Guards with D Squadron, The Life Guards, and their rearguard flew out on 26 March 1956. An administrative party remained, and at dawn on Wednesday, 13 June 1956, after seventy-four years of British occupation, the Union Jack was replaced by the green flag of Egypt, bearing the three stars disrespectfully known to British troops as 'Maleesh, Mafish and Baksheesh'.[142]

Suez (1956)

It looked like the end of service in Egypt for the British Army. But on 26 July 1956, just six weeks after the final handover of power, President Nasser arbitrarily took over the Suez Canal from the Anglo-French authorities and declared it to be nationalised. Britain and France reacted by mounting a military operation to restore the situation. This is no place to go into the details of this complex and controversial affair. This account simply shows how 'Suez' affected the Household Division – a tale mainly of preparation followed by frustration.

The Life Guards armoured car regiment at Windsor were ordered to mobilise, but never got beyond Southampton Water, though their vehicles were landed at Port Said – after the operation was over. 1st Guards Brigade mobilised as part of 3rd Division, but when the division sailed to Port Said, they were left behind, except for 3rd Bn Grenadier Guards who got as far as Malta.

The only Household Division troops finally involved were the Guards Parachute Company, and the Machine Gun Platoon of 3rd Bn Grenadier Guards in Malta, who were embarked on minesweepers as protection, while they operated off Port Said Harbour; later, they held part of the perimeter.

The fateful chain of events gathered momentum following the Israeli attack on Egypt on 29 October. The Allied air assault began on 1 November, but the ships carrying the main force from Malta did not arrive until the 5th – a four day time-lag that was to prove fatal.

On Guy Fawkes Day 1956, an airborne landing was made on Gamil Airport, Port Said, by 3rd Bn The Parachute Regiment, and within an hour it was in their hands.

The Guards Parachute Company had the special role of providing a small party to cooperate with the French paratroopers from 2nd Colonial Regiment, who were to capture two bridges over the causeway south of Port Said.

The party, nine strong, was led by Captain de Klee of the Scots Guards and dropped under fire at 0715 hours. One Guardsman was wounded and the remainder set off southwards along the causeway; they met no opposition, but had to halt after ten kilometres, because they had reached the bomb-line which was the limit of advance.

The next day the party were allowed to advance again, and reached a village a further fifteen kilometres down the causeway, where they dug in, having again reached the bomb-line.

The next few hours are best described in the words of Captain de Klee's unofficial report of events.

Our first visitors were two Egyptians on a motor bike from the south on their way to Port Said. They were dressed in white shirts and nondescript trousers and cried 'Civeelian, Civeelian' when stopped. But Lance Sergeant White noticed a bulge under one shirt. They each had a revolver, and their uniform shirts, caps and identity cards, which were replacing the stuffing inside the pillion seat, proved one to be an Egyptian commando, and the other an Air Force cadet. They offered us money, riches and their services for life if they were spared, but as it was, one became our cook, and the other our grave-digger for the following twenty-four hours.

From then on everyone coming through was searched. Next came a car. On being signalled to slow down, it stopped violently and went flat out in reverse, full toss into the Sweet Water Canal, and disappeared completely. A pause, bubbles, and eight heads appeared on the surface, screaming for mercy as they were pulled out. The bag this time included one soldier, and a member of the Secret Police, with a loaded revolver.

Little happened for the next hour or so, but then about forty people appeared. Three were soldiers, obviously deserters. The remainder were refugees, including one couple with their six-year-old daughter, with a gaping wound in her cheek.

We had used all our dressings, so I indicated to her father that I needed his shirt to bandage his daughter. He shook his head. I hardly had to look at the Guardsman near me. I nodded and in a matter of seconds I had sufficient blue cotton bandages to finish my job. The little family left us, the father in his singlet, the mother evidently grateful, and the child, mouth, hands and pockets stuffed with sweets.

Our final capture was an Egyptian complete with steel helmet, medal ribbons and brand new Russian rifle and bayonet, who somehow had escaped from Port Said.

At about 1630 hours, the main advance down the empty causeway got under way at last, and the Centurion tanks of 6th Royal Tank Regiment roared southwards past the Guardsmen, whose task was now over.

At midnight the cease-fire came into effect, the unopposed advance was halted, and the forty-two-hour campaign was over. Angry and frustrated Regulars and Reservists sorted themselves out, and life slowly reverted to normal.

So ended a decade of decidedly phoney peace, and this was to be followed by twenty years of assorted activities round the world, centred mainly on attempts to 'keep the peace', which others were actively and subversively trying to undermine.

The Guards Parachute Company.

Chapter 18

Keeping the Peace (1955–75)

hese two decades were troubled years indeed, and saw the Household Division involved in four further major counter-insurgency campaigns, in Cyprus (1955–64), Aden (1964–7), Borneo (1964–6) and, finally, Northern Ireland from 1969 onwards. This period also produced a series of smaller operational commitments in various parts of the world, and Guardsmen saw action in British Guiana, Kuwait, Kenya, Uganda, Tanzania, the Cameroons, Jordan, Oman, Mauritius, Zanzibar and Hong Kong.

It was a time of challenge, with the whole army stretched to the utmost in its efforts to 'keep the peace' in the far-flung territories for which Britain was still responsible.

In addition, there was the standing commitment of maintaining a highly trained force in Germany as Britain's contribution to NATO, a role involving the use of sophisticated equipment and an ability to wage nuclear warfare – both a far cry from the 'jungle-bashing' of Borneo.

National Servicemen helped to provide the manpower for a while, and their contribution was impressive and effective. But this was not to last much longer, for in 1957 came news of what was probably the most drastic reorganisation of the Army since the reforms of Cardwell, nearly a century before.

The changes submitted to Parliament on 5 April 1957 by the Conservative Minister of Defence, Mr Duncan Sandys, forecast the ending of National

Service by 1960, and a reduction in the strength of the Army from 373,000 to 180,000. The number of infantry battalions was to be cut from seventy-seven to sixty, and the armoured regiments from thirty to twenty-three.

The Household Division bore its share of the cuts. The Household Cavalry lost one squadron, while the Foot Guards lost two battalions out of ten. 3rd Bn Coldstream Guards were placed in 'suspended animation'[143] on 1 September 1959, and 3rd Bn Grenadier Guards met the same fate on 31 March 1961.

Other changes followed. In 1960, the Guards Depot left its renowned site at Caterham and joined the Guards Training Battalion at Pirbright. The same year, the Self Loading Rifle (SLR) was carried for the first time on the Queen's Birthday Parade, and the order 'Slope Arms' was replaced by 'Shoulder Arms'.

The next year, the Household Cavalry at Windsor were given the impressive title of 'Airportable and Training Regiment, Household Cavalry', with the role of being an armoured car regiment that could move by air at short notice to any trouble spot.

In 1965, G Squadron of the Special Air Service was also created, consisting of officers and men of the Household Division. They have served since in Europe, the Middle East and the Far East, carrying on the traditions established by David Stirling in 1942–5.

Meanwhile, the Guards as a whole were to see plenty of action during this period, starting in Cyprus.

Cyprus (1955–64)

The campaign in Cyprus began on 1 April 1955, with a barrage of explosions which caused some £60,000 of damage, and effectively highlighted the problems facing Britain in this island.

Cyprus had been in British hands since 1878, before which it had been ruled by Turkey for 300 years. It had never belonged to Greece, but eighty per cent of the population were Greek-Cypriots, speaking Greek and belonging to the Greek Church. This Greek majority of the population, led by Archbishop Makarios, demanded *Enosis*, or the Union of Cyprus with Greece. The active part played by the Church was not so unorthodox as it might seem, for the Cypriots had long looked to their Church for temporal as well as spiritual guidance.

The British Government could not agree to *Enosis*, and the Turkish minority were naturally totally opposed to the idea.

So the Greek-Cypriots set out to achieve their aims by violence, and began a campaign of terrorism against the British, the Turkish-Cypriots, and also any Greek-Cypriots who did not, in their view, support *Enosis* with sufficient enthusiasm. The military operations were led by Colonel Grivas at the head of the National Organisation of Cypriot Combatants, better known as EOKA, which also had the full political backing of Greece.

The fighting was the usual grim story of terrorist warfare with mines, bombs and booby traps, kidnappings, propaganda and intimidation. On

top of this, the troops had to contend with the frustrations of using 'minimum force' against a ruthless enemy to whom no holds were barred. There was also the impossibility of telling friend from foe, and the tedium of endless patrolling, guarding, watching, ambushing and searching, which so seldom produced tangible results.

Both The Life Guards and The Blues served during the Emergency in their armoured cars, and they also had the special responsibility of protecting the Governor, Field Marshal Sir John Harding, an association which was cemented when he became Colonel of The Life Guards in 1957.

The Guards Parachute Company also served in Cyprus, disappearing in 1956 to Suez, and two years later to Jordan, when trouble threatened there.

The Suez operation in November 1956 inevitably took priority over events in Cyprus, and there was a lull in the struggle against EOKA. But in June 1958, 1st Guards Brigade was among reinforcements flown to Cyprus to deal, not only with EOKA, but also with trouble expected elsewhere in the Middle East. The brigade was commanded by Brigadier R. G. V. Fitz-George-Balfour (Coldstream Guards) and consisted of 2nd Bn Grenadier Guards, 1st Bn Irish Guards (with one company of Welsh Guards under command) and 1st Bn Royal Scots Fusiliers.

The campaign in Cyprus ended in March 1959, when the island was granted independence (but not Enosis), and Archbishop Makarios became the first President.

But it was not the last that the Guards were to see of Cyprus. In 1964 The Life Guards and the Guards Parachute Company were sent there again, this time to keep the Greeks and Turks apart, a situation aptly summed up in a cartoon, first published in 1958 of a puzzled British soldier remarking, 'Who are we fighting today, Sarge?'

At first they were there as British troops, but when the United Nations took over on 27 March 1964, the Guardsmen came under their command and donned the pale blue beret, thus becoming the first Household troops to serve the United Nations.

Just ten years later, in July 1974, 2nd Bn Coldstream Guards were to find themselves helping the United Nations forces to keep the peace between Greek and Turkish Cypriots, following the invasion of the island by Turkey. Ironically, on this occasion President Makarios sought refuge in their area when he fled in disguise from Nicosia, and when he finally left the island by helicopter, they provided him with a Guard of Honour as appropriate to a Head of State.

(*Opposite*) Standards and Colours of the Household Division. (*Top left*) The Sovereign's Standard of The Life Guards; (*right*) A Squadron (or Union) Standard of The Blues and Royals; (*middle left*) The Queen's Colour of 1st Bn Irish Guards; (*right*) the Regimental Colour of 1st Bn Irish Guards; (*below left*) The Household Division Flag. It is in the Household Division colours of blue, red, blue (see page 138) and bears the badge 'Septem Juncta in Uno' (Seven Joined in One). This flag flies over the Horse Guards building, and other Household Division establishments; (*right*) Company Colour of the Prince of Wales Company of 1st Bn Welsh Guards. This shape is unique to the Welsh Guards, other Regiments having rectangular Company Colours. (These illustrations are reproduced by kind permission of Major N. P. Dawnay, from his book *Standards, Guidons and Colours of the Household Division, 1660–1973*.)

The ten years 1958–67 saw trouble spots developing all round the world, and the Guards found themselves campaigning in a remarkable variety of countries, some of which had never before been visited by the British Army, let alone by Household troops.

The first occasion was a classic 'small war' operation, in which 'D' Squadron of The Life Guards supported the Special Air Service against some

Here, There and Everywhere (1958–67)

255

Cyprus Patrol. The Household Cavalry make use of local transport during the Emergency in Cyprus.

rebellious Beni Ryami tribesmen in Oman in November 1958. (See Map 12.)

The battlefield was a bare, rocky plateau, 9,000 feet up the Jebel Akhdar, or Green Mountain, a sheer peak approachable only by narrow, twisting tracks, which were all too easily defended. The task of dislodging the dissidents had been allotted to the SAS on the grounds that it would need their special toughness and fitness. But The Life Guards took the Browning machine guns off their Ferret scout cars (every one of which had at some stage of the campaign been blown up on mines) loaded them onto donkeys, and set off with the SAS for the mountain top.

It was a nine and a half hour climb by night, but the peak was reached – even though the donkeys had to be pulled most of the way, and on occasions even be carried by the Troopers! The rebels were dispersed, and one more operation had been completed.

An example of the variety of places and problems facing the British Army in the 1960s is provided by the travels of 2nd Bn Coldstream Guards, who found themselves in 1961 with half the battalion in Kenya and half in Bahrain, 2,000 miles away in the Persian Gulf. When the Kuwait crisis developed, the Bahrain Detachment were the first troops flown in – being beaten only by 42 Royal Marine Commando and a squadron of 3rd Dragoon Guards who landed by sea.

That incident over, they moved to Zanzibar and established another precedent by being the first British troops ever stationed there.

Meanwhile, on the opposite side of Africa, 1st Bn Grenadier Guards did a tour in the Cameroons, while that country went through the travails of gaining independence.

In October 1962 1st Bn Coldstream Guards were sent to maintain law and order in British Guiana (now Guyana). All was quiet until the summer of 1963, when there was serious rioting following a General Strike. A lighter touch occurred when rioters occupied a building near the Guards

(*Overleaf*) The Cameroons. A Grenadier Guards patrol during internal security operations in 1961.

'Minimum force' in Cyprus as illustrated by Giles.

"*Throw one more and I'm going to ask my sergeant to ask my captain to write to Duncan Sandys to ask him to ask U Thant if I can throw one back*"

257

camp. Smoke shells were fired to evict them, and the smoke drifted into the Officers Mess, waking an officer who was enjoying a siesta after lunch. Choking, he rang for a drink, whereupon a Mess waiter (who knew his taste), appeared, carrying a glass of champagne on a silver salver – but wearing his respirator.

No sooner had the troubles in British Guiana subsided than a multiple crisis brewed up in East Africa in the shape of a series of mutinies among the troops of the newly independent countries of Kenya, Uganda and Tanzania – not to mention a 'palace revolt' in Zanzibar.

Swift action by a handful of British troops settled each of the mutinies, the Scots Guards being involved in Uganda. Zanzibar was left to sort itself out, and so 'peace' was restored all round – for the moment.

Aden (1964–7)

In 1964 British troops were withdrawn from East Africa to Aden where the next rebellion was already building up. (See Map 12.)

For 125 years, there had been no real threat to this strategic outpost of the British Empire, but various Arab countries had been watching with interest the success of the Egyptians in pushing the British first out of Cairo, and then out of the Canal Zone. The fiasco of Suez in 1956 encouraged others to try their luck at tweaking the lion's tail, and the Yemen set the pace by stirring

12 Arabia

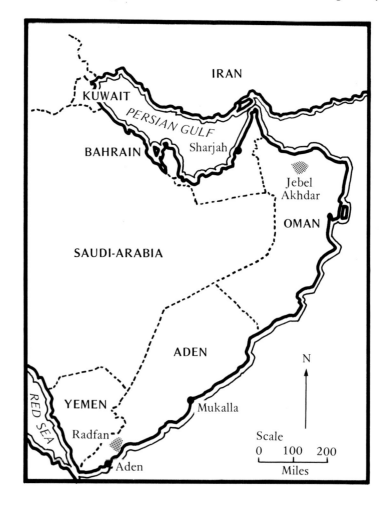

up revolt against the British in Aden from 1962 onwards.

With covert encouragement from Egypt and Russia, insurgency and terrorism were soon under way, culminating in a grenade attack against the High Commissioner, Sir Kennedy Trevaskis, on 10 December 1963. He escaped, but fifty-five others were killed or wounded, and a State of Emergency was declared the same day.

So began four years of bitter fighting both up in the mountains of Radfan and in the streets and alleys of Aden town, a ruthless insurgency campaign that was to end with Britain evacuating Aden completely in November 1967.

The campaign began with the Radfan operation, which lasted from January to June 1964. British troops succeeded in checking, but not subduing the rebels of the mountainous interior of the Aden Protectorate, and a complete brigade was still required to retain some form of control over the area for the next three years.

Operations up-country were basically guerilla warfare in steep, rugged mountains, where small groups pitted their wits against each other in patrols, ambushes and picquets. It was a war of sudden encounters, and there were many incidents and quite a few casualties. But it was active service and was welcomed as such by the battalions who were now regularly fighting there.

2nd Bn Coldstream Guards received an unexpected change of scenery when they were ordered in May 1965 to send a company for two months to Mauritius, where a State of Emergency had been declared, following riots between the locals and the Indians, who formed seventy per cent of the total population of 700,000.

But the trouble soon died down, and the company enjoyed two months of rest and relaxation. As their stay extended over June, a Queen's Birthday Parade was mounted with 'the Mauritian Navy, the Fire Brigade, two ancient saluting guns, Old Comrades of many kinds and hues; Boy Scouts, Girl Guides and Nurses on parade.'[144] A far cry from the Horse Guards, but none the less sincere.

Back in Aden the insurgency grew in intensity both up-country and in the towns, and the Guards increased the number of their units in Aden to three.

1st Bn Irish Guards arrived in October 1966 and were thrown in at the deep end indeed. Before they had even completed the customary week's acclimatisation they were embarked aboard HMS *Fearless* for an 'exercise'.

But once at sea, they learned that it was in fact 'the real thing', and the next day, they landed by helicopter and assault boat at a remote coastal village in Eastern Aden, where they successfully rounded up a budding 'liberation army'.

The constant round of guards, patrols, stand-by platoons, searches and road blocks meant that every man was required to share the heavy duties. The Pipes and Drums for instance, were usually made into a normal infantry platoon, while the Coldstream drummers were on one occasion turned into muleteers, hauling mules and donkeys laden with supplies to the peak of a mountain called 'Cap Badge'.

The last year of this increasingly grim campaign saw only the Irish Guards

still in Aden, and in June 1967, when they were enjoying a rare day's holiday
in honour of the Queen's Birthday, it was rudely interrupted by a message
ordering them to send a company at the shortest notice to Mukalla, where
the Residency was reported to be besieged by rebels. They got there, but
found the trouble had died down; they then returned to be greeted by

Radfan. An operation in the Radfan mountains of
Aden. Two forms of transport – ancient and modern.

another message, this time from the Commanding Officer, congratulating them on their 'smart turnout for the Queen's Birthday Parade 1967'.

The Battalion ended their tour by acting as dockers to help clear the stores, before returning in August 1967, three months before the final evacuation of Aden on 29 November 1967.

Borneo

Meanwhile, in the Far East, the Household Division were involved in operations 'East of Suez' almost continuously from 1964 onwards.

During 1963, Communist forces based in Indonesia began insurgency operations against the neighbouring British colony of North Borneo, and counter-action had to be taken. It involved guarding a wild and mountainous 970-mile long frontier against constant incursions by Communist insurgents from Indonesia. It also meant that a country slightly larger than England and Scotland had to be kept free of Communist domination.

The first Guardsmen on the scene were the Guards Independent Parachute Company who were committed to surveillance of the frontier.

They were followed by 1st Bn Scots Guards who were based in Malaysia, and from there carried out two four-month tours in Borneo,[145] They were made responsible for the State of Sabah, which they controlled in much the same style as in the Malayan campaign, fifteen years before.

The multi-national aspect was very much in evidence, for the Scots Guards were the only British unit in the 5th Malaysian Infantry Brigade Group. Most of their patrolling work was with the Tawau Assault Group, which contained soldiers and sailors from no less than four different nations and seven different services.[146]

The operations were typical counter-insurgency campaigning. Incessant patrolling and surveillance in the forest and mangrove swamps was carried

A Scots Guards patrol in Borneo.

out by foot, boat or helicopter, from a tented base deep in the jungle. Supplies were provided either by parachute or by helicopter – the normal vehicle for all transport. As in Aden, the battalion had its own Air Platoon of two Sioux light helicopters, named 'Bella' and 'Bertha' after the two Scots Guards cows of World War One fame. (See page 174.) They also ran their own airstrip and helicopter pad with the Pipe Major as Airport Manager, and the Master Tailor in charge of air supply back at base.

The Life Guards arrived in June 1966 as an armoured reconnaissance regiment, and when the campaign ended in September 1967, the Household Division had contributed creditably to what was described in Parliament as 'one of the most efficient uses of military force in the history of the world'.[147]

The conclusion of the Aden campaign in 1967 marked the end of an era, for it was virtually the last of the long list of 'imperial policing' tasks which the British Army had carried out with remarkable efficiency for a hundred years or more.

For the first time now in twenty-two years, British troops were not involved in active peace-keeping operations anywhere in the world. An unaccustomed lull ensued, and for once the Army was not over-committed. But the respite lasted a matter of months only. New troubles soon developed, even though they were 'only' riots and rebellions rather than prolonged insurgency campaigns.

In July 1968, racial riots flared up in Hong Kong, and among the troops called in were the Guards Parachute Company and a squadron of The Life Guards. This operation emphasised the remarkable dispersion that can be required of armoured car regiments, for The Life Guards at that time had another squadron in Singapore, 1,600 miles away, and a third in Seremban some 200 miles north of Singapore.

Trouble occurred at intervals too in the Middle East, among the Arab States along the Persian Gulf, and The Life Guards, the Foot Guards and also the Guards Parachute Company did tours in the burning sands of Sharjah, Bahrain and Oman.

Across the Atlantic, British Honduras became a Guards station, where, battalions contended with nationalism and racialism, riots and hurricanes from 1972 onwards.

On 26 March 1970, the last British units pulled out of Libya. It was a moment of some historic significance, for it was the first time since the Cape of Good Hope was garrisoned in 1806 that Britain possessed no permanent military base anywhere on the African continent. The 'wind of change' had blown fiercely and effectively indeed during the last twenty-five years.

The End of an Era

(*Overleaf*) Northern Ireland. The Life Guards, operating as infantry, are involved in a typical incident in Ulster.

Northern Ireland

The overseas commitments might now be far fewer, but further trouble was about to develop much nearer home, just across the Irish Sea.

During the immediate post-war period, Northern Ireland had been a comparatively peaceful and pleasant station. But it was in fact a quiescent volcano, which by 1969 was beginning to rumble ominously, as the Police found increasing difficulty in keeping the peace between the Catholic and Protestant communities. On 14 August 1969 Londonderry erupted, and troops of 24th Brigade were called in. The rioting spread next day to Belfast, and more troops became involved there. The 'trouble in Ireland' had begun yet again, as it had done at intervals for the last four centuries.

Reinforcements were hurried into the province, and a squadron of The Life Guards, together with 2nd Bn Grenadier Guards were among the first arrivals.

Since then, there have always been some Household Division units on operations in Ulster. Each Regiment (except the Irish Guards) has carried out several four-month tours of duty, and some have gone back four or five times. The Household Cavalry have operated both as infantry and in armoured cars.

The warfare there today is highly specialised, and also highly unpleasant. It is not unlike the terrorism of Aden, but with the added grimness that the 'enemy' who riot, snipe, mine and booby-trap are our own kith and kin. Also they are more professional, more dangerous, and even more vicious, than the unsophisticated Arabs of Crater and Sheikh Othman.

The principle of 'minimum force' in handling such terrorism places a tremendous burden of responsibility on every soldier, NCO and officer. Also, the campaign has to be fought in the full glare of publicity and propaganda, some of it hostile, biased and subversive.

A further unpleasantness is the problem of distinguishing between friend and foe. It was bad enough with Arabs and Jews in Palestine, Greeks and Turks in Cyprus, and assorted Arabs in Aden; but it is far worse when the war has to be fought in the British Isles.

It is no pleasure to return from patrol with one's combat jacket covered with spittle, placed there with taunts and curses by women and children who are citizens of the United Kingdom. It is not easy to refrain from any form of retaliation in the face of such provocation, day after day.

Such a situation calls for infinite restraint, determination and coolness, which in one word means 'Discipline'. This is a primary requirement, and it comes easily to Guardsmen.

Altogether, as at the end of 1975, units of the Household Division had carried out thirty-two tours of duty in Ulster, suffered losses of 20 killed and 87 wounded and earned ninety-five honours and awards.

(*Opposite above*) Jungle Warfare Training. No. 2 Troop of the Guards Parachute Company in Malaya.

(*Opposite below*) Winter Warfare Training. The Coldstream Guards in Norway – still in step!

Reorganisation

Despite the threat from Communist insurgency worldwide, 'defence cuts' seem to be an inevitable hazard of peacetime soldiering, and the moment the operational commitments ease, then the pressure for reductions grows.

When the Borneo and Aden campaigns were both nearing a conclusion in mid-1967, the Labour Government, which had already halved the Territorial Army, announced drastic cuts for the Regular Army, aimed at reducing the Defence Budget from seven per cent to five per cent of the Gross National Product.

The basis of the reorganisation was that the Infantry were to be regrouped into 'Divisions' each of which would consist of between three and eight Regiments under one Headquarters. It sounded reasonable, but it meant that three cavalry regiments and eight infantry battalions would have to disappear from the Army List altogether, or else amalgamate. Such a proposal cut straight across a Regimental system that had been the foundation and the strength of the British Army since 1661.

Strong emotions were aroused and bitter battles of words were waged, as Regiments fought for survival, and to preserve the identities and traditions for which men had proudly died in a hundred wars.

The Guards were called upon to lose one of the two Household Cavalry regiments and one Foot Guards battalion. The Life Guards had already been cut in 1922, and so this time the axe fell on The Blues. On 29 March 1969 they were amalgamated with The 1st Royal Dragoons, to form a new Regiment, 'The Blues and Royals' (Royal Horse Guards and 1st Dragoons).

The Foot Guards nominated 2nd Bn Scots Guards for sacrifice, which meant that they were reduced on 1 April 1971 to a strength of one company, stationed in Edinburgh. But then came a need for more infantry battalions for Northern Ireland, and on 19 January 1972, after just 200 days as a company, the battalion was officially re-formed and sent to Ulster.

The final change arising from the reorganisation was that the Brigade of Guards changed their title on 1 July 1968 to the Guards Division, and the Household Brigade became the Household Division.

So the titles change, but the character of the Guards lives on. The challenge remains of maintaining in the future the standards and traditions of the past. Fighting efficiency, courage, discipline and leadership are as vital as ever, with tasks that range from patrols in the Bogside and nuclear warfare training in NATO to peace-keeping in Cyprus or British Honduras.

At the same time, the Guards play a major part in most of the traditional occasions associated with the Monarchy, and the next chapter tells something of the ceremonial duties involved in this role.

Opposite above Trooping the Colour. The March Past at Buckingham Palace. The Queen takes the salute as the Foot Guards march past. The Household Cavalry are formed up in front of the Queen Victoria Memorial, and the Mall stretches away in the background.

Opposite below Trooping the Colour. The Escort to the Colour in the centre of the Parade are about to troop the Colour down the line of Guards. Behind the Escort are the Massed Bands. In the background in front of the Guards Memorial are the Household Cavalry with their Mounted Band.

Chapter 19

On Parade

'A soldier's life is terrible hard,' said Alice, as she and Christopher Robin watched the Changing of the Guard at Buckingham Palace.[148] Doubtless Alice's fiancé, who was on parade, had told her a story or two about the drill, discipline and 'spit and polish' involved in State duties in London and at Windsor.

He would have had some justification, for the life of a Guardsman in London is demanding. The standards required for the many ceremonial duties are not achieved without constant practice, including rehearsals which sometimes have to be carried out before dawn, so as not to disrupt London's traffic.

Drill parades are a regular feature, of course, especially in the spring, when all ranks, including the officers, undergo an exacting, intensive course in preparation for the ceremonial season ahead. For some Foot Guards officers, who may never have ridden before, but must now appear on parade mounted, it means also many uncomfortable hours in the riding school.

There are always barrack guards and fatigues and in addition, a variety of duties ranging from running the Royal Tournament to organising cadet camps or recruiting drives. Training, too, continues throughout the year, so that units are always operational, be it for service overseas or for internal security at home, as at Heathrow airport.

It is an exacting routine, particularly today when there are so many skills to be mastered and so many different types of warfare to prepare for, in

(*Opposite above*) 'God Preserve Queen Elizabeth'. The final moment of the Ceremony of the Keys at the Tower of London.

(*Opposite below*) The Garter Procession. The Queen and Prince Philip lead the Knights of the Most Noble Order of the Garter in procession from Windsor Castle to St. George's Chapel. The Household Cavalry traditionally line the route, dismounted.

273

addition to ensuring that the traditional standards of ceremonial duties are never allowed to lapse.

Alice's fiancé, being in the Foot Guards, whose privilege it is to guard the Queen at Buckingham Palace, might also have told Alice that this particular Royal Guard was the most important one in London. In fact he would not be quite right on that point, for the senior Royal Guard is actually the Queen's Life Guard, mounted by the Household Cavalry outside the Horse Guards building in Whitehall.

The Queen's Life Guard

The reasons for this precedence go back to the Stuart days, when the Sovereign's residence was in Whitehall Palace, which was guarded by the Household Cavalry.

When it was burnt down in 1698,[149] the Court moved to St James's Palace, and indeed it is still officially there. Royal Proclamations of the death and accession of the Monarch are announced from the balcony overlooking Friary Court, and Foreign Ambassadors are always accredited to the Court of St James's.

On the same basis, the Arch through the Horse Guards was, until 1841 when Trafalgar Square was completed, the only carriage entrance to the Royal Palace and Park of St James. It is still the official entrance to Buckingham Palace for State occasions, and the Household Cavalry have therefore continued to guard it for over 300 years, though other regiments and corps have on occasions taken over for short periods. Since 1973, it has been agreed that the Queen's Life Guard may be carried out by the King's Troop Royal Horse Artillery on occasions, to enable the Household Cavalry to train.

In addition to the well-known mounted sentries in Whitehall there are also two dismounted sentries. One is posted outside the Guard Room and the other is posted under Horse Guards Arch, with the special duty of preventing all but members of the Royal Family from *driving* through the Arch, unless they are in possession of an Ivory Pass.

This pass is granted only to a very limited list of people,[150] and there are many tales of disgruntled personages, who were doubtless Very Important People, but did not happen to qualify for this particular privilege. So, when they sought to drive through the Arch, they found their way barred politely but firmly by a Trooper with drawn sword, requiring to see their Ivory Pass.

When the Sovereign is in London, the Queen's Life Guard consists of one officer and fifteen other ranks, and a Standard is carried. This is called a Long Guard, and it is changed to a Short Guard of two NCOs, and ten Troopers with no Standard, when the Queen is not in residence.

The ceremony of Changing the Guard at Buckingham Palace must be one of the best-known sights in the world, watched as it is by some six million people every year. The duty of providing this guard is the prerogative of the Foot Guards, though other regiments and corps are increasingly invited to take over at times, when the Guards battalions are heavily committed on operations or training.

By day the Queen's Guard is ceremonial, but after dark it is now essentially operational, with sentries patrolling in rubber-soled boots and using small pocket radios round the grounds of Buckingham Palace and St James's. Indeed, several intruders have been apprehended by the sentries and handed over to the civil police.

Although the Queen's Guard[151] mounts each day in the forecourt of Buckingham Palace, it is still based at St James's Palace, where the Officers' Mess remains and where the Colour is lodged.

Originally the Guard used to mount regularly on Horse Guards Parade, and march from there to St James's Palace, but this practice died out during the nineteenth century. Now that procedure is carried out only on a few days in May each year (when it is often mistaken for a rehearsal of Trooping the Colour).

A Colour is always carried by the Queen's Guard, and this is the duty of the junior officer, called the Ensign. The Colour is the Queen's Colour, if the Queen is in residence; otherwise, it is the Regimental Colour. (See page 296.)

Until 1959, the sentries at Buckingham Palace were posted by day on the pavement outside the railings in front of the Palace. But the behaviour of the sightseers in pestering them finally reached the stage where it detracted seriously from the dignity of the Guard. The wretched sentry could only suffer in silence, but one day it apparently became too much for a certain Coldstream Guardsman, who, according to a female tourist, kicked her on the ankle as he patrolled his beat.

She complained to the police, and although there was much sympathy for the sentry, discipline had to be maintained, for the rules had been broken. Amid much Press publicity, the sentry was punished by an award of ten days CB (Confinement to Barracks). But all ended happily, for he received not only many messages of sympathy, but also over £100 from various supporters of his misdeed.

Soon after, it was reluctantly decided that the only answer was to move the sentry posts inside the forecourt, where they are today.

Another Royal Guard in London, and one that is perhaps less well-known than the others, is at the Tower of London, which is a Royal Palace and Fortress. The Foot Guards provide a small Guard there of one officer and twenty-two other ranks mounting each day at 11.30 hours.

It is at the Tower that the traditional Ceremony of the Keys takes place

The Queen's Guard

Tower of London Guard

'On Sentry' as seen by Giles.

every night at 2150 hours. At that moment, four members of the Guard, including a Guardsman with a lantern, form up under the Bloody Tower, to escort the Chief Warder as he proceeds on his rounds in order to lock the gates leading into the Tower.

As the party return to the Bloody Tower, they are challenged by the sentry on duty, and the following historic exchange takes place.

Sentry 'Halt, who comes there?'
Chief Warder 'The Keys.'
Sentry 'Whose Keys?'
Chief Warder 'Queen Elizabeth's Keys.'[152]
Sentry 'Pass, Queen Elizabeth's Keys. All's Well.'

The Keys then continue to the inner court, where the complete Tower Guard has turned out. As the Chief Warder and his escort halt, the Guard present arms; the Chief Warder then declares 'God preserve Queen Elizabeth,' to which the Guard and the Escort reply 'Amen.'

Exactly as the clock strikes 2200 hours, the Drummer sounds 'Last Post', and the Chief Warder then leaves to hand over the Keys to the Resident Governor for the night.

It is a simple but impressive ceremony, and it has taken place every night, in war and peace, for over 700 years. It was continued throughout the blitz on London in 1940–41, even when, on 16 April 1941 a bomb landed on the Tower, so close to the Escort that they were blown off their feet. But they picked themselves up from the ground, re-formed, and maintained the unbroken record of the Ceremony of the Keys.

276

One traditional London duty that should not be forgotten, though it is now discontinued, is the Bank Picquet, which began life in 1780, when a regular military guard was provided for the Bank of England, following the Gordon Riots (see page 71). The Directors of the Bank have over the years shown their appreciation of this service by providing dinner for the Officer of the Guard and one male guest, while the men received a cash gratuity in recognition of their contribution towards the protection of the country's gold reserves.[153]

The Picquet has always sought literally to move with the times. Originally, they marched to the City from Wellington or Chelsea Barracks, accompanied by a Drummer or Piper. But with the introduction of traffic lights, their journey caused increasing problems, and from 1963, the guard travelled by truck. Finally it was reluctantly decided that there was no longer a justification in times of manpower problems for this duty to continue, and so since 31 July 1973, the tramp of Guardsmen's feet has no longer echoed round Threadneedle Street.

The Bank Picquet

The fourth regular Royal Guard is at Windsor Castle, and is provided daily by the Foot Guards battalion quartered at Victoria Barracks, Windsor.

There is a famous story of Private Hadfield of the Coldstream Guards, who was charged in 1701 with being asleep while on sentry on the Terrace of Windsor Castle, and was court-martialled.

In his defence, Hadfield put forward the utterly improbable tale that he had not only heard the bell of St Paul's in London chime, 23 miles away, but that it had struck 13 times. His claim was naturally rejected as absurd, and he was sentenced to death, which was the normal penalty for his crime in those days. But it was then found on further investigation that the clock had indeed struck 13 that night. Whether he heard it himself or at secondhand could not be proven, but he was granted a pardon by William III, and lived to be 102.

Windsor Castle is also the scene for the historic Garter Ceremony, when The Queen and Prince Philip walk in procession with the Knights of that Most Noble Order to St George's Chapel.

Windsor Castle Duties

State Visits by foreign Monarchs and Heads of State also take place with increasing frequency at Windsor Castle, instead of in London, and this involves the whole Household Division. Two Guards of Honour are provided by the Foot Guards, and the procession then moves to Windsor Castle, a most perfect and impressive setting for such an occasion.

Most State Visits take place in London, together with many other Royal occasions and State functions, such as the Opening of Parliament. The Household Division is responsible, not only for providing troops for these ceremonies, but also for much of the planning and organisation in conjunction with the Lord Chamberlain's Office.

State Visits

(*Overleaf*) Internal Security at Heathrow. Guardsmen on patrol with the police at London's Heathrow Airport in 1974.

277

The duty of the Household troops on these occasions remains, as it was three centuries ago, to escort and guard the Sovereign and the Royal Family. So it is that when the Queen is present, the Household Cavalry provide a Sovereign's Escort of eight officers and 109 other ranks, and carrying a Sovereign's Standard.

At other times, it may be a Captain's Escort, which is smaller, and may or may not carry a Standard, depending on the person for whom it is mounted.

The Household Cavalry also provide, as appropriate, a Prince of Wales Escort for the Heir to the Throne, and an Escort for the Regalia, which is required when the Crown, the Sword of State and the Cap of Maintenance are taken by carriage to the House of Lords for the State Opening of Parliament.

The role of the Foot Guards on State occasions is usually to provide a Guard of Honour at the start and finish of the Procession; they also provide troops to line the street along part of the Royal route, the sector allotted to the Guards traditionally including the Mall, as being the approach to Buckingham Palace.

A Guard of Honour of three officers and 100 other ranks, with a Colour, is mounted for foreign Heads of State and distinguished visitors; and as a courtesy towards the person for whom the Guard of Honour is provided, it is customary for the officer to report his Guard 'Present and ready for your inspection' in the language of the guest concerned. It is a gesture that may cause complications if the conversation becomes prolonged.

The Household Cavalry also on occasions provide Dismounted Detachments, which, for example, line the staircase to the House of Lords at the State Opening of Parliament. They also line part of the route to St George's Chapel, Windsor for the Garter Ceremony, and are on duty at Investitures and other functions at Buckingham Palace. This is in accordance with the long-established custom that only the Household Cavalry have, since 1664, had the privilege of doing duty *inside* the Royal Palaces.

One exception to this tradition occurs on the death of the Monarch when the privilege of guarding the coffin until the Lying-in-State is granted to the Sovereign's Company of the Grenadier Guards, more generally known as the 'Queen's Company' or the 'King's Company', as appropriate. This select body whose 120 members have an average height of about 6 foot 2 inches is the First Company of the First Battalion of the First or Grenadier Regiment of Foot Guards, and it has a particularly close association with the Sovereign. The Company has its own unique Camp Colour, which is traditionally buried with the Sovereign. A new one is then presented personally by the Monarch on accession.

At the Lying-in-State of the Sovereign in Westminster Hall, officers of all Regiments of the Household Division pay their respects by taking their turn in the Vigil over the catafalque, resting on arms reversed, while the nation files silently past to pay its homage.

The final tribute is paid at the Funeral Procession, where the Sovereign's Company traditionally provides the Bearer Party, and the whole Household

Division is represented. Officers and Warrant Officers wear mourning bands, Standards, Colours and Household Cavalry trumpets are draped, and drums are muffled.

Such respect is normally due only to Royalty, and it was a worthy tribute to a very great Englishman, that 2nd Bn Grenadier Guards provided the Bearer Party for Sir Winston Churchill's funeral in January 1965. It was also an appropriate gesture, in that Major Churchill had served on attachment with that battalion in the trenches in 1915.

Trooping the Colour

Probably the best known parade of all is the ceremony of Trooping the Colour[154] carried out in the first half of June in honour of the Queen's Official Birthday, and so known also as The Queen's Birthday Parade.

This parade has been traced back to 1755, when there was a real need to troop the Colour in front of the soldiers so that they could recognise it as a rallying point in battle. It was in 1805 that the parade was first regarded as being carried out to celebrate the Sovereign's Birthday, and this has continued ever since, except for a period from 1811 to 1820 during the Regency, and also during the two World Wars in this century.

Wherever they may be in the world, the Guards try to celebrate the Queen's Birthday with a parade, be it in Mauritius (see page 261), Guyana, Hong Kong or Berlin.

But the Trooping on the Horse Guards in London, with the Sovereign present in person, is undoubtedly the finest ceremonial parade in the world, in a unique setting.

The Sovereign attends mounted, and wears the uniform of the Regiment whose Colour is being trooped. Other Members of the Royal Family are also on parade or watch from the Horse Guards building, and so it is very much a personal occasion for the Guards as they march past their Colonel-in-Chief.

A large part of the Household Division normally takes part, since the ceremony calls for an Escort from the Household Cavalry, as well as eight Guards, each seventy-three strong, from whatever battalions of Foot Guards are stationed in England at the time.

Also on parade are the Mounted Bands of the Household Cavalry, the Massed Bands of the five Regiments of Foot Guards, and the Corps of Drums of the battalions on parade. This makes a total of some 350 musicians in all, and it is impressive indeed to hear them and to see them march and manoeuvre across the Horse Guards Parade.

The ceremony follows a time-honoured sequence, in which the Sovereign first inspects her Household troops, and then watches as the Colour is trooped down the ranks. The Foot Guards next march past in slow and quick time, followed by the Household Cavalry, who walk and trot past. As a fitting conclusion, The Queen rides back down the Mall to Buckingham Palace at the head of her Guards for the final March Past.

At this point, the King's Troop, Royal Horse Artillery[155] join the parade before returning to their barracks at St John's Wood. They are not strictly part of the Household Division, but are Household Troops, in that they fire the Royal Salutes on this and other State occasions and thus have a special link with the Sovereign. They also ride past on the occasion of a State Visit at Windsor Castle.

The aim of the Household Division is to be 'Second to None' in every task undertaken, be it on parade or on the field of battle. We live in a time when many basic principles and beliefs such as Service, Duty, Patriotism and Discipline are being mocked and undermined by too many. It may be worthwhile therefore to end this 'story of the Guards' with an attempt to define very briefly what it is that enables them to maintain these standards that our country so badly needs, if we are to continue to be *Great* Britain.

Chapter 20

'Those must be the Guards'

Ian Hay who wrote after the First World War, 'Yes, we can safely take the Guards for granted.'[156]

Such a reputation is neither easily won, nor easily maintained. But maintained it undoubtedly is, and the reason why is a deep determination within every Guardsman that it shall at all costs be preserved, and if possible, strengthened.

This does not happen by chance. It is the outcome of a carefully planned and well-proven set of standards and of a system of training, which covers everything that every Guardsman, be he a recruit or a general, does and thinks. The process starts at the Guards Depot and continues in the Regiment, which is itself but a part of the whole, the Household Division. It lasts a lifetime.

The basic material is nothing special; 'the recruits are not braver, better, stronger or possessed of more stamina than any other young men.'[157] The only requirement is that they have the spirit and the will to last the course, which is not for the weak-hearted.

All potential Guardsmen, officers and men alike, Household Cavalry and Foot Guards, go through a training, which builds up each individual into something greater and stronger than himself. It results not in the loss of individuality, as has been suggested, but in the development of a confidence in oneself, one's comrades and one's corps that gives great strength and inspires men to achievement.

'What a man has got doesn't matter. What a man has done, and what he's stood or fallen for, that's what matters.'[158]

There has never been a lack of individuality among Guardsmen; indeed, the reverse. Audacity springs from self-confidence, and is expressed in many ways, be it by Sergeant Graham at Hougoumont or by David Stirling in Cairo; it applies equally to the Guards Parachute Company, a squadron of the SAS and indeed, to every Guards unit in Northern Ireland, Germany, or elsewhere today.

The rule is that there shall be no acceptance of anything that is in any way second rate. 'It may be good enough for others, but not for us,' sets a standard whereby the best becomes the norm.

This attitude, often called 'Guards discipline', is not always fully under-stood. An unbending insistence on nothing but the highest standards in every detail from turnout to the timing of arms drill is not an end in itself.[159] It is a means to an end, which is the achievement of self-imposed standards, such as few of us can hope to attain without help. This is, of course, the aim of all military discipline, but the Guards have always aspired to that 'some-thing extra' and have helped each other to achieve it.

External discipline, properly applied, leads to the other stronger, and also more flexible qualities of self-discipline and *esprit de corps*. It was not fear that made Guardsmen behave as they did at Lincelles, Loos, Longstop and many other places. It was the self-discipline of wanting to behave as Guardsmen are expected to behave and always have behaved.

Such an attitude is fortified by complete confidence that every other Guardsman has the same standards and the same determination to maintain them, be it on the Queen's Birthday Parade, in advancing under fire, or on a parachute drop.

The Guards approach to life extends beyond the barrack square and be-yond the battlefield. It covers qualities such as leadership, loyalty, charity and integrity. It means administrative as well as fighting efficiency. It sets standards which live on in civilian life, be it a straight back or a straight answer, moral courage or a day's work for a day's pay.

'Once a Guardsman, always a Guardsman', they say, and that means something very worthwhile.

Tradition plays a vital part too, for great achievements in the past tend to inspire similar deeds again. 'Hundreds of years of successful soldiering ends by making the Guardsman feel that he can beat the world.'[160] The result is that he can, and he does. It becomes a habit to try to set an example.

But it is not enough to look back, unless one also moves with changing times. The problem is what to retain as being of value today, and what to discard as no longer relevant.

The Guards way of doing things, based on a firm insistence on the highest standards in all things at all times, is surely needed today as much as ever in our history. It is of very real relevance to the many challenges that face us not only as individuals, but as a nation.

This book tells of Guardsmen of the past. No doubt present and future generations of Guardsmen will provide much material for further volumes.

Victoria Crosses

Crimea

GRENADIER GUARDS
Sergeant A. Ablett · Private A. Palmer · Colonel The Hon. H. H. M. Percy
Major Sir Charles Russell, Bt.

COLDSTREAM GUARDS
Major J. A. Conolly · Major G. L. Goodlake · Private W. Stanlack · Private G. Strong

SCOTS GUARDS
Sergeant J. Craig · Sergeant J. Knox · Major R. J. Loyd-Lindsay
Sergeant J. McKechnie · Private W. Reynolds

World War I

GRENADIER GUARDS
Private E. Barber · Lance Corporal W. D. Fuller · Lieutenant Colonel The Viscount
Gort, MVO, DSO, MC · Private W. E. Holmes · Colonel H. T. Paton, MC
Captain T. T. Pryce, MC · Lance Sergeant J. H. Rhodes, DCM

COLDSTREAM GUARDS
Lance Sergeant O. Brooks · Lieutenant Colonel J. V. Campbell, DSO
Lance Corporal F. W. Dobson · Captain C. H. Frisby · Lance Corporal T. N. Jackson
Private T. Whitham · Lance Corporal G. H. Wyatt

SCOTS GUARDS
2nd Lieutenant G. A. Boyd-Rochfort · Sergeant J. McAulay, DCM
Private J. MacKenzie · Lance Sergeant F. McNess · Lance Sergeant H. B. Wood, MM

IRISH GUARDS
Lance Sergeant J. Moyney · Lance Corporal M. O'Leary · Private T. Woodcock

WELSH GUARDS
Sergeant R. Bye

World War II

GRENADIER GUARDS
Lance Corporal H. Nicholls · Major The Hon W. P. Sidney

COLDSTREAM GUARDS
Captain I. O. Liddell · Company Sergeant Major P. Wright
Brigadier A. Nicholls (George Cross)

SCOTS GUARDS
Captain The Lord Lyell

IRISH GUARDS
Guardsman E. Charlton · Lance Corporal J. P. Kenneally

WELSH GUARDS
Lieutenant The Hon. C. Furness

286

Notes

1 (page 25). In *History of the British Army*, Sir John Fortescue, vol i, p. 240.

2 (page 25). They celebrate St George's Day, 23 April, as their Regimental Day.

3 (page 31). In *Early History of the Coldstream Guards*, G. Davies, p. 101.

4 (page 32). As such he sat in the Cabinet with a political appointment, something that no other serving soldier was to do until Lord Kitchener joined the Cabinet as Secretary of State for War in August 1914. *Kitchener*, Sir Philip Magnus, p. 278.

5 (page 40). The King also decreed that 'the Queen's Troop' was to rank as the Second Troop, much to the indignation of James, Duke of York, whose troop was thereby relegated to being the Third Troop. In 1685, the personal titles were dropped, and the Troops were called 1st, 2nd and 3rd Troops.

6 (page 40). A custom continued today, when men belong to, for example, 'No. 2 or Major Willoughby's Company'.

7 (page 41). In *History of the British Army*, Sir John Fortescue, vol ii, p. 236.

8 (page 42). The Regiment's title was to change over the years, as follows:
> 1751 1st or Royal Regiment of Dragoons;
> 1920 1st, The Royal Dragoons;
> 1961 The Royal Dragoons (1st Dragoons).

Dragoons originally acted as highly mobile infantry, and were armed with a musket called a 'dragon', from which comes their title. They wore no armour and so had smaller horses than the Heavy Cavalry, though this distinction soon disappeared.

9 (page 42). The Scottish Regiment of Foot Guards received theirs three years later. The 'grenadier company' should not be confused with the Grenadier Guards of today, with whom there is no particular link.

10 (page 42). In *Treatise on Military Discipline*, 1684.

11 (page 46). Their composition was:

1st Guards Brigade:	2nd Guards Brigade:
1st Bn First Guards;	2nd Bn First Guards;
2nd Bn Third Guards;	1st Bn Coldstream Guards;
2nd Bn Dutch Guards.	1st Bn Third Guards.

12 (page 47). This honourable title was to be bestowed nearly 250 years later on another Guards general, Sir Bernard Freyberg, whom Winston Churchill called 'Salamander of the British Empire'. It was fully deserved, for General Freyberg fought in both World Wars, won a Victoria Cross and a Distinguished Service Order with three bars, and was wounded no less than eleven times. He served with the Grenadier Guards from 1918 to 1929.

13 (page 48). Chamberlayne's *Angliae Notitia*.

14 (page 50). The 'Battle of Blenheim' by Robert Southey.

15 (page 51). Battalions of the Line are those other than the Foot Guards.

16 (page 51). 2,000 more than on the entire D-Day landings.

17 (page 51). The Royal Marines have an outstanding fighting record worldwide, but they still show 'Gibraltar' as their only Battle Honour.

18 (page 56). The French version, ascribed to Voltaire, is that Lord Charles Hay added, 'Gentlemen of the French Guards, fire first,' to which he received the retort, 'No, gentlemen, we never fire first.' In fact it seems clear they did.

19 (page 59). He was later court-martialled and 'adjudged unfit to serve His Majesty in any military capacity whatever'. But he later became Secretary of State for the American Colonies, and in that capacity was partly responsible for their loss.

20 (page 61). It was commanded by Colonel E. Mathews, (Coldstream Guards,) and in 1777 was reorganised as a brigade.

21 (page 67). Moore was to become Sir John Moore, father of the Light Infantry, and hero of the Retreat from Corunna.

22 (page 67). Major General the Hon George Ludlow (First Guards).

23 (page 70). Buckingham House was made a Royal residence by King George III in 1762, but was not called a Palace until 1837, when Queen Victoria made it her main home.

24 (page 71). The Horse Grenadier Guards are still commemorated by the scarlet 'flash cords' worn on the white pouch-belts, and also by the grenade fastening the neck of the officers' cloaks.

25 (page 74). Winston Churchill, 4 June 1940.

26 (page 75). Lord St Vincent.

27 (page 75).

1st Guards Brigade	2nd Guards Brigade
1st Bn First Guards	1st Bn Coldstream Guards
3rd Bn First Guards	1st Bn Third Guards

28 (page 77). Later Earl of Uxbridge and 1st Marquess of Anglesey.

29 (page 77). In *History of the British Army*, Sir John Fortescue, vol iv, p. 375.

30 (page 78). This is not the present Lord's, which was opened in 1814.

31 (page 79). Tom Crane of the Coldstream was Huntsman to the pack with which Wellington used to hunt.

32 (page 79). In *Reminiscences and Recollections*, R. H. Gronow, p. 64.

33 (page 79). *ibid.*, p. 63.

34 (page 79). It was commanded by Major General W. T. Dilkes (Third Guards) and consisted of:
Six companies, 2nd Bn First Guards;
Three companies, 2nd Bn Coldstream Guards;
Three companies, 2nd Bn Third Guards.

35 (page 79). He was created Baron Lynedoch in 1814, and was one of the founders of the United Services Club in Pall Mall. He is also credited with introducing Cleveland horses and Devon cattle into Scotland, not to mention playing in the first cricket match in Scotland in 1785.

36 (page 80).
1st Guards Brigade (Major General K. A. Howard, Coldstream Guards);
1st Bn First Guards;
3rd Bn First Guards;
Composite Bn of Coldstream and Third Guards.
2nd Guards Brigade (Major General The Hon E. Stopford, Third Guards):
1st Bn Coldstream Guards;
1st Bn Third Guards.

37 (page 80). He was Colonel of The Blues 1813–27.

38 (page 82). In *Last Recollections*, R. H. Gronow, p. 23.

39 (page 84). Wellington to Lieutenant General Lord Stewart, 8 May 1815.

40 (page 84). At that time he was in the 7th Hussars, but was, as Lord Anglesey, to be Colonel of The Blues from 1842 till his death in 1855 at the age of 85.

41 (page 84). Their composition was:
1st Guards Brigade (Major General Peregrine Maitland, First Guards):
2nd Bn First Guards;
3rd Bn First Guards.
2nd Guards Brigade (Major General Sir John Byng, Third Guards):
2nd Bn Coldstream Guards;
2nd Bn Third Guards.

42 (page 85). In *Malmesbury Letters*, ii, pp. 445–6.

43 (page 86). *ibid.*, p. 447

44 (page 92). It was reported in Wellington's Official Despatch that Lt. Colonel Home took over command at Hougoumont. This was incorrect, but was never publicly corrected, because Wellington resolutely refused to amend any of his despatches.
Major General Byng, the original commander of 2nd Guards Brigade, had left to take over command of 1st Division from General Cooke, who had been wounded.

45 (page 92). In *Passages from my Life*, Baron von Müffling.

46 (page 97). The Royals also took part in this charge, as part of the Union Brigade, and they captured the Eagles of the French 45th and 105th Infantry Regiments, a feat commemorated by their Regimental badge of an eagle, still worn as part of the uniform of The Blues and Royals.

47 (page 101). In *Reminiscences and Recollections*, R. H. Gronow, pp. 69–72.

48 (page 101). Copenhagen.

49 (page 101). In *Reminiscences and Recollections*, R. H. Gronow, pp. 190–91.

50 (page 102). *Ibid.*, p. 69.

51 (page 102). This is the moment at which Wellington is supposed to have uttered the historic but uncharacteristic cry of 'Up Guards and at 'em.'

52 (page 104). A similar tale is told of the future Lord Raglan (First Guards) who, having had an arm amputated, is said to have remarked to a friend, 'Excuse me, my dear fellow, but would you mind bringing me my arm from over there. It has a ring on, which I value highly.'

53 (page 105). In *Creevey Papers*, pp. 236–7.

54 (page 105). The Battle Honour for Salamanca (1812) was not granted until 1951.

55 (page 106). He was knighted soon after Waterloo.

56 (page 110). Brigade Order of 6 March 1844.

57 (page 110). *Soldiers of London*, R. Money Barnes, p. 179.

58 (page 111). Brigade Order of 6 March 1844.

59 (page 119). The brigade was commanded by Brigadier General Bentinck (Coldstream Guards) and consisted of 3rd Bn Grenadier Guards, 1st Bn Coldstream Guards and 1st Bn Scots Fusilier Guards.

60 (page 122). Lieutenant Robert Lindsay Victoria Cross (afterwards Lord Wantage)
Lieutenant Arthur Thistlethwayte
Sergeant James McKechnie Victoria Cross
Sergeant W. Lane   Killed
Sergeant W. Bryce
Sergeant Angus McLeod   Killed.

61 (page 123). The last occasion when the Standards of The Life Guards were carried into action was at Fontenoy (1745), but The Blues and The Royals both had theirs at Willems in 1794.

62 (page 124). Later Sir William Russell.

63 (page 125). Grenadier Guards 4; Coldstream Guards 4; Scots Fusilier Guards, 5.

64 (page 134). In *Not Worth Reading*, Sir George Arthur, pp. 28–30.

65 (page 135). It is of interest that between 1856 and 1868, the Foot Guards were in fact called a Division, a term that was to be revived as a peace-time title in 1968, exactly a century later.

66 (page 135). The title has varied, i.e.
1862–80	*Journal of the Household Brigade;*
1888–99	*Brigade of Guards Magazine;*
1899–1968	*Household Brigade Magazine;*
1968 onwards	*Guards Magazine.*

It was not published between 1880 and 1888, nor during the Great War.

67 (page 143). It consisted of:
Household Cavalry Composite Regiment;
7th Dragoon Guards;
Four Guns of 'N' Battery, Royal Horse Artillery.

68 (page 143). It consisted of
2nd Bn Grenadier Guards;
2nd Bn Coldstream Guards;
1st Bn Scots Guards.
The new title of Scots Guards had been granted to the Scots Fusilier Guards by Queen Victoria on 4 April 1877.

69 (page 144). It was in fact a nondescript greyish colour rather than the khaki drill of today.

70 (page 146). Rudyard Kipling, whose son served in the Irish Guards and was killed in the Great War, celebrated the formation of the Regiment with a poem which began:

> We're not so old in the Army list,
> But we're not so young at our trade,
> For we had the honour at Fontenoy
> Of meeting the Guards Brigade.
> (The Irish Guards)

This verse refers to the Irish Brigade which was formed in 1690 to support James II while in exile. It then fought for France as a mercenary force, and fought against the Guards Brigade at the Battle of Fontenoy in 1745.

71 (page 150). It was commanded by Major General Sir H. Colville (Grenadier Guards), and consisted of:
3rd Bn Grenadier Guards from Gibraltar;
1st Bn Coldstream Guards from Gibraltar;
2nd Bn Coldstream Guards from England;
1st Bn Scots Guards from England.

72 (page 150). It consisted of:
2nd Bn Grenadier Guards;
2nd Bn Scots Guards;
1st Bn East Yorkshire Regiment;
1st Bn Leicester Regiment.
The Royals also fought in South Africa from 1900 to 1902, and were among the first troops to enter Ladysmith.

73 (page 153). In *The Micks*, Peter Verney, p. 76.

74 (page 153). The Scots Guards sought permission in 1964 to bring back to England as regimental mascots two lion cubs presented to them while serving in Kenya. The request was refused, and the cubs were then given to Joy Adamson. They later achieved a different sort of fame as Boy and Girl in the film 'Born Free'.

75 (page 156). In *Twenty Five Years*, Viscount Grey of Fallodon, vol ii, p. 20.

76 (page 157). The brigade joined the Cavalry Division under General Allenby, who later became Colonel of The First Life Guards (1920–22) and of The Life Guards (1922–36).

77 (page 157). *1st Guards Brigade* (Brigadier General F. I. Maxse, Coldstream Guards):
1st Bn Coldstream Guards;
1st Bn Scots Guards
1st Bn Black Watch;
2nd Bn Royal Munster Fusiliers;
4th Guards Brigade (Brigadier General R. Scott-Kerr, Grenadier Guards):
2nd Bn Grenadier Guards;
2nd Bn Coldstream Guards;
3rd Bn Coldstream Guards;
1st Bn Irish Guards.

78 (page 158). Kaiser Wilhelm in an Army Order of 19 August 1914.

79 (page 159). *7th Cavalry Brigade* (Brigadier General C. M. Kavanagh, The Life Guards):
1st Life Guards;
2nd Life Guards;
The Blues.
20th Infantry Brigade (Brigadier General H. G. Ruggles-Brise, Grenadier Guards):
1st Bn Grenadier Guards;
2nd Bn Scots Guards;
2nd Bn The Border Regiment;
2nd Bn The Gordon Highlanders.

80 (page 160). He ended the war as a Major in the Connaught Rangers.

81 (page 161). It was a precedent in those days for the Commanding Officer to act as Captain of the King's Guard, but it has since become accepted practice on special occasions.

82 (page 162). *1st Guards Brigade* (Brigadier General G. P. T. Feilding):
2nd Bn Grenadier Guards;
2nd Bn Coldstream Guards;
3rd Bn Coldstream Guards;
1st Bn Irish Guards.
2nd Guards Brigade (Brigadier General J. Ponsonby):
3rd Bn Grenadier Guards;
1st Bn Coldstream Guards;
1st Bn Scots Guards;
2nd Bn Irish Guards.
3rd Guards Brigade (Brigadier General F. J. Heyworth):
1st Bn Grenadier Guards;
4th Bn Grenadier Guards;
2nd Bn Scots Guards;
1st Bn Welsh Guards.

83 (page 164). In *The World Crisis 1916–18*, Winston Churchill, vol. iii, p. 179.

84 (page 168). In *The Irish Guards in the Great War*, Rudyard Kipling, vol ii, pp. 1–2.

85 (page 170). In *The World Crisis*, Winston Churchill, vol iii, p. 412.

86 (page 172). Later 1st Viscount Astor of Hever Castle.

87 (page 172). No longer so on either score. Indeed, in 1975, the Guards Club closed down, and its members joined the Cavalry Club, to form what is now the Cavalry and Guards Club.

88 (page 172).

The Life Guards	President's Bodyguard of Pakistan	1965
The Blues and Royals	Royal Canadian Dragoons	1929
	Governor General's Horse Guards of Canada	1941
Grenadier Guards	Canadian Grenadier Guards	1930
	1st Bn Royal Australian Regiment	1952
Coldstream Guards	Governor General's Foot Guards of Canada	1929
	2nd Bn Royal Australian Regiment	1952
Scots Guards	Winnipeg Grenadiers of Canada	1934
	3rd Bn Royal Australian Regiment	1951
Irish Guards	4th Bn Royal Australian Regiment	1965
Welsh Guards	5th Bn Royal Australian Regiment	1966

These are the original titles, some of which have since changed.

89 (page 173). In *They Die with their Boots Clean*, Gerald Kersh, p. 179.

90 (page 175). They were replaced by one only in 1953.

91 (page 175). In Official Report, House of Commons, vol 130, col 1061.

92 (page 183).

Grenadier Guards	Windsor;
Coldstream Guards	Pirbright;
Scots Guards	Pirbright;
Irish Guards	Lingfield;
Welsh Guards	Colchester.

93 (page 183).

April 1940	20th Guards Brigade;
January 1940	24th Guards Brigade;
October 1940	30th Guards Brigade (later 6th Guards Armoured Brigade);
October 1941	32nd Guards Brigade
October 1941	33rd Guards Brigade (disbanded October 1943)

94 (page 185). *1st Guards Brigade* (Brigadier M. B. Beckwith-Smith, Welsh Guards):
3rd Bn Grenadier Guards;
2nd Bn Coldstream Guards;
2nd Bn Hampshire Regiment.
7th Guards Brigade (Brigadier J. A. C. Whitaker, Coldstream Guards):

1st Bn Grenadier Guards;
2nd Bn Grenadier Guards;
1st Bn Coldstream Guards.

1st Guards Brigade joined 1st Division, which was commanded by Major General Alexander (Irish Guards), while 7th Guards Brigade was in 3rd Division under Major General Montgomery.

The Commander-in-Chief of the British Expeditionary Force was General Lord Gort, VC, DSO, MC (Grenadier Guards).

95 (page 187). In *The Micks*, Peter Verney, p. 85.

96 (page 188) The brigade was commanded by Brigadier W. A. F. L. Fox-Pitt (Welsh Guards), and consisted of 2nd Bn Irish Guards, 2nd Bn Welsh Guards and 5th Bn The Loyal Regiment.

97 (page 189). They had joined the British Expeditionary Force from Gibraltar in early 1940, and had the role of guarding Lord Gort's headquarters.

98 (page 190). By Lance Corporal H. Nicholls, 3rd Bn Grenadier Guards and Lt. The Hon. C. Furness, 1st Bn Welsh Guards.

99 (page 192). In *Second World War*, Winston Churchill, vol ii, p. 539.

100 (page 193). They all formed part of XXX Corps under Lieutenant General Sir Willoughby Norrie.

101 (page 194). The brigade in fact had two changes of title in three months. On 14 February 1942 it was changed from 22nd to 200th Guards Brigade, and then became 201st on 21 May 1942.

102 (page 194). In *Rommel Papers*, edited by Liddell-Hart, p. 222.

103 (page 197). The Royals were also present at the Battle of Alamein, as an armoured car regiment, and they fought not only in North Africa and Italy, but also in North West Europe 1944–5.

104 (page 198). In *'G' Patrol*, Michael Crichton-Stuart, p. 27.

105 (page 199). In *Special Air Service*, Philip Warner, p. 32.

106 (page 199). In *Ill Met by Moonlight*, Stanley W. Moss.

107 (page 202). *1st Guards Brigade*:
3rd Bn Grenadier Guards;
2nd Bn Coldstream Guards;
3rd Bn Welsh Guards.
24th Guards Brigade:
5th Bn Grenadier Guards;
1st Bn Irish Guards;
1st Bn Scots Guards.
201st Guards Brigade:
6th Bn Grenadier Guards;
3rd Bn Coldstream Guards;
2nd Bn Scots Guards.

108 (page 205). 4th Indian and 4th Mixed Divisions, 6th and 7th Armoured Divisions.

109 (page 212). Now Viscount De L'Isle. He was the son-in-law of Field Marshal Lord Gort, VC (Grenadier Guards) who was present when Field Marshal Alexander (Irish Guards) gave him his medal.

110 (page 212). The Order of Battle from April 1944 to February 1945 was:
1st Guards Brigade:
    3rd Bn Grenadier Guards;
    2nd Bn Coldstream Guards;
    3rd Bn Welsh Guards.
24th Guard Brigade:
    5th Bn Grenadier Guards;
    3rd Bn Coldstream Guards;
    1st Bn Scots Guards.

111 (page 215). He had been made a Field Marshal after the capture of Rome.

112 (page 215). In *The Welsh Guards at War*, L. F. Ellis, p. 245.

113 (page 216). The organisation from February to May 1945 was therefore:
1st Guards Brigade:
    3rd Bn Grenadier Guards;
    3rd Bn Welsh Guards;
    1st Bn The Welch Regiment.
24th Guards Brigade:
    2nd Bn Coldstream Guards;
    1st Bn Scots Guards;
    1st Bn The Buffs.

114 (page 216). Two DSOs; one MC; two DCMs and ten MMs.

115 (page 219). Rex Whistler was killed in Normandy in July 1944.

116 (page 219). *5th Guards Armoured Brigade:*
    1st (Motor) Bn Grenadier Guards;
    2nd (Armoured) Bn Grenadier Guards;
    1st (Armoured) Bn Coldstream Guards;
    2nd (Armoured) Bn Irish Guards.
Reconnaissance Regiment:
    2nd Bn Welsh Guards.
32nd Guards Brigade:
    5th Bn Coldstream Guards;
    3rd Bn Irish Guards;
    1st Bn Welsh Guards.

117 (page 220). The brigade was commanded initially by Brigadier Gerald Verney (Irish Guards) who was promoted a month later to command 7th Armoured Division; he was replaced by Brigadier Sir Walter Barttelot (Coldstream Guards), who was killed six weeks later. Brigadier Douglas Greenacre (Welsh Guards) then took over for the rest of the campaign. It consisted of:
    4th Bn Grenadier Guards;
    4th Bn Coldstream Guards;
    3rd Bn Scots Guards.

118 (page 221). Deputy Leader of the Conservative Party in 1975.

119 (page 222). In *Hugh Dormer's Diaries*, p. 149.

120 (page 222). *Ibid.*

121 (page 222). The Regimental Groups were:
Grenadier Group:
    1st (Motor) Bn;
    2nd (Armoured) Bn.
Coldstream Group:
    1st (Armoured) Bn;
    5th (Infantry) Bn.
Irish Group:
    2nd (Armoured) Bn;
    3rd (Infantry) Bn.
Welsh Group:
    1st (Infantry) Bn;
    2nd (Armoured) Bn.

122 (page 224). In *The Coldstream Guards 1920–1946*, Howard and Sparrow, p. 284.

123 (page 225). Rommel covered 150 miles in one day during his advance to Cherbourg, 17 June 1940.

124 (page 227). In *A Bridge Too Far*, Cornelius Ryan, p. 119.

125 (page 228). A British fighter aircraft used to give close support to ground troops, particularly against tanks.

126 (page 228). The Irish Guards War Diary records that their Intelligence staff 'spent the day in a state of indignant surprise; one German regiment after another appeared which had no right to be there'.

127 (page 228). In the United States Army, a 'Regiment' is roughly equivalent to a 'Brigade' in the British Army.

128 (page 229). Conservative Secretary of State for Defence, 1970–74.

129 (page 230). The Commander of 84 Medium Regiment reported at this point that he had guns facing north, south, east and west.

130 (page 231). A modern instance of 'for want of a nail, the shoe was lost; for want of a shoe, a horse was lost, and for want of a horse, the rider was lost'. (*Poor Richard's Almanac*, 1758.)

131 (page 231). The supply situation had been eased by the capture on 20 September of a vast German food dump at Oss. The division drew supplies from it each morning, and were made to sign for them by a meticulous Dutch clerk. They were intrigued to discover from his books a day or two later that he was in fact issuing supplies to the British in the mornings and to the Germans to the north in the evenings.

132 (page 236). The occupants were: *First Vehicle:* Major General Adair, Commanding Guards Armoured Division; Field Marshal Montgomery, C-in-C 21st Army Group; Lt General Sir Charles Loyd, Commanding the Brigade of Guards. *Second Vehicle:* Lt General Sir Miles Dempsey, Commander, Second Army; Lt General J. T. Crocker, Commander I Corps; General Brian Horrocks, Commander XXX Corps.

133 (page 241). After Arnhem, 1st Airborne Division amalgamated with 6th Airborne Division in November 1945.

134 (page 241). It was commanded by Brigadier E. H. Goulburn (Grenadier Guards) and consisted of:
3rd Bn Grenadier Guards;
3rd Bn Coldstream Guards;
1st Welsh Guards.

135 (page 243). In *The Micks*, Peter Verney, p. 174.

136 (page 243). It now consisted of:
1st Bn Grenadier Guards, replacing their 3rd Bn;
1st Bn Coldstream Guards, replacing their 3rd Bn;
1st Bn Irish Guards, from 6th Airborne Division.

137 (page 244). In *Menace in Malaya*, H. Miller, p. 97. The author's own comment was 'They made a great reputation . . . took their job of fighting the bandits more seriously than did some others . . .'

138 (page 245). In *The Scots Guards 1919–1955*, David Erskine, p. 476.

139 (page 246). *1st Guards Brigade:*
3rd Bn Grenadier Guards;
3rd Bn Coldstream Guards;
1st Bn Queen's Own Cameron Highlanders.

140 (page 246). *32nd Guards Brigade* (re-formed 1951):
1st Bn Coldstream Guards;
1st Bn Scots Guards;
1st Bn Bedfordshire and Hertfordshire Regiment

141 (page 246). In June 1948, all airborne forces were reduced, and 1st (Guards) Parachute Battalion became 1st (Guards) Independent Company, The Parachute Regiment, with a Pathfinder role for the airborne forces.

142 (page 248). This might be broadly translated as: 'Don't Care, Don't Have, and Don't Forget Me.'

143 (page 252). A state which is one step short of disbandment, and means that the battalion will be re-formed when any expansion of the Army occurs.

144 (page 261). In *Guards Magazine*, Autumn 1965.

145 (page 264). January–May 1965 and September 1965–January 1966.

146 (page 264). Royal Navy; British Army; Royal Australian Navy; Malaysian Army; Royal New Zealand Navy; Malaysian Police; Royal Malaysian Navy.

147 (page 265). Mr Denis Healey, Minister of Defence (1964–70).

148 (page 273).
'They're changing Guard at Buckingham Palace,
Christopher Robin went down with Alice,
Alice is marrying one of the guard,
A soldier's life is terribly hard,
Says Alice.'
'*Buckingham Palace*', by A. A. Milne.

149 (page 274). Only the Banqueting Hall, situated across Whitehall from the Horse Guards, still survives today.

150 (page 274). The List includes:
Ambassadors and Ministers of Foreign States
Archbishop of Canterbury
The Prime Minister
Lord Chancellor
Defence and Service Ministers
The three Chiefs of Staff
General Officer Commanding London District
Speaker of the House of Commons
Clerk and Deputy Clerk of the Privy Council
Commissioner of the Metropolitan Police
Lord Chamberlain
Earl Marshal
Certain members of the Royal Household
Permanent Under Secretary of the Home Office

151 (page 275). 3 officers and 40 other ranks, which is reduced to 3 officers and 31 other ranks when the Queen is not in residence.

152 (page 276). Varied, of course, according to the title of the Sovereign at the time.

153 (page 277). The amounts in 1973 were:
NCO in charge of the Picquet 75p
Other NCO's 50p
Guardsmen 25p

154 (page 281). Sometimes incorrectly referred to as the Trooping *of* the Colour.

155 (page 281). They received the title of 'The King's Troop' from King George VI in 1947, and retain it even when a Queen is on the throne.

156 (page 283). In *The King's Service*, p. 236.

157 (page 283). In *Fighting with the Guards*, Keith Briant, p. 13.

158 (page 284). In *They Die with their Boots Clean*, Gerald Kersh, p. 197.

159 (page 284). Ian Hay called it 'Scrupulous punctilio in the performance of routine duties . . .'

160 (page 284). In *Fighting with the Guards*, Keith Briant, p. 21.

Glossary of Military Terms

| | Organisation and ranks | It is difficult to understand any military book fully without some knowledge of the Army's rather complex organisation, and a guide is therefore set out below, showing the various military units, their approximate size, and the title of the officer who normally commands them. |

<table>
<tr><td colspan="2">. UNIT</td><td></td><td></td></tr>
<tr><td>Infantry</td><td>Cavalry or Armoured</td><td>Approximate Strength</td><td>Rank of Officer Commanding</td></tr>
<tr><td>Platoon</td><td>Troop</td><td>10–30</td><td>2nd Lieutenant (Ensign or Cornet) or Lieutenant</td></tr>
<tr><td>Company</td><td>Squadron</td><td>100</td><td>Captain or Major</td></tr>
<tr><td>Battalion</td><td>Regiment</td><td>5–800</td><td>Lieutenant Colonel</td></tr>
<tr><td>Brigade</td><td>Brigade</td><td>2–3,000</td><td>Brigadier or Brigadier General</td></tr>
<tr><td>Division</td><td>Division</td><td>5–15,000</td><td>Major General</td></tr>
<tr><td>Corps</td><td>Corps</td><td>Variable</td><td>Lieutenant General</td></tr>
</table>

The Household Division

This consists of both Household Cavalry and Foot Guards, i.e.

Household Cavalry
The Life Guards
The Blues and Royals

Guards Division
Grenadier Guards
Coldstream Guards
Scots Guards
Irish Guards
Welsh Guards

The Guards Division

This is the collective title of the five Regiments of Foot Guards, who were till 1968 called 'The Brigade of Guards'.

It is not the same as '*A* Guards Division', which is an operational formation, formed only in wartime, and consisting of two or more Guards Brigades.

A Guards Brigade

An operational formation consisting of two or more Guards Battalions and commanded by a Guards officer.

This is not the same as '*The* Brigade of Guards', which was until 1968 the title of the present 'Guards Division'.

294

A most confusing word with several meanings. The two most important are:

(a) A non-operational term used to describe a military body composed of one or more units of battalion level, e.g. The Grenadier Guards are a Regiment consisting of two battalions.

(b) An operational cavalry or armoured unit of battalion level.

There are other meanings too, but to avoid adding to the confusion, they are not mentioned at all in this book!

Regiment

A title held by the Sovereign in respect of certain selected Regiments of the British and other Armies.

Colonel-in-Chief

Each Regiment of the British Army has a Colonel, who is normally a senior distinguished retired officer, not necessarily a former officer of that Regiment. It is an honorary appointment, involving an overall care of the affairs of the Regiment.

Colonel of a Regiment

Each Foot Guards battalion has a Corps of Drums, under a Drum Major. The Scots and Irish Guards have Pipers in addition, and a Pipe Major as well as a Drum Major.

The Drummers are also Buglers, and sound all calls in barracks, just as they were originally used to sound calls in battle.

Unlike the Regimental Bands, the Drums are part of a battalion, and accompany it overseas, where they also carry out operational duties.

The uniform, embroidered with fleur-de-lys, dates back to the Stuart times.

All Drum and Pipe Majors are appointed as Household Drummers and Pipers to the Sovereign.

Corps of Drums

The term 'grenadiers' applies to two quite different bodies.

The Grenadier Guards are the senior Regiment of Foot Guards, and are sometimes referred to as 'The Grenadiers'.

They should not be confused with the 'grenadiers' who were special assault troops in the British Army from the seventeenth to the early nineteenth century.

Grenadiers

An honour awarded to a regiment in recognition of distinguished service at a particular battle.

Battle Honours

Standards and
Colours

Standards and Colours were originally used as rallying points in battle, but today they are consecrated emblems of a unit's history and achievements. They are inscribed with selected Battle Honours, and are on certain days decked with laurels to commemorate those Battle Honours.

The *Household Cavalry* have a Sovereign's Standard for each Regiment, which is carried by the Escort to The Queen on State occasions. They have also Squadron Standards, which are carried by The Queen's Life Guard when The Queen is in residence in London. The Standards are carried by a warrant officer or non-commissioned officer, whereas Foot Guards Colours are carried by the junior officer on parade, called the Ensign.

The Blues and Royals also have a Regimental Guidon which replaces the former Regimental Standard of The Blues and the former Regimental Guidon of the Royal Dragoons.

The *Foot Guards* have in each battalion a King's (or Queen's) Colour, and a Regimental Colour. The latter is a Union Flag, unlike the remainder of the Army, where the Union Flag is the King's (or Queen's) Colour. The Queen's Colour in a Guards battalion is red.

The Grenadier, Coldstream and Scots Guards also have very special State Colours used only on Royal occasions when the Sovereign is present in person. The State Colours are somewhat larger than the battalion colours, i.e. five feet ten inches by four feet ten inches with a ten feet five inch pike as against three feet nine inches by three feet with a pike of eight feet seven and a half inches.

Each company within a Foot Guards battalion also has its own Company Colour, dating back to Stuart times.

See also pages 254 and 255.

Acknowledgements

I wish to express my humble thanks to Her Majesty The Queen for gracious permission to reproduce the pictures from the Royal Collection on pages 93, 129 (Uniforms 1821), 44, 55, 63, 98, 109, 110, 146; and to Her Majesty Queen Elizabeth The Queen Mother for the picture on page 253 (The Vigil).

I would also like to express my very sincere thanks to all those who have allowed me to reproduce the pictures on the pages shown:

Bank of England, 73
Beaverbrook Press, 257, 276
Chaucer Press, 262
Mr E. J. Collings, 155, 163
Colonel R. J. V. Crichton, 124
Major M. Crichton-Stuart, 197, 198
Major N. P. Dawnay, 254
Governor, Royal Hospital, Chelsea, 159
Guards Club, back cover
Imperial War Museum, 158, 166, 184, 224, 225 (two), 230, 234
Major General, Commanding the Household Division, front cover, 17, 18 (two), 20, 23, 27, 35 (two), 181 (two), 193, 232, 239, 253 (Guards Chapel), 264, 271 (two), 272 (two)
National Army Museum, 96 (Waterloo)
National Maritime Museum, 40
National Portrait Gallery, 26, 59, 142
Officer Commanding, Grenadier Guards, 57, 213
Officer Commanding, Coldstream Guards, 22, 36 (two), 165, 269 (winter warfare)
Officer Commanding, Scots Guards, 96 (Talavera), 129 (Alma), 130, 132 (Normandy)
Officer Commanding, Irish Guards, 153, 279
Officer Commanding, Guards Parachute Company, 247, 250, 269 (jungle warfare)
Osprey Publishing, 127, 200
Parker Gallery, 53, 64, 68, 114, 118, 120, 123, 126, 132, 133, 135, 136, 139, 140, 151, 156, 176, 177
Major A. Philipson, 90, 91
Pitkin Press, 258, 266
South African Embassy, 216
Victoria and Albert Museum, 92

Bibliography

Anglesey, Marquess of, *One Leg* (1961)

Arthur, Sir George, *Story of the Household Cavalry* (4 vols) (1909–26)

Aubrey-Fletcher, Major H. L., *A History of the Foot Guards to 1856* (1927)

Barnes, R. Money, *The Soldiers of London* (1963)

Blaxland, Gregory, *The Regiments Depart* (1971)

Brett-James, Anthony, *The Hundred Days* (1964)

Briant, Keith, *Fighting with the Guards* (1958)

Coldstream Guards, *Coldstream Guards (1650–1950)* (1950)

Crichton, Richard, *Coldstream Guards (1946–1970)* (1972)

Crichton-Stuart, Michael, *'G' Patrol* (1958)

Crofton, Sir Morgan, *Household Cavalry Brigade in the Waterloo Campaign* (1912)

Churchill, Winston, *The World Crisis* (1923); *Second World War* (1960)

Davies, G., *Early History of the Coldstream Guards* (1923)

Dawnay, N. P., *The Colours of the Guards Division* (1975)

Dormer, H., *Hugh Dormer's Diaries* (1947)

Ellis, L. F., *The Welsh Guards at War* (1946)

Erskine, David, *The Scots Guards, 1919–1955* (1956)

Forbes, Patrick, *6th Guards Tank Brigade* (1946)

Fortescue, Sir John, *History of the British Army* (1899–1927)

Grenadier Guards, *The Grenadier Guards, 1939–1945* (1946)

Gronow, R. H., *Reminiscences and Recollections*, (1862)

Hall, Sir John, *Coldstream Guards, 1885–1914* (1929)

Hamilton, General Sir F., *History of the Grenadier Guards* (1874)

Household Division, *Guards Magazine* (1864–1974)

Headlam, C., *The Guards Division in the Great War* (2 vols) (1924)

Hill, Colonel E. R., *Colours & Customs of the Coldstream Guards* (1951)

Hills, R. J. T., *The Life Guards* (1971); *The Royal Horse Guards* (1970)

Howard and Sparrow, *The Coldstream Guards, 1920–1946* (1951)

Howarth, David, *A Near Run Thing* (1968); *Waterloo – A Guide to the Battlefield* (1974)

Kersh, Gerald, *They Die with their Boots Clean* (1941)

Kipling, Rudyard, *The Irish Guards in the Great War* (1923)

Legge-Bourke, Henry, *The King's Guards* (1952)

Liddell-Hart, Sir Basil, *Rommel Papers*, (1953)

MacKinnon, Colonel D., *Origin and Services of the Coldstream Guards*, (1833)

Magnus, Sir Philip, *Kitchener* (1958)

Maurice, Major General, Sir F., *The Scots Guards 1642–1914* (2 vols) (1934)

Moss, W. S., *Ill Met by Moonlight* (1950)

Nicholson and Forbes, *Grenadier Guards in the War 1939–45* (1949)

Orde, Roden, *2nd Household Cavalry Regiment* (1953)

Paget, Julian, *Counter-Insurgency Campaigning* (1967); *Last Post – Aden 1964–67* (1969)

Quilter, David, *No Dishonourable Name* (1947)

Ross, Sir John, *Coldstream Guards 1815–1895* (1896)

Rosse, Lord, and Hill, E. R., *Story of the Guards Armoured Division* (1956)

Ryan, Cornelius, *A Bridge Too Far* (1974)

Sutherland, John, *Men of Waterloo* (1967)

Verney, Gerald, *The Guards Armoured Division* (1955)

Verney, Peter, *The Micks* (1960)

Ward, Dudley, *History of the Welsh Guards* (1920)

Warner, Philip, *Special Air Service* (1971)

Whitworth, R. H., *The Grenadier Guards* (1974)

Wyndham, E. H., *First Household Cavalry Regiment* (1952)

Young, Peter, *The British Army 1642–1970* (1967)

Index